Praise for *I Saw 1*

MW00803615

"Debbie Gendler takes us on a ma␣ ␣ ␣␣ accompany her on one fascinating adventure after another. If you're a Beatles fan (and who isn't?) you'll thoroughly enjoy this book. There's never been a more engaging telling from a fan's perspective." —*Andrew Solt*, Founder, SOFA Entertainment (*The Ed Sullivan Show*)

"In this heartfelt, personal, and engaging memoir, Debbie Gendler has perfectly captured the fun, the passion, the insanity, and all of the raging hormones surrounding 1960s Beatlemania. Having lived through it myself, this book was a thoroughly enjoyable—and accurate—trip back in time." —*Bob Gale*, co-writer, *I Wanna Hold Your Hand* and *Back to the Future*

"Sixty years after they conquered the world, The Beatles' fandom still numbers in the millions. And not one of these fans wouldn't trade places with 13-year-old Debbie Gendler. If there's a title for first American Beatle fan, Debbie qualifies. Long before the 1964 *Ed Sullivan Show* debut, she was tuned in. This is her story—the closest any of us will get to trading places. Written with immediacy, passion, and an observant eye, she shares her life-changing journey that took her from small-town New Jersey to the group's inner circle. Stories like this are no longer possible, but thankfully Debbie shares hers beautifully with us, the present-day fans." —*Robert Rodriguez*, author, *Revolver: How The Beatles Reimagined Rock 'n' Roll*; creator/host of the Something About The Beatles podcast

"Debbie, I remember you at the Ed Sullivan Show!" —*Harry Benson*, CBE, official photographer for The Beatles' 1964 first visit to America

"An engaging, vivid account of a first-generation Beatles fan, *I Saw Them Standing There* lets readers vicariously experience everything, from Ed Sullivan to Shea Stadium and beyond, through Deb's eyes. Her account helps reclaim the voice, savvy, and reputation of the female fan after generations of dismissive portrayals." —*Erin Torkelson Weber*, author of *The Beatles and the Historians*

"When the Beatles arrived in the United States in early February 1964, their critics deemed the Liverpool band a passing fad—certain that the exuberant, female-led fandom that followed them would soon fade away. While history has proved otherwise, it is only more recently that this first generation of fans has come forward to share what the Beatles have meant to them. As a leading participant in the earliest days of American

Beatlemania (complete with a ticket to the band's debut on *The Ed Sullivan Show*), Debbie Gendler gifts readers with a page-turning memoir that vividly depicts how the twentieth century's most joyful cultural phenomenon has shaped her life in meaningful and often surprising ways." —*Christine Feldman-Barrett*, senior lecturer in sociology at Griffith University, Queensland, Australia; author of *A Women's History of the Beatles*

"With a one-of-a-kind, front-row perspective, Debbie Gendler shares what being a part of Beatlemania truly felt like from the beginning until today." —*Augie Max Vargas*, Emmy Award–winning producer of *The Night That Changed America: A Grammy Salute to the Beatles*

"As a last-minute stand-in for the ailing George Harrison during the historic *Ed Sullivan Show* rehearsal, I felt the excitement, frenzy, and screams that Debbie conveys so enthusiastically in this story she is finally ready to share. Deb tells it like it was!" —*Vince Calandra*, talent executive, *The Ed Sullivan Show*, 1962–1971

I SAW THEM STANDING THERE

Remembering February 9, 1964, and walking through those doors to see The Beatles fifty-five years earlier. It was magical.

AUTHOR'S COLLECTION

I SAW THEM STANDING THERE

ADVENTURES OF AN ORIGINAL FAN DURING BEATLEMANIA AND BEYOND

Debbie Gendler

Backbeat
Books

Essex, Connecticut

Backbeat Books

An imprint of Globe Pequot, the trade division of
The Rowman & Littlefield Publishing Group, Inc.
4501 Forbes Blvd., Ste. 200
Lanham, MD 20706
www.rowman.com

Distributed by NATIONAL BOOK NETWORK

Copyright © 2024 by Debbie Gendler

All photos are owned by the author unless otherwise noted.

All rights reserved. No part of this book may be reproduced in any form or by
any electronic or mechanical means, including information storage and retrieval
systems, without written permission from the publisher, except by a reviewer
who may quote passages in a review.

British Library Cataloguing in Publication Information available

Library of Congress Cataloging-in-Publication Data

Names: Gendler, Debbie, author.
Title: I saw them standing there: adventures of an original fan during
  Beatlemania and beyond / Debbie Gendler.
Description: Essex, Connecticut : Backbeat, 2024. | Includes bibliographical
  references and index.
Identifiers: LCCN 2023038512 (print) | LCCN 2023038513 (ebook) | ISBN
  9781493079742 (paperback) | ISBN 9781493079759 (ebook)
Subjects: LCSH: Gendler, Debbie. | Rock music fans—United States—Biography.
  | Beatles. | LCGFT: Autobiographies.
Classification: LCC ML429.G413 A3 2024 (print) | LCC ML429.G413 (ebook) |
  DDC 780.78—dc23/eng/20230816
LC record available at https://lccn.loc.gov/2023038512
LC ebook record available at https://lccn.loc.gov/2023038513

∞™ The paper used in this publication meets the minimum requirements of
American National Standard for Information Sciences—Permanence of Paper
for Printed Library Materials, ANSI/NISO Z39.48-1992.

For my parents, who endured the ridicule
to indulge my unreal dream;
I wish you had known how it worked out.

The Macs . . . and Cheese
My friend Michael McCartney and his family enjoyed Kraft
macaroni and cheese that was available only in the States.
One day my daughter and I decided to pop a
few boxes in the mail for a surprise.
At the post office the clerk looked strangely at the package addressed to
"The McCartneys."
I thought for sure he recognized the name,
especially with an address in England.
Instead, he picked up the box only to hear the contents rattle.
"What's in this?" he questioned.
I cautiously responded, "Boxes of macaroni and cheese."
"Sending macaroni and cheese all the way to England?"
"Well, it's an important package," my daughter added with pride.
"How good of you to be sending food to a 'needy' English family,"
he responded.

CONTENTS

ACKNOWLEDGMENTS

If it wasn't for ardent Beatle enthusiast Gay Linvill who shouted out from the back of the Clive Davis Theater at the Los Angeles Grammy Museum "where's your book?" and Sue Steinberg's persistent—in a good way—urging to keep on going, this book would have never happened. Thank you, Sue, for always believing in the viability of these adventures.

I spent nine years writing this book to have it ready for the sixtieth-anniversary celebration of the Beatles' first live performance on *The Ed Sullivan Show*. With each sentence I hoped that I would be around to celebrate this milestone anniversary.

There are so many people to thank for their encouragement, support, and participation over the years, and surely some will be missed, but please know that you are part of this book and contact me . . . I want to include you.

Big hugs to Lee Sobel my super literary agent who vowed he was going to sell this book and John Cerullo at Backbeat Books who embraced Lee's vision—I am eternally grateful as you made a dream come true. Thank you is too simple to describe my indebtedness to Barbara Claire also at Backbeat Books who saw to every detail, Della Vache, Chris Chappel, Laurel Myers, Joanne Foster, and Emily Jeffers who were always available to answer my many questions. It has been a joy to work with you.

To the Fan Club members of Beatles (U.S.A.) Ltd., Club #28 in Oakland, New Jersey, we came together . . . Michele, Sharon, Pam, Alice, Bev, Linda, Andy, Sue, Wendy, Elaine, Karen, Cheryl, Patty, Donna, Betty, Barb, Marilyn, Carolyn, Roz, Joyce, Joanne, Trudy, Kathy, Adele, Eileen, Louise, Nancy, Sari, Sherri, Lynda, and the many who joined from the Tri-State area, we all agreed that these four guys from Liverpool had talent above all others.

There are friends who accompanied me on many adventures and shared the highs and lows . . .

Sharon Mercer Machado, we had so much fun together and always found a way to get to JFK to welcome the Stones, the Animals, Herman's Hermits, and others to America.

Mikal Gilson Berry, what an overnight at the Delmonico!

Andy Wirkmaa, our lone brave male Fan Club member, we nearly incited a massive demonstration.

Beverly Don, when others questioned my intentions, you were my greatest supporter, cheerleader and still are! I remember how excited I was when you, Michele de Medici, and Linda Guldemann Kelly saw me off to London for what proved to be a pivotal lifetime adventure.

Photographer extraordinaire Jill Jarrett, you have photographed the super famous, but have always found time for me—thank you for your diligence, kindness, and love in making sure every photograph is perfection. Also, a hug to Kevin Winter for permission to use one memorable photograph.

Brigitte Sarnoff, Adrianna Smits and Patty Nazzaro—my Beatle sisters—we shared a very special night!

And to more recent Beatle sisters and one brother—Carol Tyler, Allison Bumsted, PhD., Christine Feldman-Barrett, PhD., Erin Torkelson Weber, Candy Leonard, and Robert Rodriguez, I appreciate your friendship, and advice.

Many thanks to Mark Lewisohn, Simon Weitzman, and Susan Ratisher Ryan who came to my aid to provide details where my memory went blank.

Thank you to Aaron Bremner, Apple Corps Ltd., for easing the permission process and to Tom Adams and Jo O'Mahony Adams of *Beatles Book Monthly*—your publication was the best! To Sujata Murthy at Universal Music a huge thank you for encouraging me to continue writing after a few chapters.

For the too many now gone who played significant roles during these adventures my forever appreciation: Walter Shenson, Brian Epstein, Wendy Hanson Moger, Walter Hofer, Sid Bernstein, Murray "the" K, Bernice Young, Sue Friedman, Mr. and Mrs. H. Harrison, Ray McCullough, Felice Lipsky, Jeannie Sakol, and Ed Sullivan.

Vince Calandra, you would have been my BFF back in 1964, but at the very least we share great memories today—much love. Wendy Heller-Stein thank you for your never-ending willingness to help me out.

Heartfelt thanks to Andrew Solt and Josh Solt who so graciously welcomed me into the SOFA family where I get to enjoy not only the Beatles, but the legendary Ed Sullivan Show roster of talent each day.

To Robb Weller and Gary Grossman who for many years not just tolerated all the Beatle antics, but participated in a few—forever thankful, you guys!

To Vivian Green Korner, roommate and confidante, who saw me through all of life's challenges and will always be there as I will for her.

To Michael McCartney and family "Thank U Very Much" for all the fun times we shared, the visits, the photographs, the scouse, and the escapades. Your edits were much appreciated.

To my family Kate, Max, Teddy, and Noah, I wrote this for you. Always remember, make time for fun adventures!

And to my husband Paul, I married you despite your name and I'm glad I did.

FOREWORD

From the moment I walked into my typically quiet eighth grade classroom at St. Francis Cabrini Catholic School, you could feel the tension. Something big had happened, and it had gripped every girl in the class. They were gathered in one corner of the room like a rugby scrum. Only this convocation, whatever it was, had not a lick about sports to it. There was crying, shock, disbelief all bundled into a near hysteric group of schoolgirls. Instead of spending this precious time before first period ratting their hair into a bouffant and gazing intently into the one small mirror in the room, self-grooming time was cast aside. No famous celebrity had died. No plane had crashed. No nuclear bomb drill would require "duck and cover" exercises. Something much bigger had occurred. A rumor in a popular teen magazine had it that Paul McCartney had secretly married his girlfriend, Jane Asher, which meant, of course, that none of my classmates had a chance.

Our teachers, the poor Sisters of the Holy Names, were always desperate to keep pubescent early teen girls from ever thinking about boys, love, or even worse . . . sex. However, that morning they realized nearly a decade of holy influence had vanished thanks to scruffy, long-haired musicians from a far-off land ruining their girls, like the devil incarnate. Hormones were running higher than heaven, and the good Sisters didn't stand a chance.

But the girls' reactions didn't seem odd to any of us students because we all had been swept up by the Beatles tidal wave. We were "all in" and wanted more. Good news finally came: the Beatles would be coming to Seattle on their summer tour, and my own Beatles moment was about to happen.

A neighbor miraculously procured one too many tickets and called me at the last minute to travel to the Seattle Coliseum for the third stop on their American concert tour. Positioned only a few rows behind the thrusted stage and way off to the side, I had the perfect angle to see most of their backsides. Wow, what great tickets, I guess. After the packed house waited and waited, finally the local radio DJ came onstage, and the place erupted. His first duty was to introduce the warmup acts. The Righteous Brothers, Bill Black Combo, then Jackie DeShannon. Jackie was gorgeous, blonde, wearing a two-piece, light-colored yellow suit. I'll never forget. She tried her hardest to get that audience's attention, but what a futile situation, trying to perform with thousands of rabid fans only waiting for the main act.

Then it happened. The DJ yelled those improbable words, "The Beatles," and my hearing has never been the same. The lads hustled onstage and broke immediately into their first song. Not a clue what it was. All I remember now is that their sound system was incredibly meager with just a few guitar amps; it didn't stand a chance against the screams of more than fourteen thousand fans. Each time they started a new song, you could barely hear what they were singing. Every time they turned their heads, hundreds of girls would stand up and shout. At twenty-nine minutes, a relatively short concert, it was worth every second.

To truly understand Beatlemania's impact, we need to go back in time to the critical moment when the band captured seventy-three million Americans in a few minutes—a magical moment when the gestalt of American music became total prisoner and surrendered to the British Invasion. It was an easy victory for the Brits, as the battle front was in our own living rooms.

Triumph was THE appearance on the Sunday night *Ed Sullivan Show*, the biggest variety program on the air. There they were. The Beatles singing to us. Maybe we'd seen brief newsreel footage or consumed still photos from a newspaper of the Beatles doing something, somewhere. We had heard their songs on a never-ending rotation over our transistor radios wanting to hold hands, or sending all my loving, but they had not performed in America. What I didn't know at the time, as my older sisters screamed at the Beatles on our family TV set, was that one of my greatest friends to be, Debbie Gendler, was in the audience of that historic performance, so lucky to be just feet away from the boys from Liverpool.

Now, finally Debbie's Beatles adventures have come to life. It is the story of how a thirteen-year-old fan became associated with the group, their families, and their early management that has survived decades.

To begin to understand Debbie's story, first it is important to understand this: you are getting an inside look at the earliest times from a fan's frontline viewpoint. Before the boys set foot on American soil, Debbie had traded correspondence with their manager Brian Epstein, via his New York attorney. You'll learn how she discovered their music before most teens in America had heard one note of a Beatles song.

When I mentioned earlier a fan's frontline viewpoint, it represents a lifetime of love, dedication, work, promotion, and friendship. Debbie could easily have cashed in on her knowledge and insights decades ago. She once told me that in 1966 *Seventeen* magazine offered her money for a Beatles insider story, from which she walked away. And at a young age Debbie was a trusted adjunct to the New York–based official fan club, where she represented the club at the Beatles' behest on television and in print.

In reading all the author puts forth, here are a few things you should know.

In the early 1990s Debbie came to work with me as vice president of development and talent at Weller/Grossman Productions. I quickly learned that she has a memory like a steel trap. As we worked together, I cannot tell you how much easier and faster it was than Google to just ask Debbie. During our time together, we produced more than nine thousand episodes of television for thirty-six different cable, broadcast networks, and animation. Debbie was involved in every one of those productions.

Next, you should know that Debbie seems to have an internal talent crystal ball. Her training at CBS and her duties at ABC required the ability to identify talent and make good choices. She literally discovered individuals who went on to become major stars. And she found them in the most unusual ways. She consistently brought obscure talent into our offices and convinced us they had the right stuff. And they did. Designers, chefs, experts, spokespeople, announcers, actors, entrepreneurs, and complete amateurs rose to success because of Debbie. She embraces people's abilities in a very special nonjudgmental way and isn't threatened to push for their success.

How lucky we readers are to finally hear the adventures of how a girl from New Jersey nurtured a decades-long connection to the Beatles. This once-young teen relates it all, just for you.

Robb Weller

INTRODUCTION

Everyone has a story to tell about where they were when the Beatles first appeared on *The Ed Sullivan Show*. Mega-celebs credit the band's performance that night for their artistic inspiration; accountants, artists, designers, hairdressers, and lawyers recollect gathering with family in front of their television sets to watch the phenomenon; older brothers grudgingly let their younger sisters take control of the dial for this one hour only; moms and dads scowled at the Beatles' hair; nurses neglected their patients for a brief moment to catch a glimpse of the four mop tops; schoolteachers tuned in to see what the fuss was all about; and seventy-three million other Americans joined in on a blustery Sunday night at 8, February 9, 1964, to witness this seminal moment in history.

I get it. I was there that night—inside Ed Sullivan's Studio 50—seated in the mezzanine, screaming, breathless, and bouncing in my seat. Who cared that we couldn't hear the Beatles sing? Or that Ed tried desperately to quiet us down? I was breathing the same air as my heroes, reaching out, practically touching their shoulders. Beatles 4 Ever!

Even before taking my seat, I was in love with the guys, and soon everything mod and British became my style—Yardley pale-colored lipsticks, listening to the BBC's *Top of the Pops* via shortwave radio, a Mary Quant dress that still hangs in my closet, ghillie shoes, an English school scarf, Pattie Boyd knee-highs, a John Lennon cap, and every piece of Beatles merchandise I could buy with my fifty-cents-a-week allowance. I even showed up in a column in *Seventeen* magazine where they acknowledged that fans in Oakland, New Jersey, set their clocks five hours ahead to be on London time. I received a C on a book report because I refused to change the spelling of "favourite" to "favorite." It was sheer madness, much like the fans running toward the train platform at the opening scenes of *A Hard Day's Night!* And I loved every moment during this wacky time when all I craved was to catch a glimpse of the Beatles. I plotted intricate schemes on how to meet my "favourites" and devised innovative ways to politely deceive. It was always for the betterment of the Beatles.

Being a first-generation Beatles fan, as we have come to be known, bears a responsibility to younger fans. I've discovered that second- and now third-generation fans admire the times in which we lived and wish they, too, could have experienced the unencumbered excitement, adulation, screams, and raw love we felt for these four guys who touched our hearts and souls. The wait for the next album to be released was excruciating. And when they married, painful. For many, like me, this love is forever.

In 1964, Oakland, New Jersey, where I grew up, was a semirural, insular, blue-collar town of about eleven thousand residents. New York City, although only twenty-six miles away, seemed a foreign land for many of the town's citizens. Until a school trip to the Cinerama Theater in Times Square to experience the epic film *How the West Was Won*, many classmates had never crossed the George Washington Bridge. That wasn't my life. I viewed the city as a place of endless opportunity where everything was possible if you tried. I needed to associate myself with something extraordinary, and the Beatles were it.

This book was written entirely from memory only supplemented by my scrapbook, a trip diary of my visit to Swinging London, and connecting with friends who might remember additional details. Beatles historians may take exception to the dates, facts, or commentary, but this is how I lived and remember it. My memorabilia collection has had very few additions since the early days of Beatlemania. When I hear that people have paid extraordinary amounts to own items, that is not the kind of fan I envision myself. For me, it is not about the acquisition, but more about the times, the experiences, and the love for these four guys who rocked our world.

My journey to *The Ed Sullivan Show* is where this adventure starts and how that February night defined my life and the lives of so many others.

MY HEART WENT BOOM

For girls, between the ages of eleven and thirteen is an awkward time. Changes occur, and you may seem more adultlike, but no one, not even you, is confident about how to react. My mom still thought I needed a babysitter after school at age thirteen, so she asked her best friend's daughter, Frances, to fill the job. Frances was a typical bobby socks teen; she loved playing records on her hi-fi; sneaking her boyfriend, Dave, over to my house (I was sworn to secrecy, but how could my parents not detect the lingering scent of Canoe?); and watching Dick Clark's *American Bandstand* from Philadelphia every weekday after school.

One evening in late April 1963, there was a knock at our front door, and waiting there were Frances's parents, with two bags brimming with packages. They had just returned to New Jersey from a trip to England. Fran's mom handed over several boxes of assorted leaf teas and biscuits purchased at Fortnum & Mason, and my mom started up the kettle, anxious to savor the taste of an authentic cup of tea rather than Lipton. She was raised in Winnipeg and Montreal and always appreciated a good cup of tea. Was there a gift for me, I hoped?

I sat patiently, listening to tales about their pedestrian nightmares of not remembering to look right, and eating ghastly steak and kidney pie, but time was short because I had a test the next day. I had just turned thirteen, and I took my seventh-grade schoolwork seriously. As the brewed tea was poured through strainers into dainty English porcelain cups, I was presented with an odd-looking square souvenir wrapped in shiny brown utility paper. It was simply taped, with no bows or ribbons, and didn't come close to the elegance of my mom's gift.

Out of respect for my parents' friends, I carefully opened the package, prepared to act surprised and sincerely thankful for being remembered. Precisely unfolding the coarse paper, I could see that it was a record album. Who was singing . . . the Beatles? I didn't know them; they hadn't even been on *American Bandstand*. I took one fast glance at the cover, stopped, gasped, and shouted so loudly that my dog started barking.

1

"These are the cutest four guys I've ever seen!" I thought, *How could anyone ever guess . . . I LOVE this record*, clutching the album next to my heart. Our friends explained that they had no idea what to buy for me, but when they passed a record store in London's West End, the Soho Record Centre, they remembered that I routinely watched *American Bandstand* and assumed that I loved rock 'n' roll. The shop clerk said this was the record to take back to America, *Please, Please Me* by the Beatles, a sensation from up north. I was later told that our friends only wanted to buy the single of the title song, but the record opening seemed oddly shaped, and they worried that it couldn't play on an American record player.

The next afternoon with Frances I finally listened, and my heart went boom.

The following day, two friends came over after school to see the album after I had told them how good the songs were and how cute the singers were with their long hair. They weren't impressed and quickly left to pick up a pizza. One of them was into scary horror films and during a sleepover at her house, while watching the movie *House of Wax*, I silently vowed never again to stay there overnight. Vincent Price, star of the film terrified me, and years later living in Los Angeles, my husband and I were assigned Price's former landline telephone number. Individuals would phone at all hours asking for Vincent or Vinny, among them art collectors and Hollywood stars such as Virginia Mayo. Every time I heard the name Vincent Price, it gave me a frightening chill and reminded me how my longtime friend had turned her back on the Beatles.

Frances tolerated their music, but they didn't have Bobby Rydell's or Fabian's drop-dead looks. She got so tired of hearing me play the only Beatles record I had that a few weeks later she told my mom I was old enough to care for myself, and she quit.

Desperately wishing for a friend to love the Beatles like I did, I reached out to many of the girls in my seventh-grade class. Most thought I was all wrong about the Beatles. With perseverance I finally found someone who got excited—Sharon Mercer. She was pretty, blonde, and open to new ideas and fun. Her mom had been married previously, and she had an older half sister who lived and worked in New York City. Her sister did fabric graphic design and had a real creative spirit, as did the entire family. Sharon's aunt, Marian Mercer, was a talented comedic actress and Broadway star who lived in the famed Dakota apartment building where I visited once with Sharon, long before John and Yoko ever moved there.

Together we would spend hours listening to the album. We could never decide which Beatle was our favorite because our opinions changed each day. One afternoon while devouring the liner notes, I noticed a small sticker attached to the cardboard inside of the album cover with the torn receipt from Soho Record Centre. It said if you love the Beatles, join their fan club, with the address. What a great idea! I could write letters to girls across the Atlantic who loved the Beatles. This was more exciting than going to Girl Scouts or digging for fluorescent minerals with my pick and shortwave ultraviolent light at the Franklin, New Jersey, quarry. Maybe my piano teacher, Mrs. Schifter, would let me learn to play Beatles music instead of Czerny?

That night I wrote to the Beatles Fan Club at 13 Monmouth Street, London, and waited excitedly for a response.

SECRET OBSESSION

For two months I raced to the mailbox with the highest hope of seeing my name on a letter from England, but nothing arrived. The Beatles became my secret obsession. To save my questionable reputation, I retreated to idolizing Richard Chamberlain, television's Dr. Kildare, but those Beatles' faces still had my heart. Until I received the Beatles album, I was a devoted Dr. Kildare fan. From age eleven, NBC on Thursday nights was appointment television, where I could be found swooning over Dr. Kildare. My bedroom walls were filled with magazine photos of the show's star at the beach, at work, and on holiday. When he won the Golden Globe for his portrayal of Dr. Kildare in 1963, I embroidered a gold-colored polishing cloth for his new statuette with his initials in black floss and mailed the gift to his attention care of the MGM lot in Culver City, where the show was filmed.

The series left a powerful impression on my young psyche. Even today, I can still feel the passion of the two-part Kildare episode costarring Yvette Mimieux as the doctor's only true love, dying in his arms on the beach. Decades later living in Los Angeles, I discovered by chance that Richard Chamberlain and I shared the same hairdresser, Mac on Melrose. I asked Mac if he would schedule us for back-to-back appointments, which he gladly arranged. The next time I arrived at the second-floor salon, there was Richard Chamberlain seated facing the mirror, and he and Mac were engrossed in conversation. As I gingerly approached the two men, Mac motioned me over to be introduced. It was a little embarrassing, but I had handled situations like this before. Richard was beyond gracious, and when I asked him if he remembered receiving the embroidered polishing cloth, he kindly admitted that it must have found its way to someone else's statue. For an instant, I felt remorse that I had dumped him for the Beatles, frantically ripping his photos from my bedroom walls and replacing them with a six-foot color Beatles' poster. But, hey, time in the spotlight is fleeting.

The school year ended, and I was headed to eighth grade with no response from the Beatles Fan Club. I was shipped off for eight weeks to Camp Naiad in Turner, Maine. My parents agreed that camp was the best place to keep me challenged for the summer. I had become a handful to control. My dad grew up on New York's Lower East Side, and the concept of sleepaway camp was reserved for the wealthy. His tears overwhelmed the goodbyes as they deposited me in my new home for two months.

Camp was right out of Allan Sherman's "Hello Muddah, Hello Faddah" Camp Granada. I wanted to go home. My mom, on the other hand, grew up in Canada, relocating to New York City with her family during high school. She was loving but tough, and I couldn't pull the wool over her eyes *ever*. She had three older siblings, and none had children, so I grew up in a communal atmosphere where I benefited from the indulgence of multiple sets of parents, yet I had way too many people to please.

While packing for the two-month adventure, I secretly placed the Beatles album cover under my clothes, which were stored in a footlocker in my bunk. Some girls hid cigarettes; I hid a Beatles album. When no one was looking, I'd take a quick peek to be sure those Beatles were still as cute as ever! I was also missing my friends and our antics around Oakland inciting trouble at the local Grand Union supermarket, repositioning items on shelves or taunting one of the male clerks we thought was cute.

Every letter home asked if I had gotten any mail. Every response back was negative. But I never gave up hope. During an overnight field trip to Ogunquit, when others bought postcards to mail home, I bought one to send to 13 Monmouth Street, London, an address etched in my head, to remind them that I was still waiting to join the Beatles Fan Club. "Remember me . . . Debbie Gendler, Oakland, New Jersey, U.S.A." I bought three five-cent stamps, affixing them to the postcard to be sure it would get to London, and scribbled "Air Mail" in big letters. The card probably got lost, because when I arrived home, nothing was waiting for me in the letterbox.

It was September, time to head back to class. We were the big shots on campus, eighth graders and soon high school. I wondered if friends would ask about the Beatles, and I figured probably not. As I was getting my new outfit prepped for the first day back, I turned on my red Sony transistor radio nestled in its black suede pouch. Playing was Skeeter Davis's huge 1963 hit, "The End of the World." I sang along not realizing that in approximately eight weeks the world as my friends and I knew it would end and what seemed like an impossible dream might be fulfilled.

HEART AND SOLES

One of my earliest BFs along with Sharon, who also appreciated Dr. Kildare but *loved* the Beatles more, was Pamela Jayne Hardon. Pam and I were kindred spirits; neither of us quite fit into the milieu of small-town life in Oakland, New Jersey, in the 1960s. Her mom came from New Jersey, and her dad was from Holland. Pam was born in Germany and had a worldly outlook, which was what I appreciated most about her. She also shared her old-school wisdom when I felt down in the dumps, not hearing back from the English fan club. She had lived in Maracaibo, Venezuela, before moving to Oakland, and part of my mom's family lived in Lima, Peru. We connected on the South American thing.

One of the first people I showed the *Please, Please Me* album to was Pam, who really got excited. Pam lived on Lakeshore Drive right on Crystal Lake, and I lived a few streets away with a brook running alongside the bottom of the property, which fed into the lake. We enjoyed each other's friendship and gossiped regularly. We played guitars together, hers electric and mine co-classical, imitating folk singers. A few years later when the show *Shindig!* hit the air, we talked about becoming a singing group called The Mods along with another friend, Sue Grygus. Saturdays were spent together, usually at Pam's house, eating thickly buttered Wonder Bread with sardines, flattening the sandwiches down before taking big bites. Pam had two brothers—Jeffrey, older, and Neil, younger—and when New Jersey Beatles Fan Club #28 started, she was among the most enthusiastic members despite Jeffrey's anti-Beatles stance. Pam wrote poetry for our club newsletters; her poems were always illustrated with funny pencil drawings.

One Saturday while enjoying our sardines, Pam let it slip that they were on the move again. This time, Brussels. I was sad to see Pam leave Oakland. She was always there to support my crazy schemes, and we shared good times.

It wasn't until the mid-1970s that I stumbled on Pam again. I knew noted film director Brian De Palma casually because there was a connection through the apartment building on lower Fifth Avenue where I lived. One evening there was an issue, and a few of us tenants joined him to discuss the problem. On a table were piles of headshots of attractive young actresses. I spotted a familiar face: Pam Hardon, now called PJ Soles! Pam had gotten married and was studying at the famed Actors Studio. Pam had read for a film that Brian was casting called *Carrie*; she and her husband, Steven Soles, lived only blocks away.

I was blown away. There was a show happening at the Fillmore East that Pam was involved with, and I planned to surprise her there, but I never made it. When I went to see Pam star in *Rock 'n' Roll High School* with the Ramones, it was a trip back to our Indian Hills High School days when we rocked it down the hallway. I've only seen Pam once since she left Oakland, at the Golden Globes at the Beverly Hilton when she was married to Dennis Quaid. Pam was startled to see me in this setting. Dennis wanted to know how we knew each other, of course: "Oakland and the Beatles." He was not surprised. We exchanged phone numbers, and she invited me to their house. Hers was an 818 area code, so somewhere in the Valley. Maybe on Mulholland? Before I got around to calling, they had separated, and Pam had moved.

I valued Pam for her worldliness and for being so supportive. I remember her parting comment that night as I headed back to my assigned table across the Hilton ballroom: "You look so much prettier than I remembered you." Pam, in my memory, will forever be a dedicated Beatles pal, holding her red electric guitar.

THANK YOU, MR. HOFER, ESQ.

Six months had passed since writing that letter to the fan club with no response, but my love for the Beatles hadn't faded.

Halloween was a big night in Oakland, but an even bigger night was the evening before, Goosie Night. It was intended for the older kids to get the Halloween spirit out of their system by prowling the streets and overturning trash cans or soaping car windows. I loved the night and canvassed the streets with a pack of friends on the prowl, looking for intrigue. If trouble presented itself with a homeowner turning on the front lights to check his lawn, my friends and I would run in the opposite direction. We never did any damage to the property of others, but we certainly made a lot of noise.

The day after Halloween when I arrived home from school, my mother was waiting at the door holding a Western Union telegram sent to my attention. The message instructed me to call a phone number in New York City to schedule a meeting for the following week regarding the Beatles. The telegram wasn't signed by the fan club or really by anyone. "Law Office" was as close to a human that I could find. A meeting? In New York City? Was it with the Beatles? Would I meet them?

My father was at work, and I ran to the phone, shrieking that I was going to meet the Beatles. I also ran next door to our neighbor, Ellen Williamson, to show her the telegram. When the initial excitement ended, I grew a little curious. The only meetings I knew were those my parents attended such as parent-teacher conferences or our Mayor Potash's Advisory Committee. Then it hit again. The BEATLES? I started to cry I was so happy—feelings I had not experienced before.

My patience was paying off. They must have gotten my letters or card from camp. It was a late Friday afternoon, and my mom said we should wait to discuss this with my dad and call on Monday. I wished I hadn't stopped at the de Medicis' house to sort through everyone's Halloween candy because then I would have been home early to phone the office. After an unbearably long weekend, my mom phoned the number on the telegram. All day during class I was ready to bust. What did my mother learn that I didn't yet know? Would I be going? Or did she mess the whole thing up?

I raced home. My mom was waiting, and so was Mrs. Schifter, ready for my weekly piano lesson. Mom said the discussion was brief. Executives would be arriving from England to discuss the Beatles' trip to America, and they were looking for fans to welcome the group at appropriate locations to stir up excitement and be available for other activities as the need arose. Except for Sharon and Pam, no other kids I knew had even heard of the Beatles except those who brushed me off as weird. Realistically, no parents in Oakland would permit their kids to gather in support of an unknown band. When asked a few questions about me and the Beatles, mom told them there was a no more devoted fan than me. Mom repeated that line for years. I was in for the meeting. The piano lesson was shortened because Mrs. Schifter was heavily into astrology, and I begged her to review my chart to see if the Beatles were in my future.

On a November morning, my dad drove me from Oakland across the George Washington Bridge and down the West Side Highway to an office at 150 West Fifty-Fifth Street in Manhattan for the meeting. It was Veterans Day, and school was closed. Deciding what to wear was my greatest challenge. I selected a simple, conservative outfit; a John Meyer of Norwich plaid skirt and a blouse with a Peter Pan collar, paired with my favorite circle pin, all the rage at the time. Arriving at the building, the first impression I remember is that it was old, and the elevator rattled and smelled. A gruff elevator operator seemed like he had been there for a century.

We went up a few floors to a busy office; two women were seated at adjoining desks. Beyond was a room with an oval table where four men stood chatting. I would come to learn that they were Brian Epstein, the Beatles manager; Walter Hofer, Brian Epstein's New York–based lawyer; Nicky Byrne (maybe), who was hired to handle licensing deals for merchandise; and a well-dressed gentleman with a British accent. Years later, I heard that that gentleman most likely was Geoffrey Ellis, a friend of Brian Epstein's who lived in New York and eventually returned to England to assist Brian with his business affairs. Another of Brian's stable of talents who traveled with him to New York, Billy J. Kramer, could have been present, but I don't remember him at all.

The meeting was in the law office that obviously was the signature on the telegram. Brian was well dressed, elegant, and soft spoken with a slight smile and, as I would describe it now, preoccupied and distracted at the same time. What I remember most was his accent and glistening gold cuff links. I think it was the first time that I had heard people in my presence speak with a British accent. How educated the men sounded! I wanted to talk just like them. I shook Brian Epstein's hand first and then Walter Hofer's, followed by the other two men, as did my dad. I had not seen Brian Epstein before, not even in a photo, or understood his importance to the Beatles. But when he spoke, there was no mistaking that he was in charge. I could tell from the look on all their faces they were quite startled to see a curious thirteen-year-old standing before them ready to declare her love for the Beatles. I was nervous. A woman offered coffee to my dad, but he declined. It was around 11 a.m., and with Brian and Walter getting down to business, they dismissed the woman.

Walter Hofer had an accent (German?). He was short, and his clothes looked like he had slept in them the night before, but he could get away with it because we were in his office. Mr. Hofer said they were looking for young fans. I went on to tell them that I was a fan and really, truly loved the Beatles and could prove my devotion. That was an obvious fact that no one in the room doubted. When Brian Epstein said that they needed a full-time person to manage the Fan Club office, I shook my head and said, "Mr. Epstein [Ep*stein*, not Ep*steen*], I need to go to college!" They glanced at each other, we shook hands again, and the meeting was over in fifteen minutes. It seemed weird that looking at me these four men thought I could be ready for a job in a few months' time. Later I learned that in Britain many people assumed full-time jobs at age fifteen. I looked older than my thirteen years, so maybe their assumption wasn't that off.

As we left the office, the secretary said that Mr. Hofer had asked for my address again and phone number. He thought there still might be a need for me and would send me a ticket to see the Beatles perform on *The Ed Sullivan Show* once they had an agreed on a deal, probably by the end of the day. The secretary's name was Evelyn Klein, and she whispered that the show would probably happen in February—the ticket was a "thank-you" for my time and effort, she explained. Months later I came to know Ms. Klein as the doorkeeper to Walter Hofer's busy office.

By late February 1964, Hofer and his wife, Sondra Hofer, had become directors with Brian Epstein of a new business entity called Beatles (U.S.A.) Ltd. This arrangement necessitated that the Hofers move their office to 221 West Fifty-Seventh Street. The location would become the first home of the Official Beatles Fan Club and Mr. Hofer's law practice.

The meeting was my introduction to the business world, and I left feeling accomplished and proud. My dad wasn't a fan of Ed Sullivan as he much preferred the more cerebral Jack Paar and Steve Allen. But I thought, *if this meeting gets me to the Beatles, I LOVE Mr. Ed Sullivan.*

CBS TELEVISION NETWORK

A Division of Columbia Broadcasting System, Inc.

485 MADISON AVENUE, NEW YORK 22, NEW YORK · PLAZA 1-2345

December 6, 1963

Mr. Henry Zaccardi
Assistant to the President
American Federation of Musicians
425 Park Avenue
New York, New York

Dear Henry,

No doubt you have heard of the tremendous popularity
of a group of young men known as the "BEATLES" in
Europe, particularly in London where they created
such a sensation at the Palladium. We have been
fortunate to have booked them for "THE ED SULLIVAN SHOW"
of February 9, 1964 for both a live performance, and
a taped performance to be shown at a future time.
In addition, we are planning to present them in another
live performance during our Miami Beach origination
on February 16, 1964.

These four young men both sing and play guitars, and
as aliens are not members of the A. F. of M. Ed and
I would appreciate a waiver from the Federation in
order to present this very "hot" musical group to our
American and Canadian audiences.

Please advise me of the Federation's decision on this
matter.

Sincerely,

RHP/bls
p.s. I didn't call you back on the Moscow State Circus problem
in Minneapolis because we were able to resolve it by hiring
another technical unit for the job. Thank you, nevertheless,
for your understanding and willingness to cooperate.

This letter from Sullivan Show producers requests that the American Federation of Musicians waive its requirements for the Beatles.
THE ED SULLIVAN SHOW © SOFA ENTERTAINMENT

THE CENTER OF ATTENTION

Eleven days after this amazing meeting, unparalleled tragedy struck America and the world with the assassination of our president. For me, even the Beatles were put on hold as I grappled with the horror and sadness that befell our country. *CBS Evening News with Walter Cronkite* on November 22, 1963, had been scheduled to broadcast a filmed segment about the Beatles and how this remarkable group of long-haired musicians was sweeping the United Kingdom and Europe. But the story was shelved and eventually aired on December 10, although the nation was still reeling with disbelief as the details of the assassination unfolded nightly. The segment received little attention except from a few very attentive fans who began getting the word out about the Beatles.

Through the darkness came the beginnings of some light and hope. Radio stations began to play Beatles records, and the demand exploded instantaneously. So, Capitol Records in the United States, decided to release the group's debut single, "I Want to Hold Your Hand," the day after Christmas 1963. The Beatles were catching on, and DJs played their music on frequent rotation. Beatlemania, although not a term yet, was beginning to take hold. *Meet the Beatles*, their first Capitol album, was released on January 20, 1964, and went right to #1! Vee-Jay's album, *Introducing . . . The Beatles*, which previously couldn't draw any interest, overnight rode the wave, skyrocketing up the charts. Newspapers, magazines, and special-interest publications began to report on these four lads from Liverpool, and the PR machine went full blast. Word hit the street that the Beatles were coming to America and would be guests on *The Ed Sullivan Show* on February 9. CBS was flooded with fifty thousand requests for tickets to the live show in New York and close to that number for the following week in Miami.

Kids in my eighth-grade class who had laughed at me months earlier now wanted to be my Beatles buddy. A teacher, C. Tucker Platt, who heard that I had a Beatles album from England, asked me to bring it to school to play at lunch. On our eighth-grade field trip to Washington, DC, girls who never spoke to me wanted to share a room so we could swap Beatles stories through the night.

I didn't tell anyone, even my closest friends, that I had had a meeting with their manager and was given an opportunity to work for the Beatles. That could wait. Months of snide comments ceased, and virtually overnight I found myself the center of attention.

THE TICKET

"The ticket is in the mail."

That is what they told me when I called Walter Hofer's office, inquiring about my ticket to see the Beatles at *The Ed Sullivan Show*. The Beatles, who in two months had become the biggest sensation to hit America, were due to land in New York City in a week, and my promised ticket hadn't arrived. Deep down, I was preparing for disappointment, trying not to let it show except for private bedroom conversations with my dog. At the same time, I wasn't sitting idle. In early January 1964, I began writing to CBS for tickets for the February 9 show that by then was common knowledge to all who listened to WINS, WMCA, or WABC Radio. I had to increase my chances to be in that audience.

Each day I would charge out of school and race home as fast as I could, crossing Ramapo Valley Road, which bisected Oakland, continuing down Powder Mill Lane to check the mailbox. By now it was apparent that for me to succeed in life, mail delivery was a priority. After weeks of high anxiety, there it was—finally—in the mailbox—an envelope with the return address "Law Office of Walter Hofer," and inside, a single ticket to *The Ed Sullivan Show*. I was really going to see the Beatles! I dialed my dad's work number, TW1-8947, as fast as I could to share the best news ever. My screams were so loud that he didn't understand what was happening until my mom took the phone as I danced off to another room. Even my dog was barking from all the excitement.

With just one week to go before *the really big shew*, in Ed Sullivan's famous words, I needed to plan everything, including letting my friends know I was headed to see THE BEATLES! Everyone was just getting to like me again, and I didn't want to make them jealous, but I also desperately wanted to let them know I had a ticket.

The following day was picture day for our eighth-grade yearbook. The photo of me looks weird. It's because I was ready to explode from excitement and had barely slept the night. I dreamed that a Beatle would spot me (any of them would do) and take me away to England so I could have a beautiful accent.

I desperately wanted to go to the newly renamed JFK Airport to welcome the Beatles to America, but Long Island was too far away. I didn't want to ask my parents; they were already letting me go out on a Sunday night, never questioning how I would make it to school on Monday morning.

The Beatles' arrival prompted a massive amount of television and newspaper coverage, and I began to cut out the news stories to start a scrapbook. Sixty years later I am still adding to the scrapbooks, which now number forty-nine volumes packed with clippings dating back to December 1963.

Life could never be better.

THE COUNTDOWN

On Friday, February 7, the Beatles landed at JFK at 1:20 p.m. on Pan Am Flight 101. I was glued to the radio hidden inside my bookbag as all three New York stations gave listeners a minute-by-minute rundown of their arrival. "I Want to Hold Your Hand" had reached #1 on the charts just six days earlier, selling one million copies in three days. Three thousand screaming fans were at JFK airport to welcome the group to America. (Brian Epstein and Walter Hofer must have been relieved.) The Beatles were shuffled through immigration and customs, specially prepped for them, and to a press conference in the arrival hall, packed with media armed with some of the worst questions ever asked of the Fab Four. Here are just three:

Reporter #1: Are you a little embarrassed by the lunacy you cause?

John: We like lunatics.

Reporter #2: Are those English accents?

George: It's not English. It's Liverpudlian, you see.

Reporter #3: How many of you are bald, that you have to wear those wigs?

Ringo: All of us.

Paul: I'm bald.

I was embarrassed that the reporters asked such dumb questions trying to make the guys seem unworthy of the hysteria surrounding their arrival. After the questioning, they were off to the Plaza Hotel, where they were met at the fountain in front by a few hundred screaming fans.

During lunch in the school cafeteria, I shared with a few friends my secret that I was going to see the Beatles on Sunday. Although I was pounded with questions about how I got the ticket, our forty-minute lunch period was over. After only one more class, we could all go home and listen to Murray the K. They made me promise to give a detailed report on Monday, same time, same table, and they all wanted me to say hi to the Beatles for them. Eileen, a friend since kindergarten, could not believe how lucky I was that my mom let me do so many things. Eileen was forbidden to mention the Beatles.

Murray the K had booked a room at the Plaza and broadcast the entire night to the fans outside the hotel and across the New York Metropolitan area. I was glued to my radio until I fell into a deep sleep.

Saturday, February 8, the day before *The Ed Sullivan Show*, I went with my mom into New York to help my grandmother, who needed to have her new eyeglass prescription filled. We were listening to WINS on the radio following the Beatles' every move during the drive into the city. Murray, who wasn't due on the air for a few hours, interrupted the broadcast to report that George Harrison had fallen ill and was unable to make the Sullivan rehearsal. The other three Beatles were going to Central Park for an impromptu press briefing before heading to the studio. After hearing this latest development, I asked my mom to drop me in front of the Plaza Hotel in hopes that I could help George feel better.

My mom was overly concerned that I wasn't dressed properly for the frigid February weather, but I begged. Despite her concern, instead of heading to the West Side Highway, we made a fast turn and drove up Fifth Avenue, at the time still a two-way street. As we made another left turn onto Central Park South, I saw that the fountain area across from the Plaza entrance was overflowing onto Fifty-Ninth Street with kids my age screaming, gazing upward at the windows. Everyone had the same idea. Photographers were there, too, alongside the NYPD patrolling on foot and horseback. I charged out of the car, hoping to catch my first glimpse of the Beatles.

Rumors spread that the Beatles were staying on the twelfth floor, so we kept counting the floors up from the street, glued to every movement. We tried to figure out whether the ground floor counted as the first floor, or the first floor was one above that. When a maid opened a window to shake out a mop, we were convinced that it was the Beatles' room. I later read that the maid intentionally opened the window to capture our attention and get us all excited as a favor for one of the DJs broadcasting live inside the hotel.

Some fans had transistor radios, so we were able to closely follow all the action as reported by Cousin Brucie Morrow at WABC or Dandy Dan Daniels, a WMCA "Good Guy." At one point we heard that three Beatles were back from a photo op and leaving for rehearsal. About half the kids in front of the Plaza took off along West Fifty-Eighth Street headed for Studio 50 on Broadway and Fifty-Third Street, home of the Sullivan show. It was cold and windy, like my mom said, but love for the Beatles kept us warm. After screaming "We Love You Beatles" for a few hours, I took a crosstown bus to my grandmother's apartment, and together with my mom, headed back to New Jersey. I didn't dare tell anyone standing outside of the Plaza that I had a ticket for *The Ed Sullivan Show* the next day. I was concerned about my safety in the huge crowds that swayed in every direction from the sheer force of people scrunched together behind the police barricades.

When I got home, the first thing I did was check my jewelry box: the ticket was still safely stashed away.

I SAW THEM STANDING THERE

The day had finally arrived. I finished my homework, took a short walk with my dad and dog, and got ready to return to New York. My mom would be driving me to the show. I couldn't decide what to wear, but I selected a light-colored blouse with a necklace my mother let me borrow for the occasion. I wanted to look grown-up, not thirteen years old, in case any of the Beatles spotted me from the stage. The night before I had put curlers in my hair to give the usually straight style some flair. Driving along Route 4 past Stern's Department Store and Bamberger's in Garden State Plaza, we stopped for gas before reaching Fort Lee. The George Washington Bridge looked very imposing set against the darkening February sky. It felt like snow. I thought about what my mom would do during the show because I had only received one ticket. She told me not to worry; she would find a place to keep warm.

With the ticket tucked safely in my mom's purse for easy access, we parked in the same lot my dad always used on West Fifty-First Street. As we walked to Studio 50, just two blocks up on Broadway and Fifty-Third Street, a bunch of kids ran past us. We assumed they were headed to see the Beatles, and I asked my mom to walk faster. When we reached Broadway, the street was blocked off, and we were told to take a detour because the other side of the street was reserved for arriving ticket holders only. I was a ticket holder! My mom had to dig into her purse to show the police officer on horseback the ticket because he was giving us a hard time. He inspected the printed ticket closely. Did he think I was counterfeiting tickets? He called over another officer stationed next to a barricade, who asked to see identification. At thirteen years old, I didn't have an official ID. I had no proof that I was the rightful holder of the ticket. The officer asked us to step aside. At this moment, a Beatles-approved photographer, Harry Benson, pointed his camera at us. I hoped this moment was being captured for posterity. He laughed at my comment. Meanwhile, taxis and cars were pulling up, dropping off people who could breeze right into the theater. I was worried that the studio was filling up. My mom had to get aggressive.

It made sense why she came with me and not my dad; my mom would speak up. Mom had ties to then New York City Police Commissioner Michael Murphy. Commissioner Murphy grew up in Queens next door to my mom's friend, who I called Aunt Betty. My mom, at 5'2", approached the police officer, gazing up at him on his horse, and they spoke briefly. She let the officer know that in one phone call she could reach Commissioner Murphy. Minutes later the other officer on foot returned and said reluctantly, "Go ahead." I looked at my mom, and she motioned me onward alone, the ticket clenched firmly in my gloved hand.

As I maneuvered around the steel and wood barricades, two kids began to tug on my coat. I had to push them away forcefully. "Sorry," I said. I wasn't really sorry; I was excited and blasted through the front door, entering the drafty vestibule. My ticket was yanked from my hand. I wanted to keep it as a souvenir but was told they needed it. I think there was a place to check our coats, and then I was led up the stairs and instructed to sit in this seat on the mezzanine level. A minute later I was shown to a different seat, where I sat down obediently. I wanted to be close to the stage, but seeing that others were sitting farther back, I just listened to what I was told and sat down in my designated place. More audience members arrived and took their seats. Adults seemed to be well-dressed, as were most teens. Dress codes were still the norm in 1964, and the unspoken rule was that going to any theater required respectful attire. I was totally taken in by all the activity onstage as people carrying clipboards rushed across the stage. Photographers, including the man I had met outside, were positioned to the left and right of the stage, getting ready to memorialize this big event. The girl behind me was bouncing in her seat before the show even began.

Then everything seemed to fall into place. I don't really remember much about the show's introduction, except hearing a countdown off to the side. Music, and then some chatter, and then Ed Sullivan asked us to be quiet. I could see the commercials playing on the studio monitors. I remember one for Anacin for pain relief. The studio crew probably needed an Anacin from all the screaming. The excitement escalated as I heard familiar music behind the curtain. Being there alone was a little scary, and I wished my mom had been by my side. I thought I had to abide by special adult behavior code, but when the Beatles were introduced, it was impossible not to shriek. It was the moment I had dreamed about since November, and it was happening now! Mr. Sullivan mentioned something about Elvis, Col. Tom Parker, and a telegram sent to the Beatles, but many in the audience screamed so I really couldn't hear. I distinctly remember thinking that these people really liked using telegrams and at that moment . . .

Right before my eyes were the Beatles. They looked BEAUTIFUL! It felt like I was suspended in a strange unreal space, where I was unable to breathe. I remember those first notes; it was my favorite song, "All My Loving" from *Meet the Beatles!*

The screams, the excitement, the adulation filled the studio; it was overwhelming. I, too, had to scream and bounce in my seat. I desperately tried to focus on each Beatle for just a moment to capture a distinct memory: John looking up toward us with a smile, George checking out the audience with a sideways glance, Paul grinning broadly, and Ringo shaking his mop top as he drummed away. I lost all control and with it, all composure. The Beatles sped through two other songs, "Till There Was You" from the Broadway show *The Music Man* and my other favorite song, "She Loves You." The first set was over.

The Beatles left the stage to our shouts and applause. Those few minutes flew by in an instant. Ed Sullivan desperately tried to quiet us down again. It was impossible. We were asked to sit quietly through other acts until the Beatles returned. How could Ed Sullivan make us wait? The Beatles were here breathing air we all shared, so close we could practically touch them! Poor Fred Kaps, the magician who had to entertain us right after the Beatles, and . . . English Music Hall performer Tessie O'Shea, so passé. Then came the little British kid from the Broadway musical *Oliver!* He was OK. Two years later we all learned who he was: Davy Jones, part of a new television series and band called The Monkees, patterned after, of course, the Beatles. Coincidentally, shortly thereafter Lionel Bart, who wrote the book, music, and lyrics for *Oliver!,* based on the Dickens novel, became a close friend of Brian Epstein.

The show seemed to go on and on; up next were Mitzi McCall and Charlie Brill, the husband-and-wife comedy team who flew from Los Angeles to New York City for their big career break on Sullivan; they shouldn't have bothered, because Ed changed their act during dress rehearsal. He felt their routine was too mature for his teen audience and suggested they do something else. All they could think of was the act where a producer is looking to cast a young female in a role, and there was no time to rehearse. Years later, Mitzi told me that she was so caught up in the Beatles that she left her dressing room for the wings to catch a glimpse during the group's performance. It would take fifty years until I saw, and this time spoke, with Mitzi and Charlie. More later.

I don't remember many details about the other performers. All I can share is that it was painful waiting for the Beatles' return. When Ed Sullivan introduced them for the second time, my heart beat rapidly. We screamed even louder than before. Two boys sitting a few rows away didn't even move. I wondered who they were because they seemed so bored and unhappy. The final two songs, "I Saw Her Standing There" and "I Want to Hold Your Hand," were over in what felt like a mere second. By the time I could fully comprehend the enormity of what I was experiencing, the show ended with Ed Sullivan telling us it was late, and we should get home safely. It was difficult to leave our seats; many of us were stunned. As I gathered my composure, with the same resolve as months before, I reasoned that maybe it was over for now but *not* forever.

WHITEHALL/ PILLSBURY	THE ED SULLIVAN SHOW AIR: FEBRUARY 9, 1964		REF # 1
ACT	AGENT/CONTACT	NOTES	
THE BEATLES FR: Bud Hellerwell CI 7-4896 Plaza - PL 9-3000 arr. 2/7 Pan Am #101 - 1:40	Nems Enterprises Brian Epstein - / 227 Plaza 9-3000	Min. of 3 nos. Equal star billing 1) "She Loves You" - 2:15 "I Want To Hold Your Hand" 2:20 2) "All My Loving" 2:00 "I Saw Her Standing There" 2:45	
THE BEATLES VTR AIR: FEB 23, 1964	PL 5-6400	1) "Twist and Shout" "I Wanna Be Your Man" 2) "I Want to Hold Your Hand"	
GEORGIA BROWN	Gloria Safier TE 8-4868	"As Long As He Needs Me" Sun. only 2:05	
BOYS FROM "OLIVER" CI 5-9374 Home JU 2 7096	Jack Schissel David Merrick office LO 3-7520	"I'D Do Anything" Sun. only	
TESSIE O'SHEA	GAC Ken Martel X 8953	"Hello Good People" Medley	
FRANK GORSHIN 276-7234	GAC Ken Martel X 8953		
McCALL & BRILL (Mitzi)(Charlie)	GAC Ken Martel X 8953		
WELLS AND THE FOUR FAYS (Christine Fay: RA 9-7244 or ST 4-7848)	GAC Sonja Weinberg X 8953	Sun. only	

Each show has a rundown composed by a producer for the crew's use. This one is for Ed Sullivan's February 9, 1964, episode.

THE ED SULLIVAN SHOW ©SOFA ENTERTAINMENT

Research reports that seventy-three million people (the country's population was 191 million in 1964) watched that evening across the country, meaning that 60 percent of all televisions turned on were watching the Beatles. Amazing numbers for 1964: New York City police reported that not one crime was committed during the 8 to 9 p.m. hour when the show aired, although more recently that has been disputed. For this generation, it wasn't only where were you when you first heard JFK was shot, but now where were you when you first saw the Beatles on *The Ed Sullivan Show.*

Dazed, I walked out of the theater into the bitter February cold. Crowds lingered, although the Beatles had already left the studio. I later read that they went with Murray the K to the Playboy Club for dinner and then on to Joey Dees' Peppermint Lounge, the disco where the Twist originated, which was owned by the notorious Genovese family. News photos the next day showed Ringo twisting into the early morning hours and Paul hanging with actress Jill Haworth. It was the night that changed America.

On the far street corner across Broadway, I spotted my mom, standing patiently waiting. She looked frozen in her navy-blue cloth coat. I ran toward her, falling into her arms with tears running down my face. I couldn't talk. We held our gloved hands together and quickly walked back to the car. There was school in the morning.

BEATLEMANIA IS HERE

When I got to school the next morning, I was greeted by the vice principal, who wanted to know how it was; he had watched. So did the safety patrol monitor at the door and the school nurse. Everyone watched Ed. In homeroom, classmates who NEVER spoke to me were all over the Beatles.

At lunch word spread, and some kids passed by with their trays, wanting to hear Beatles details. Those who didn't own a copy of *Meet the Beatles* were anxious to get one, and my friend Wendy brought her copy of the single to class and pasted the sleeve on her notebook cover.

We passed the time deciding which of the four Beatles we liked the best. Ed Sullivan let us know each of their names by displaying them beneath their faces during the show. There were the George girls, Paul girls, John girls (he's married), and of course, everyone LOVED Ringo! The classmates whose parents hadn't let them see the show made plans to watch at a neighbor's house the following Sunday's performance from Miami. Sharon Mercer came to my house to watch the show from Miami, and we jointly screamed at the television set as if it would respond. Now during class girls would scribble on lined notebook paper . . . The Beatles . . . The Beatles . . . The Beatles or write the Beatles' names in ink on their palms. I was no longer in this alone.

Critics blasted the Beatles as a passing fad, but Madison Avenue took them seriously. Magazines were on the newsstands overnight; my first one was *Around the World*, with the Beatles depicted in color on the cover. Every detail of the Beatles' bios was scrutinized: their birthdays—oh, yeah, George was a Pisces, like me. Paul had hazel eyes, Ringo's real name was Richard Starkey, and John was 5'10". We fell in love with the Beatles' boots and, of course, their mop tops. That's what had captured me back when I received the *Please, Please Me* album only ten months earlier, which now seemed like long ago.

With all this activity, I barely had time for school. My basement became the hub of the action, where we gathered to talk, play the album, and love our Beatles. Brian Epstein was right: an organized fan club was essential, and I decided to phone Evelyn Klein in Walter Hofer's office to check on its status.

The fans at the Plaza and crowds at Studio 50 were one thing, but now kids in Oakland, who in my mind were out of the loop before, had overnight become Beatles crazy.

Beatlemania was here.

P.O. BOX 505, RADIO CITY STATION

This Beatles adventure began with a letter to the British Beatles Fan Club, and there is a special place in my heart for fan gatherings. Many years ago, I had a job on a television show working out of an office building in Burbank where the rock radio station KROQ was housed. One morning I arrived at the office to find twelve girls camped at the building's backdoor, trying to gain access because the band Depeche Mode was at the station for a live interview. Building security kept moving the fans away, but I understood their desperation to meet the band. Calling upon my past adventure, I approached the girls and told them to casually follow me to the garage, where I used my elevator pass to get them up to the radio station to see their heroes. I knew their frustration; we spoke the same language.

Walter Hofer's new, sedate fifth-floor law office at 221 West Fifty-Seventh Street became my personal Mecca. The office was so under the radar that the front door bore no identification. This is where Beatles (U.S.A.) Ltd., the Official Beatles Fan Club, was originally housed. It was very different from Mr. Hofer's office on West Fifty-Fifth Street, where I had met Brian Epstein briefly and was promised the ticket to the Sullivan show. Walter was a preeminent entertainment attorney referred to Brian Epstein through his London-based solicitor, David Jacobs. I quickly understood that Mr. Hofer was overseeing all things Beatles, especially the merchandise. How I loved all those items plastered with the Beatles' names and images. Walter Hofer's new location in more recent years became the Hard Rock Café and was demolished, making way for retail and the new Nordstrom's on West Fifty-Seventh Street.

The best and, strangely, the only way to connect with the Fan Club and, in turn, the Beatles was by mail through their official address: Beatles (U.S.A.) Ltd., P.O. Box 505, Radio City Station, New York, New York 10019. The address was legendary and treated with reverence among Beatles fans. Secrecy of the club's office location was always of supreme importance. The director tried to keep the address under the radar for fear too many fans would stop by or organize a vigil in front. In addition, decorum was needed because the fan club was housed in a functioning law office.

I never shared the street address with anyone, primarily fearing that divulging this might be traced back to me. For this reason, I always went alone to the fan club and its related activities. I wanted to share my experiences going to the club, but I was instructed to keep the location private. I would have enjoyed inviting a friend along with whom I could share the excitement afterward, but it never happened. On numerous occasions being a Beatles fan was lonely, and it shouldn't have been that way. Too many parents prohibited their daughters from partaking in the fun of being a fan and looked for excuses to curtail their children's involvement with me and the fan club. I wasn't wild, didn't run around with a bad crowd or get in trouble. Nights were spent doing my homework before any Beatles activities, yet classmates' parents did not see it that way. Some even labeled me a bad influence on their daughters.

From my vantage point, it was Brian Epstein who appreciated the fans. He realized early on the power and influence we had in charting a band's success. Maybe it was the lunchtime crowds at the Cavern Club or what he experienced while managing his record store, NEMS, in Liverpool. For whatever reason, Brian seems to have valued fans and our importance for a band's success. Brian understood that establishing a strong fan base in America was key to the group's initial and ongoing success. That was part of setting that early planning meeting with me back in November 1963, before all the hysteria. It is unfortunate that today the label "fan" all too frequently is a pejorative. Brian would have taken great exception to calling Mark David Chapman "a fan," albeit deranged, as so many in the media do today. I feel the fan stigma never seems to fade; I cringe when called a fan in a certain tone and manner.

Understanding firsthand that a fan club was essential, I called Evelyn Klein in Walter Hofer's office, and she suggested I stop by the next time I was at my grandmother's apartment during the week. That was a serious invite. The first time I went to the law office, I saw very little and remembered even less, but by my next visit the fan club was up and running. It was late March 1964. The Beatles were filming *A Hard Day's Night*, and I had celebrated my fourteenth birthday.

It was also a terrifying time in New York. Kitty Genovese had been brutally murdered in the courtyard of her apartment building as thirty-eight neighbors watched or listened to her screams and did nothing. New York was paralyzed at the inhumanity of this vicious act, and it left an indelible imprint in my mind. My parents were skeptical about in-person fan club visits after this incident. So, at first, I corresponded with innumerable office helpers, who had been hired to work out of a large supply closet, fitted with shelves, in a corner of the law office. By my next visit, the closet was permanently transformed to house the official fan club headquarters of Beatles (U.S.A.) Ltd., and the work area now extended beyond the closet.

I remember one large desk to the left as you entered the space. Two smaller tables to the right held typewriters, black phones, and storage cabinets that housed stacks of fan club materials: membership cards, letterheads, and the official magazine sent out when people joined. Mail was scattered all over the desks, and in the middle of the room were large canvas bags filled to the top with letters. A few years later, there were boxes of "flexies"—the special Christmas messages sent out to members on a flexible cardboard that could be played on your record player, which now sell for hundreds of dollars. The cabinets stood right outside the closet door.

An outside mail fulfillment service was hired to collect the letters at the post office and sort through them, retaining the applications for club membership and processing the $2 membership fee. The service would then send out directly to the new member a welcome letter, membership card, a quarterly newsletter, and the official Beatles Book sold at their concerts. A Beatles fact sheet also included was free for members and twenty-five cents for nonmembers. The printout had a short biography of each Beatle and a chronology listing details about the formation of the group. All other mail was then forwarded to headquarters for answering. Those letters included requests to start chapters, inquiries about when the next Beatles album or single would be released, and how could they meet the Beatles.

The demand for glossy photographs of the Beatles was big. There had never been a photographic sitting for the American Fan Club. Legendary photographer Dezo Hoffmann in England took the photographs that the club offered during the Beatles' early days in 1963. They never had the full Beatles look we loved. These photographic images became familiar because they were reproduced on millions of pieces of Beatles memorabilia and used in magazines and newspapers for years. Fifteen shots in total were available, but the most popular was the 8 x 10 group shot and four individual photos available to fans for one dollar each.

What I couldn't understand is that every time I wrote to the fan club, I received responses from a revolving door of signatures by the person in charge. First there was Marjorie Minshull, then Feather Schwartz, then Charlotte Sharkowitz, followed by Lynn Hargrave (aka Bernice Young), and later Sandi Morse (aka Bernice Young), Sue Clark, Joanne Maggio, and Frances Fiorino who a few years later was the receptionist at Nemperor. Nemperor was Brian's joint venture with attorney Nat Weiss after the departure of Walter and Sondra Hofer from the Beatles (U.S.A.) Ltd.

board of directors. The fan club continued functioning until 1970, when George and the other Beatles abruptly ordered all operations to halt.

Other names were in use, such as Rusty Rahn and Laura Cayne. Check out those signatures: they all look like Bernice Young's writing. The signatures of these various women directors of the club were strangely scribbled on letters and were as confusing as the names themselves. Letters dated less than one month apart in my collection from Feather Schwartz have differing signatures. As a devoted fan, I carefully examined every detail. This was my life. Finally, a woman named Bernice Young responded to my mail, and I visited her at headquarters. By this time, I had organized many of the girls in my high school and started Beatles Fan Club #28. Each chapter across the country was given a designated number.

Because of the TV appearances I later did on behalf of the National Fan Club and other speaking engagements, chapter #28 grew to encompass not just New Jersey but parts of Connecticut, Long Island, Pennsylvania, and upstate New York. Correspondence to my house became so overwhelming that the postman refused to deliver the bags of mail. I was ordered to rent a P.O. box, which I happily did with my saved allowance.

Bernice Young (aka Lynn Hargrave) was a very personable yet officious woman about thirty-five years old. She seemed ancient to be involved with the Beatles. Bernice could not be manipulated by anyone; and as the paid director, she let everyone know she was in charge. Bernice had the best job in the world, and I was set on making her my friend. Bernice had never married and lived with her sister in an apartment on East Thirty-Fourth Street in Manhattan. Our first meeting was short and to the point, but at the end she gave me additional copies of the fan club magazine for the members and told me to keep in touch: big plans were looming, and I would be needed to help. I let Bernice know that I was available day and night.

A few classmates weren't allowed to join the fan club because their parents were opposed to the Beatles and what the group represented. Plotting how they could still be part of the club fell to me. One parent even told my dad he thought the Beatles were subversive communists with long hair. I arranged with those friends that they pay the fee to join, but all mailings would be sent to my house instead of theirs. If they couldn't afford the monthly dues of twenty-five cents to fund our club activities, I would contribute my allowance for each friend to remain in the club. Two friends used my home address, and I used my meager allowance— by now a dollar per week—to keep their dues and membership current. At our fiftieth high school reunion, we all joined together and laughed about the ridiculousness of their parents' fears—mild in comparison to the concerns of today.

Going to the fan club to see Bernice was one of the highlights of the Beatles experience. The place hummed, and I was given simple tasks to perform—sort and respond to correspondence or reply to vendors. I even saw Brian Epstein there twice when he visited with other talent he managed.

Being part of the network of fans was very important. With no internet, we kept in contact through written correspondence. First-class letters were five cents, and what I didn't spend on friends' club dues went for postage. Chapter presidents were sent lists of the other chapter organizers across the country. This is how I learned geography. I had friends from Livermore, California, to Tucson to Shaker Heights and Hollywood, Florida. Ping Tom, were you in Albuquerque? Leslie Cannon, who headed the Hartford club, became a good friend.

Fan club headquarters also established a pen pal exchange with the British fan club. I received my first pen pal's name and address on July 13, 1964, the day before the special *A Hard Day's Night* preview screening. My first pen pal was Vivien, who lived just north of London. Her favorite Beatle was John; in 1966, she visited with my family; and then, in 1967, I saw her in London. I exchanged letters and established friendships with other Beatles fans, too: John Muszynski, from Sherwood Rise in Nottingham; Sue Cooper, in Derby; and Mike Kemble from Merseyside and Eamonn Duncan from Dublin.

I'm still friends with Vivien sixty years later and exchange messages via Facebook. More on Mike Kemble later. As for Sue Cooper, she will always be remembered for sending me the early release of *Beatles for Sale*, which wasn't available here, and a pair of knee-high mod socks identical to the ones Pattie Boyd wore in a photo before becoming George's wife.

With so much happening and the fan club growing, they needed additional office help. Two terrific assistants were hired part-time. Still in high school in Queens, they came to the office after school or dance class and most Saturdays. They were June Taylor dancers who appeared on *The Jackie Gleason Show* that was broadcast from New York before it moved to Miami Beach. Their names were Pam Barlow and Sue Friedman, and they deserved respect for always being considerate. I wrote way too many letters to them and would casually stop by the club unannounced. Yes, they seemed to be Beatles fans, yet they had a life beyond the Beatles, too. Pam's father was a noted musicologist in Manhattan, and through his connections, the friends attended the Beatles Cerebral Palsy fundraiser concert at the Paramount Theater in September 1964. At a post-concert champagne cocktail party, the two women learned the secret location of the fan club. Together they went to the office, where they met Bernice, and learning that the fan club was in dire need of part-time help, Pam and Sue were hired! After I met the Beatles, I made copies of the press

Beatles (U.S.A.) Limited

P. O. BOX 505, RADIO CITY STATION, NEW YORK, NEW YORK 10019

BEATLES FAN CLUB
OFFICIAL HEADQUARTERS

November 15, 1965

Dear Debbie,

Sorry we missed you on Friday, but it was our day off. Thanks a million for the pictures! They bring back such great memories. We didn't expect you to pay for them, and you were much more generous than you needed to be. If there's anything we can do, please tell us. Thanks again — Love, Pam & Sue

Beatles (U.S.A.) Limited

221 WEST 57TH STREET, NEW YORK, N. Y. 10019

3 sets for
Pam, Sue + Bernice

Pam Barlow and Sue Friedman were the two paid assistants to Bernice Young at the fan club. I bothered them a lot. Here's a thank-you note for the photos from the Warwick press conference. Note the address on the small letterhead: it's the fan club's actual street address.

AUTHOR'S COLLECTION

conference photos for each one, hoping that they would add them to the collection that they surely were keeping.

Among the things I remember about Pam and Sue is that each was given a Beatles pendant for Christmas that they wore around their necks. The pendants were beautiful and engraved with "luv from Brian and the Beatles." Many years ago, I connected with Pam, who was also living in Southern California. After sharing remembrances and reminding her who I was, I mentioned the pendant. Pam sorrowfully shared that hers had been stolen. Sue Friedman stayed on with the club longer than Pam and ended up dancing for entertainer Sylvie Vartan across Europe. Sue sadly passed away a few years ago. Pam and Sue were very kind and understanding about my Beatles passion, never ridiculing or demeaning my devotion.

MURRAY THE K, aka THE FIFTH BEATLE

No weeknight was ever complete without hearing the resounding call of DJ Murray the K blasting from the radio—"This meeting of the *Swingin' Soiree* is now in session!"

In New York City, 1010 WINS was the most popular station in bringing Beatles news to their fans. Most fan club members listened to WINS in the evening, especially Murray the K and his *Swingin' Soiree*. The other popular AM stations such as WABeatleC, with most notably "Cousin Brucie" Morrow and Scott "Scottso" Muni, and WMCA with B. Mitchell Reed and Charlie Greer "The Good Guys," perpetually battled for supremacy in covering the Beatles phenomenon. In time, all the top DJs worked at WMCA, but the race was always Murray's to lose. Perhaps Murray took the lead because he was more aggressive and pushier than any of the other DJs. Yet this made Murray the most listened to and respected Beatles DJ.

Murray the K Kaufman had New York City energy and even his own language, "Meusurray," which inserted portions of his name into words. In school we would use his secret language to communicate among ourselves. Originally, Murray promoted many of the doo-wop bands as he moved from station to station, but he lucked out when he joined WINS just as famed DJ Alan Freed was indicted for tax evasion and was forced off the airwaves. Coincidentally, Cousin Brucie was also at WINS at the time, but Murray was given Freed's evening slot from 7 to 10 p.m., and Cousin Brucie moved on to an even more powerful station with greater broadcasting range, WABC.

Besides his radio work, Murray was famous as a concert promoter at small venues. At the Brooklyn Paramount theater during school holidays, Murray with TV presenter and actor Clay Cole would introduce the latest groups and performers to young audiences. Some of the top names he worked with were Dionne Warwick, Smokey Robinson, Little Anthony and the Imperials, Bobby Vinton, and what proved most strategic, The Ronettes.

I say The Ronettes, because it was Ronnie Bennett from The Ronettes (later Mrs. Phil Spector) who gave Murray the inside edge with the Beatles when they landed in New York City on February 7, 1964. Murray always booked The Ronettes for his holiday shows, and the group had enduring loyalty to Murray. So, when they left for England in January 1964, to headline a tour of the United Kingdom (I've read that the Rolling Stones were their opening act), Ronnie met and partied with the Beatles. When Murray heard that Ronnie knew the Beatles, he wasted no time in asking her to arrange an exclusive meeting upon their arrival at the Plaza Hotel. Ronnie worked her magic, because by the time the Beatles spent their first night at the Plaza, Murray was in their suite broadcasting live.

With this special consideration, Murray traveled on the train with the Beatles and entourage to their Washington, DC, Coliseum concert, then to Miami and back to New York with the band. By now he was known as the "Fifth Beatle." There is a discrepancy about how Murray got the Fifth Beatle name. Some reports say that he gave himself the name; Murray said that George Harrison referred to him as Fifth Beatle on the train to Washington because he was always around; Ringo called Murray the Fifth Beatle during an interview. Whatever the source, it was a good tactic to keep other DJs away from the Beatles and Murray's supremacy tops.

We fans didn't care about the radio stations' battles for ratings; Murray brought us exclusives and not just Beatles info. He had the inside track to all the groups that were part of the British Invasion. Accurate information mattered most. It just wasn't all about the songs anymore. We needed to know upcoming tour dates, TV appearances, and the latest gossip. In retrospect, Murray's radio show was the early nonvisual version of Twitter meets celebrity websites.

WINS was always welcoming to listeners stopping by. Several times, I visited the austere old-looking building that sat facing Columbus Circle and Central Park West. A guard who seemed like he had been sitting at the same desk in the lobby for years was also the greeter. Gladly he would phone the office you wanted to visit and direct you to the proper staircase. During school holidays and in the summer of 1964, I would stop by to see Murray the K. Sometimes my friend Sharon came along, but she remembers always waiting outside. He would be doing his radio show, wearing a signature hat—in the summer straw and in the winter a Russian-looking Persian lamb cap—not politically correct these days. Murray was larger than life and spoke his special language, and I would answer right back. I never realized that Murray was the age of my parents.

Murray seldom mentioned his family. In mid-1981, and living in Los Angeles, I heard that Peter Altschuler, Murray's son, was also in LA, and I invited him to dinner. I had originally contacted Peter to participate in the class I was teaching on the Beatles at UCLA. Peter couldn't make it, but we had the chance to meet and talk four years later at Michael McCartney's photographic exhibit that I had arranged in Los Angeles. Murray, Peter explained, was complicated. He had attended a military boarding school as a young man and later served in the army. He had six marriages, including to Jackie Zeman, the actress from the daytime soap *General Hospital* who played the older sister to Luke of "Luke and Laura" fame.

Another question: how does a son have Altschuler as a last name when the K in Murray's name stood for Kaufman? I really got no answer to that one, but he probably was legally adopted by the man his mom subsequently married. I shared with Peter the great times I had had with his dad at the radio station or when I saw him at concerts. It felt awkward because it became apparent that I had had more fun with his dad than he had growing up.

Murray never let anyone leave the station empty-handed. There were WINS bumper stickers and free singles for the asking, and always Murray the K Fan Club (of which I was a proud member) pins and photos.

I remember that it came as a total shock when in February 1965 Murray did his final show on WINS. The station's format was going all news; WINS would no longer be the source for all Beatles and British Invasion information. It was heartbreaking to hear him sign off for the last time. Murray eventually resurfaced at WOR-FM in a brand-new FM format, where he could finally play cuts that ran longer than three minutes and enjoy more creative freedom, but it never had the raw excitement of the WINS broadcasts. Listening to Murray into the night by dim light from the fireflies I had caught in a jar was forever gone.

The last time I saw Murray was at the premiere of the 1979 feature *I Wanna Hold Your Hand* in Westwood, California, in a theater adjacent to the UCLA campus. Murray played himself in the movie. It had been twelve years since I had last seen him in New York. I shook his hand firmly but wanted to hug him. Just seeing Murray made me feel like I was home and safe. Los Angelenos didn't appreciate the importance of Murray in the Beatles' story. They didn't listen to him and his play-by-play nonstop narration of the Beatles' arrival in America in 1964 and summer 1965. Some people standing in the theater lobby couldn't comprehend what all the commotion was about when Murray made his grand entrance.

Peter didn't share with me that Murray was terminally ill when we spoke briefly one afternoon. Murray passed away from cancer in February 1982. To end on a sad note would not be Murray the K appropriate. Murray was about fun and good times. Wanting to dazzle his fans, from time to time, Murray would share something amazing. I'll never forget one afternoon while visiting the station, I picked up a Bobby Darin 45 that was on the console. I was with a friend and commented that Bobby Darin was old school. Murray turned around and said, "Hey, I wrote that song!" We looked closer at the record label, and sure enough Murray had cowritten with Bobby Darin his first big hit, "Splish Splash." Murray was so much more than just the Fifth Beatle.

BEATLES VERSUS ROLLING STONES

The battle started when I told my parents I couldn't go back to sleepaway camp. It was spring 1964; I was already fourteen years old, and I had too much to do that summer. Until then, I had gone for eight weeks every summer to Camp Naiad in Turner, Maine, as I mentioned earlier. It was on a beautiful, serene Maine lake, but I felt like I would just perish for eight weeks looking at fish swim.

Beatles Fan Club would keep me busy along with the highly antici-pated premiere of the Beatles film *A Hard Day's Night* scheduled for July and the group's return to New York City in late August as part of their 1964 cross-country summer tour. I had heard from Murray the K that they would be staying at the Delmonico Hotel on Park Avenue, and I planned to hold a vigil in hopes of getting a slight glimpse of my idols. My parents couldn't ship me off; my camping days were over! After I pleaded my case, Mom and Dad agreed.

Classes ended, and I graduated on June 18, finally heading to high school. While most kids in the class along with their families were rejoic-ing in their child's accomplishments, I was secluded in my bedroom celebrating Paul's birthday with the radio and a cupcake from a Duncan Hines cake mix! Murray the K on WINS was talking Paul's birthday nonstop. My graduation gift was tickets to see that raging bad-boy band the Rolling Stones at Carnegie Hall two days later and a reel-to-reel tape recorder.

Recently I reread in Bill Harry's famed Liverpool music newspaper *Merseybeat* an article on the comparison between the early Beatles and Stones. To paraphrase, the Beatles were supposed to be the clean-cut guys but were drinking madly, carousing, and hanging with the prostitutes in Hamburg, while the bad boys—Brian Jones living the proper country life in Cheltenham and Mick Jagger studying at the London School of Economics—were not the rowdy band painted by the press. History has had much to say on this.

It had been four months since the Beatles made their Carnegie Hall debut, and although I couldn't get tickets to either of the two shows, I was looking forward to seeing the Rolling Stones at that prestigious venue. I didn't comprehend then that having attended the Beatles at *The Ed Sullivan Show* would, in later years, be considered a historic event. At the time, I believed I missed a BIG opportunity not being at Carnegie Hall.

Two people I went with to the Stones' concert, Laura Grygus and Dana Dolan, both older sisters of girls with whom I graduated, gave me some assurance. Pulling up in front of Carnegie Hall, we jumped out of the taxi, only to see Murray the K get out of his car.

Being deeply offended that Murray was sponsoring this rival concert (not comprehending that I was there, too) we three shouted at him, "You stink, Murray!" "If you think so," Murray replied as he tipped his signature straw hat. How could the supposed Fifth Beatle be so betraying? The battle between the Stones and the Beatles had just begun, and parents started to prefer their daughters be Beatles fans rather than chase after Mick, Keith, and Brian. Funny that Bill and Charlie always seemed to be relegated to backup.

As much as I was a self-proclaimed Beatles person, the concert was exciting—in Beatles terms, fab. Forever etched in my head is Mick Jagger wearing a fashion-forward pink shirt, singing "Not Fade Away," and crisscrossing the Carnegie Hall stage playing the maracas. Nearly sixty years later, Mick's prophetic lyrics still ring true. Neither he nor the band has faded away.

A HARD DAY'S NIGHT AND DAY

I was visiting fan club headquarters when a flyer arrived with dates for preview screenings of *A Hard Day's Night*. Tickets would be held for some fan club chapter presidents to attend. Unable to control myself, I asked Bernice Young if I could be included in the group. "Of course," she replied. I returned home dreaming about the film. I couldn't wait. I shared the great news with my club members. They seemed excited, but not in the way I was. Looking back to evaluate why I was always in a state of anxiety, perhaps it was because I was an only child. Life in this insular community in New Jersey was dull and monotonous, and I was simply lonely. Family activities filled the downtime for most of my friends, whereas I was home alone. Beatles activities filled the vacuum and afforded me the opportunity to think beyond the recently opened bowling alley or the after-school hangout, the Wigwam, where many kids congregated, devouring shakes and greasy burgers.

The few times I did enter the Wigwam, I was bullied and taunted by one of the older guys. I don't want to name him, but he was later drafted and sent off to Vietnam, where he was killed in action. This young man has been honored by the town and on the Vietnam Veterans Memorial in Washington, DC. I have stood before his name on the wall with very mixed emotions. Though thankful for his service and for giving his life to what he believed in, I am left wondering what there was about me that made him so mean. Never sharing my fears with anyone, I would walk as fast as I could whenever I saw him approach. So, instead of hanging at the Wigwam, I would pass the building quickly in hopes of not being seen and pause at the adjacent depot where the Short Line bus to New York's Port Authority Bus Terminal would idle, waiting for its final return trip. I wanted to be on that bus.

A Hard Day's Night was shot over a few weeks' time between March and April 1964, after the Beatles returned from their monumental success in the States. The back story of the film is widely known. United Artists asked London-based American film producer Walter Shenson to make a movie with the Beatles so that United Artists could own the soundtrack. They cared little about the film's content, only the music. They had found a loophole in the Beatles' contract with Parlophone that excluded movie soundtracks from their record agreement. Walter always took special delight that this Richard Lester-directed film met with overwhelming critical and everlasting success. I thought surely this masterpiece was Oscar worthy.

One week before the private screening, my mailman delivered the oversized letter containing a large yellow rectangular ticket with the fun logo of the film. Printed in black lettering was "Admit One," Beacon Theatre, Broadway at Seventy-Fourth Street, July 14th at 2:30 p.m. This would be something special; the week couldn't pass fast enough.

Tuesday, July 14, was another hot, humid day, but that didn't deter me from leaving the cooler suburbs of New Jersey for New York. I arrived at the Beacon Theatre three hours early for the first of two preview screenings. A long line had already formed. I found out that other girls had been there since 9 a.m. I took my place, falling into line with fans who loved the group as much as I did. It was fun swapping Beatles stories, and it made the time go quickly. At 2 p.m., the doors opened. We swarmed in, rushing to get a good seat. After securing my place, I felt confident to check out the lobby, never knowing who could show up. People were arriving in limousines and casually taking their seats. Many of the seated fans were screaming even before the film began.

Returning to my seat, I saw that Frank Sinatra Jr. and his female guest had taken the two seats next to me. Everyone in the theater recognized him because seven months earlier, in December 1963, he had been the subject of a huge news story. Sinatra, just nineteen years old, had been kidnapped at Harrah's in Lake Tahoe and held for ransom. His photo had been everywhere. Released two days later after his father paid the demanded $240,000 ransom, his abductors were soon captured and convicted but served only short sentences. He seemed calm after going through such an ordeal.

The lights dimmed, the G7 chord with an added 9th and suspended 4th brought the house down, and the girls didn't stop screaming! I sat there absorbed in the sheer beauty of the Beatles up close and larger than life. The film was even better than expected. I swayed in my seat to the music, and Frank Sinatra Jr. seemed annoyed. In 1984, when the film's producer, Walter Shenson, asked me to participate in the rerelease of *A Hard Day's Night*, I shared details about seeing the film for the very first time. To Walter it seemed like I had just watched the film a few weeks earlier. Curiously, he asked when *was* the last time I had seen *A Hard Day's Night*?

I thought for a moment and replied, "Seventeen years ago."

That is the impact that the film had on devoted fans. We knew the dialogue word for word, especially Grandfather's lines. During that same visit Walter mentioned that *A Hard Day's Night* was the first film in the history of the motion picture industry to ensure a profit while filming was still in progress due to the number of theaters that wanted prints.

The eighty-eight minutes went by so quickly that I wanted to see it again. The ushers tried to move out the resisting fans. I gathered my things and headed for the door. Outside, I spotted a long line. It was for the 6 p.m. showing. If only I could get a ticket. It was almost as if someone had heard my wish because at that minute Charlie Greer, a DJ from WABeatleC Radio, turned and asked, "Would you be interested in seeing the film again? I've got an extra ticket that's not being used."

"Of course, I'd love to see the film again!"

He handed me a pink ticket with 6 p.m. replacing 2:30, and I was in. Watching the film for the second time let me focus on the movie's details, listing the songs on a notepad I always carried for autographs.

Returning to New Jersey that night, I got on the phone to share the details with the fan club members. They would have to wait nearly one month until 7 p.m., Tuesday, August 11, for the big premiere. Tickets would go on sale at the Astor Theatre box office on Wednesday, July 22, $2 for the orchestra and $2.50 for the loge. Continuous performances began across the country on Wednesday, August 12, for $1.75 per ticket. Of course, my friend Sharon and I would be there.

Two days after the preview screenings I attended, I received a telegram from Mike Hutner, director of publicity at United Artists. The studio requested that I mobilize the fan club to camp out on the street in front of the Astor Theatre on July 21, the night before the presale of tickets for the premiere of *A Hard Day's Night*. The studio promised to supply any materials needed to make it a big event worthy of media coverage. At first it seemed like a senseless publicity stunt; something out of an episode of *I Love Lucy* when Lucy and Ethel landed on the top of the Empire State Building dressed as Martians to promote a film so they could each earn $500. We were receiving no payment.

The following day I called Mike's office, as he asked in the telegram. After talking a few minutes, Mike convinced me that no harm was intended; we would be properly cared for with hot chocolate, blankets, and New York's Finest in attendance all night. I promised him that I would be there with friends. The most difficult part was to get our parents' permission. The Times Square area was the worst, populated with prostitutes, drugs, and porn. New York City in 1964 was more dangerous in that area than any other. After much begging and pleading, one friend had a sister in her early twenties who said she'd go with us for protection.

With that assurance, six of us set out for an overnight pajama party on the sidewalks of Times Square.

Sleeping bags in tow, we arrived at the theater in two station wagons, each driven by a parent. By the time we pulled up to the theater entrance around 6 p.m., a few fans were in line. Some were singing Beatles songs from the movie, and others were napping under blankets that the United Artists people handed out. By 9 p.m., as it was growing dark, two guards patrolled the sidewalk as drunken reporters stopped by to cover the event after Happy Hour. The feeling that we were on display began to take shape when the Grey Line sightseeing bus returning from its mid-night nightclub tour stopped to photograph us. Taxicabs cruising down Broadway slowed to gawk, and vagrants saw a good opportunity for a free cup of cocoa and a Chock full o'Nuts whole wheat doughnut topped with powdered sugar.

The night was long and drawn out. I was miserable, as were the friends I had assembled. The sidewalk was hard and cold even though it was summer, and the police were ridiculing us like we were subhu-man creatures. I could tell they didn't appreciate the Beatles. One officer was disgruntled because he could have been home watching *The Beverly Hillbillies* and that sexy Elly May Clampett. One of my friends who joined us but wasn't in the fan club never forgave me for talking her and her parents into participating in this caper. Some friends still talk about it as "the night they will never forget!"

At 7 a.m., we were instructed by a representative from United Artists to line up single file for the ticket sale. We were exhausted and could barely smile, feeling grubby in the same clothes from the previous day. One of the girls managed to stay inside the theater, curled up on the disgusting rug outside of the bathrooms that they had opened for our use.

The following day, the press went for the wrong story when reporting about the Beatles movie campout. One reporter wrote, "Beatle fans and local residents took to the streets last night to celebrate ticket sales for *A Hard Day's Night.*" The article was illustrated with a photograph in the *Daily News* not of fans purchasing the first tickets when the box office opened at 11 a.m., but of two transients sipping cocoa with the fans in the background.

I thought for sure that this masterpiece would win an Oscar. To my disappointment and that of many others, *A Hard Day's Night* wasn't even nominated for Best Picture. The year 1964 proved very competitive for movies, with *My Fair Lady* winning Best Picture pitted against *Becket, Dr. Strangelove, Mary Poppins*, and *Zorba the Greek*.

There was cause for some celebration though. Glued to my TV for the Academy Awards broadcast on April 5, 1965, live from the Santa Monica Civic Auditorium, my friends and I closely followed *A Hard Day's Night.*

Writer Alun Owen, who was nominated for writing the original screenplay, did not prevail; nor did George Martin, who received an Oscar nomination for the film's music, losing to Andre Previn for *My Fair Lady*. The only long-term winner in this overnight fiasco was me, who forever has this crazy story to share.

RINGO FOR PRESIDENT

Summer 1964 was busy with the release of the movie and the excitement of the Beatles' upcoming August return to our shores.

Just as I was recovering from the July excitement of the back-to-back private screenings of *A Hard Day's Night* and the campout in front of the Astor Theatre, I received a phone call from Bernice Young at the fan club.

Would I be willing to represent the National Beatles Fan Club on the *Clay Cole Show*? The appearance would be in connection with the promotion of a new novelty single called "Ringo for President." How exciting! It became obvious to me that these requests were the favors that attorney Walter Hofer had in mind when we met back in 1963.

Clay Cole was a New York tri-state teen phenomenon. His weekly TV show was seen all over the metropolitan area. It differed from Dick Clark's *American Bandstand* in that Clay would dance and perform. In 1961, he played himself in the Chubby Checker film *Twist around the Clock* that also featured Dion DiMucci. Clay Cole was way ahead of his time: he was one of the few white performers to appear at the Apollo Theater in Harlem and bring on show acts ranging from Little Anthony and the Imperials to the Rolling Stones even before their first appearances on *The Ed Sullivan Show*. He was also associated with Murray the K and Beatles impresario Sid Bernstein introducing talent to new audiences at the Brooklyn Paramount during vacation breaks. Always at the cutting edge, the last professional TV show Clay Cole produced was in 2002, in San Remo, Italy, featuring Alicia Keys, Shakira, Kylie Minogue, and Britney Spears, among others. An amazing lineup. Clay Cole passed away at age seventy-two from a heart attack in 2010, at his home in North Carolina. We had just reconnected and become Facebook friends two months before.

Representing the Beatles on TV sounded great, but I had one problem. I had to be at WPIX Channel 11 in New York City at 3:30 p.m., on Friday, August 28, 1964, the same day I also had tickets to see the Beatles perform live at Forest Hills Tennis Stadium in Queens. I had been planning for months to attend. I wasn't sure how to work it all out because the concert began at 8:15 p.m., and the television show taping could go as late as 6 p.m., per the producer.

I needed my parents' guidance. My mother came to the rescue because she was driving my friends and me to the concert in Forest Hills. We would just leave earlier do the TV show and then see the Beatles. My friend Sharon Mercer would come along and wait at the studio during taping.

As Bernice requested, in the confirming letter, I was to gather Ringo items from my collection, to which she would add Ringo mementos to display on the show. I sorted out pictures, a poster, flashing "I Love Ringo" pins, and so on. This was all working out—August 28 would be a fun day.

I can't say I liked the song "Ringo for President." Truthfully, I thought it was dumb. But if the Beatles needed me to represent the fan club, that was my responsibility, and I would see it through no matter how ridiculous I thought it was.

Now, 1964 was a presidential election year. Songwriters Bob Hilliard and Mort Garson who had a #1 hit in 1963, with "Our Day Will Come" for Ruby and the Romantics, caught the Beatles bug and wrote a novelty song, "Ringo for President." Thinking they could cash in quickly on the Beatlemania craze, they wasted no time in getting two labels to release the song. Two versions were recorded. For the British/Australian audience on Columbia Records, Rolf Harris of "Tie Me Kangaroo Down, Sport" fame sang the song.

The stateside version came out on Decca Records, sung by The Young World Singers. The Singers were brought together just to record this novelty song.

I was very nervous when we arrived at the studio on East Forty-Second Street. Following Bernice Young's written instructions, I asked for Terry Bennett. Mr. Bennett was nowhere to be found. Finally, an assistant came forward and brought us all to a waiting room. After a short while, it was my turn for makeup. I don't remember meeting Terry Bennett this first visit.

Walking down the long corridor was excruciating, and my heart was beating rapidly. I looked around the corner, and there were celebrities I recognized: Jay and the Americans—they had hit records. After makeup, I was brought into another room and given a large black-and-white printed poster to carry onto the set. I would join The Young World Singers marching in a circle, parading the sign "Ringo for President."

We rehearsed it once or twice, and then the taping began. Clay Cole's sidekick and announcer, Chuck McCann, made a few jokes, and I remember little more about the show except that I loved seeing Jay and the

Beatles (U.S.A.) Limited

P. O. BOX 505. RADIO CITY STATION. NEW YORK. NEW YORK 10019

BEATLES FAN CLUB
OFFICIAL HEADQUARTERS

August 25, 1964

Miss Debbie Gendler
34 Dacotah Avenue
Oakland,
New Jersey

Dear Debbie:

It was good talking to you today, and I thank you
for agreeing to represent the National Beatles
Fan Club on the Clay Cole show. Just in case
you were too excited to remember, you are to
report to Mr. Terry Bennett at 220 East 42nd
Street in New York City on Friday (August 28) at
3:30 p.m. And take with you as much Ringo
material as you have - I am including with this
letter a photo of him to add to your collection.

While I'm ... I'm going to answer
your le ... ay, as well. The
plans ... ood to me - have
you d ... an to support?
Need ... portunity, I
sha ... attention. It
is ... have their
fan

Unf ... e to arrange
for ... et with the
Beatl ... tell you how much
we wou ... e to arrange it, but
time wou ...

Have fun on Friday, be yourself, and let us know
all about how it came out.

Bernice Young, director of Beatles (U.S.A.) Ltd. phoned me in late August 1964 about representing the Beatles on a TV show to promote the novelty record *Ringo for President*. Here is the letter that confirms the details of my participation. In spite of all the publicity, the record was a flop.
AUTHOR'S COLLECTION

Americans in person. I knew them from *American Bandstand*. Simultaneously, I received the news that the Beatles had arrived at the Delmonico Hotel on Park Avenue and were holding a press conference in the Crystal Ballroom before leaving for the first of two concerts at Forest Hills. As usual the press asked the Beatles ridiculous questions, and fortunately, the Beatles responded in the same tone.

For example, one reporter asked, "It's been said that the Beatles are a threat to public safety. Could you give me your reaction to that, any one of you?"

John responded, "Well we're no worse than bombs, are we?"

And for a follow-up question, "Who do you like for president?" Paul chimed in, "Ringo . . . Johnson's second choice."

Not only was the song inane, but marching in a circle while singing carrying the sign was embarrassing even for a fourteen-year-old and beneath the Beatles' dignity. I was cringing the entire time, hoping that people in my town would not be watching this show.

Still clutching the sign "Ringo for President" as the performers finished the song, it was my turn to answer questions about the fan club and why Ringo should be elected president. I gave a crazy answer that Ringo was smart and so cute. Then with a laugh Chuck McCann said that Ringo couldn't be president because he wasn't born in this country.

Not knowing what to say, I responded, "Isn't England the mother country?"

They must have liked that response because I was invited back several times to answer fans questions about the Beatles in my own reoccurring segment. Sometimes my friend Sharon even came along to be on TV, too.

And, by the way, the record "Ringo for President" was a flop.

SEEING DOUBLE

THE BEATLES AT FOREST HILLS TENNIS STADIUM

The late Friday afternoon drive from WPIX TV Studios on East Forty-Second Street where I had just finished an interview representing the Beatles Fan Club and "Ringo for President" to Forest Hills Tennis Stadium in Queens was slow. My friend Sharon and I kept asking my mom to drive faster, but traffic was at a standstill with people heading leaving the city for the final weekend of summer. Sharon and I were finally on our way to see the Beatles in concert, so truly nothing else mattered.

I had closely followed the Beatles' arrival earlier that month at Los Angeles International Airport. After a few press questions, they boarded their rented jet for San Francisco, where ten thousand fans gathered to welcome them to the city. There had never been a tour like this anywhere in the world. By the time the tour was over, the Beatles had stopped in twenty-four cities in thirty-four days, covering forty thousand miles and playing thirty-two concerts.

It had been reported that the San Mateo County sheriff's office had been prepared for the overwhelming crowd that showed up, but when Paul McCartney mumbled "Hello" into a microphone, the entire five-foot fence built for the Beatles' protection gave way to pushing fans. The 180 police deputies on hand to control their arrival could not manage the hysterical fans, so the Beatles dashed to a waiting car and on to the Hilton Hotel. The evening after the Beatles' arrival in San Francisco, they made their first appearance on this tour at the Cow Palace. The giant auditorium's seventeen thousand seats had been sold out for more than three months. Several thousand fans showed up without tickets, hoping to catch a glimpse of their idols. This was reenacted at every concert performance the Beatles gave.

Now it was our turn to welcome them back to New York City. Fortunately, I was able to buy four tickets to the first of two concerts scheduled for Friday, August 28, and Saturday, August 29. As my mom pulled up to the stadium entrance through a residential area, it didn't look like a typical stadium venue. Beautiful trees lined the street along with very impressive Tudor-style brick homes. My mom would wait for us at the apartment of my aunt's best friends who lived on Austin Street just two blocks away. Sharon and I walked into the stadium. Neither Sharon nor I remember who the other two friends were.

Forest Hills was the home of the US Open Tennis Championships where Billie Jean King and Jimmy Connors would play. The stadium with nearly sixteen thousand seats was a complete sellout. It wasn't just the Beatles I was excited about seeing that night. I had made friends with other fan club chapter presidents, one of whom was Leslie Cannon from Hartford. Leslie and I wrote continuously to each other about club activities. When we discovered that we were both coming to this show, we made plans to finally meet in person.

Leslie had brought several of her fan club members along, but one special member was Buddy Bailey of Wethersfield, Connecticut. Buddy was older than we were, but what really stood out was that he was a Paul McCartney look-alike. Wherever Buddy went, people would chase him thinking that he was Paul. This night was no different. Leslie and I were to meet near Gate B at 7:45 p.m. and had exchanged photos so we could recognize each other. I stood there waiting and finally saw her with Buddy. Hordes of girls were chasing Buddy and Leslie. I tried to catch them by shouting out who I was, but Leslie was too busy running after Buddy to protect him from the fans who thought he was Paul McCartney. The police joined in the chase. It was a scene right out of *A Hard Day's Night*.

By now it was just past 8:15 p.m., and the show was beginning. The first act, the Bill Black Combo, was starting their set. I was desperate to meet Leslie but was told to take my seat, which I did obediently. Next came The Exciters, Jackie DeShannon sporting a bright yellow suit that I clearly still remember, followed by the Righteous Brothers. Fans were just as intolerant as at the Sullivan show six months before. We had come to see the Beatles, and instead we were sitting through an hour and a half of other acts. Through this I kept a lookout for Leslie but couldn't see her. All of us in the stands grew restless because it was getting late, and the Beatles still hadn't arrived. It wasn't until about 9:50 p.m., when we all looked up, first heard and then saw a helicopter hovering over the grass courts. The Beatles had arrived, and the stadium went crazy with screams. We later heard that the Beatles were delayed because the pilot was not *properly* cleared for departure.

A moment later, out came the Beatles onto the stage, and they played the first few notes of "Twist and Shout." It seemed like the stadium lights came up, but it was just flashbulbs going off. Girls were running to the stage, most captured by the police before they made it close to the Beatles. One girl whose name I later read as Mary Smith made it to the stage and tightly held onto George until the police pried her away, hauling her off the stage. I was enjoying the show and the screams but was distracted looking for Leslie. And then out of the darkness, right by the gate where I was to meet Leslie, stood Buddy Bailey surrounded by two police officers. He was being escorted out of the stadium, with Leslie following him closely. The Beatles played twelve songs, the entire show lasted thirty minutes, and it was over. What a concert. I had a sore throat from screaming, as did probably every person in attendance.

I didn't get to meet Leslie or Buddy that night and sadly, they both missed a great show. Even Nora Ephron, who was sent to cover the concert for the *New York Post*, reported that a Paul look-alike had caused a near riot. Eventually Leslie and I lost touch, but I forever kept Buddy Bailey in mind. Whenever I traveled through Connecticut, I would look for the Wethersfield exit and keep a lookout. With the help of the internet, I finally located Buddy after fifty-four years of searching. In September 2018 we met at a New York City restaurant for dinner. Although he looked nothing like Paul, it was still an enthralling evening.

Buddy later shared that Leslie has passed away, as had our other friend, Gene Milbier, who ran the Springfield, Massachusetts, fan club. Buddy still is an avid Beatles fan, and we spent the evening reminiscing. Although I barely heard the Beatles play a single note that night, it was my favorite Beatles concert of all. The venue was intimate despite the eight-foot-high fence topped with barbed wire, and not hearing them sing seemed unimportant. If fans wanted to listen to the Beatles, they could play their records at home. Sharon and I were in heaven.

VIGIL ON PARK AVENUE

The momentum was in high gear! The day after the *Clay Cole Show* taping and the Beatles' Forest Hills concert, the craziness continued. I discovered that fans would spend the next day outside New York's Delmonico Hotel where the Beatles were staying on the nineteenth floor. It was widely reported that the Plaza didn't want them back. Brian Epstein had a difficult time trying to find a hotel that would welcome the Beatles. With time running out, Brian turned to Ed Sullivan. Mr. Sullivan had his permanent residence in the Delmonico. It was only due to his influence with the management that the Beatles were welcome to stay there.

When I arrived at the Delmonico at the corner of Fifty-Ninth Street and Park Avenue early Saturday morning, the conservative, upper-crust sophistication of the exclusive area was under Beatles siege. Girls running down the sidewalk with their transistor radios up against their ears were desperately trying to get the latest Beatles news updates. Many wearing "I Love the Beatles" pins from the concert the night before were shrieking, retelling their stories of seeing the Beatles. A few were beyond excited because they were going back to Forest Hills to see them in a second concert that evening. We were all instructed to congregate across the street from the hotel, where additional barricades had been set up, and the police were ready for action. All eyes were focused on the nineteenth floor. What we didn't know is that inside the hotel after the concert, the Beatles had met Bob Dylan and, if reports are correct, enjoyed marijuana and other goodies that he had brought to share.

At one point a few girls came out of the hotel. They were so lucky. In another suite was Cousin Brucie Morrow of WABeatleC. The station was broadcasting live, and we all tried desperately to get his attention from the street. He described what the Beatles were having for lunch and how they were passing time in their suite. At one point I heard reports that more than ten thousand fans were crowding the surrounding streets.

While keeping vigil, I met two girls from Brooklyn who also had been at the concert the night before and were also members of the Fan Club.

They spent their entire summer staking out Radio City Station Post Office to catch a glimpse of anyone retrieving Beatles mail in hopes of following them to the secret office. When I heard that, I decided I had better not share too much information.

Queued up along Park Avenue we were singing Beatles songs, screaming each Beatle's name, and doing anything to get their attention. We were all asking each other, "Who's your favorite Beatle?" George fans blasted John fans. Ringo fans shouted back at Paul fanatics. I couldn't get enough of the fun. My friends back in New Jersey were really missing out by not being here.

Girls kept trying to sneak into the hotel. I heard about one girl, Angie McGowan, who crossed the barricades in the early morning hours when the Beatles returned to the hotel after the first Forest Hills concert. Angie caught up with Ringo and pulled his St. Christopher medal and chain from his neck. It was a devastating loss for Ringo, who cherished the medal because it was a gift from an aunt. St. Christopher is the patron saint for travel; losing that medal on a trip was scary.

Cousin Brucie, firmly entrenched in the hotel to interview the Beatles, heard about the loss of the St. Christopher medal and broadcast what happened to the fans. Angie realized that what she had taken was meaningful to Ringo. So, after a telephone conversation with Cousin Brucie, she and her mom returned to the Delmonico the following day to give Ringo back his chain and medal.

He was very gracious and kind, posing for photos and giving autographs to Angie and the friends she had brought along. Jeez . . . she got to meet Ringo. I was learning that being polite and obeying the rules weren't always rewarded.

FANS HELP OTHERS TO SOMETIMES HELP THEMSELVES

PART 1—THE DANCE

It already had been the best summer ever: *A Hard Day's Night* preview screening, staging a sleep-in on Broadway to promote the sale of movie tickets, the official film premiere, and the anticipation of going to seeing the Beatles perform at Forest Hills at the end of August.

About two weeks before the Forest Hills concert, I had received a letter from Bernice Young to let me know that she had given my name to Norman Kimball of the United Cerebral Palsy Association of New York. Mr. Kimball, director of public relations and fundraising, would contact me about "An Evening with The Beatles" planned for September 20 at the Paramount Theatre in New York City to benefit United Cerebral Palsy. Steve Lawrence and his wife, Eydie Gorme, who had emceed the cerebral palsy telethons for the previous four years, were again going to host.

"How exciting. I wanna go."

This letter was the first I had heard about the Beatles performing again in New York. There was no publicity yet, and I needed to find out how to get tickets. Sure enough, the following day, just as Bernice wrote me, I received a call from Mr. Kimball asking for help in trying to get fans to buy tickets. He said they would sell the more expensive seats to supporters of the organization, but they needed fans to be in the audience, too. I assured him that would be easy to do because it was the Beatles. Then he shared the bad news: tickets were selling from between $100 and $25 each. Beatles' seats for Forest Hills or other venues on this tour averaged $5 each. Some lesser-priced seats had already been reserved for select groups. *How could any of us afford that*, I wondered? I told Mr. Kimball I would call him back the next day with some ideas. I had to think.

At fourteen years old, all I knew about charity fundraising was Jerry Lewis's annual telethon to raise money for the Muscular Dystrophy Association. Every Labor Day weekend my mom would watch the show throughout the night. I remembered that people would come on and donate proceeds from their local fundraising efforts to the national organization. The organizer of the charitable event would present a check to

Jerry Lewis, and he would be most appreciative and shake their hand, sometimes even give the donor a hug and kiss. How could the fan club raise money quickly so we could go onstage and present our check to the Beatles?

The next day I phoned Mr. Kimball back and cautiously asked if substantial money could be raised, would it be possible to present a check directly to the Beatles at the charity show? Mr. Kimball agreed that was a well-thought-out plan where he would be certain of having fans there. "Do it," he assured me, "and then we can arrange for you and your club members to meet the Beatles." It was a dream come true. Now all I had to do was come up with a way to get donations fast.

A day later, another letter arrived. It was a form letter announcing the sale of tickets to fan club chapter presidents and their members with an RSVP card to be returned with a check or money order. The letter was signed Jane Pickens Langley. Mrs. Langley, originally from Georgia, had been a popular singer who had appeared on TV, Broadway, and radio. She lived on posh Park Avenue and was a noted socialite and philanthropist who enjoyed regularly being featured on the society pages. After her first husband, a stockbroker, passed away, she married Walter Hoving, who had owned Tiffany's and the department store Bonwit Teller. As a charitable organization, United Cerebral Palsy particularly interested Mrs. Langley because her daughter suffered from the affliction.

I called an emergency meeting of the club. Fortunately, it was summer, and most members were home. We only had five weeks to raise a significant amount money to donate. The pressure was on. How a dance came up I can't quite remember, but we all felt we could accomplish this before school started right after Labor Day.

We split up into committees—advertising, organizing, refreshments, cleanup, finding a band and a venue, and getting a celebrity to attend. With our parents help and the community pitching in, we were confident this could be a success. First, we secured the location. The Veterans of Foreign Wars (VFW) a few years earlier had opened a meeting place, American Legion Hall Post No. 369, on Oak Street in Oakland, with a large space perfect for dancing with an elevated stage. It was surrounded by an easily accessible parking lot. The veterans donated the location to our cause. The Embers, a local band headed by a fellow high school student, agreed to play for free. We would serve lemonade, homemade cookies, and pound cake slices that would sell for twenty-five cents each. The entrance fee for the dance would be seventy-five cents per person. We made posters and designed flyers that we printed in my basement on the trusty mimeograph machine that I had purchased to produce a newsletter. My dad, his pal, and additional friends, "Special" Civil Defense (CD) police officers who volunteered in Oakland, would provide security for the dance. The only thing missing was a celebrity. Finding one fell to me.

I needed a known talent who was interested enough to attend a teen dance and had a connection to the Beatles. Inviting a DJ from a radio station was an obvious choice. I frantically made phone calls to several New York City stations we all listened to daily. First, I contacted 1010 WINS's Murray the K, then WABC's Cousin Bruce Morrow and "Scottso," Scott Muni. Then I contacted WMCA looking for one of their "good guys" to attend.

Nothing shocked me more than getting a call back from Scott Muni's assistant, who told me he that would love to drive out after his radio show ended at around 10 p.m. He hoped that wouldn't be too late. Were they joking? Dana Dolan, the older sister of one of my classmates, was instrumental in getting Scott Muni to agree to attend. Dana had guts, ambition, and foresight. She showed up at the radio station in person and backed up my initial request using her special talents. Scottso took a liking to Dana and agreed on the spot to do it. This would be the biggest event ever to hit Oakland, New Jersey, and we were just a few weeks away from getting a hug from a Beatle.

We had presold about one hundred tickets and were feeling good about the dance because throughout the week Scott Muni promoted that he would be in Oakland at the Beatles Fan Club dance on Friday night. The stage was set. At around 8 p.m., the kids rolled in. I couldn't believe the numbers. The ticket takers kept selling tickets even as the line grew longer and longer. By 9:30 p.m., they had sold an additional two hundred tickets. The Embers blasted their music, and the kids danced madly, anticipating Scott Muni's arrival. The local veterans who hung out at the American Legion Hall also were waiting for Scott Muni. They all congregated in the basement of the building where the bar was located, and they were having a good time in their own special way.

With the radio blasting on WABeatleC, Scott Muni signed off for the evening right at 9:55 p.m. and told his audience he was headed to Oakland. Oakland is about twenty-six miles from the George Washington Bridge, the last western outpost of Bergen County. Set in the valley adjacent to the Ramapo Mountains and river of the same name, the population of Oakland was just about twelve thousand in 1964 and considered a working-class town; many of the residents were employed at the Ford plant in Mahwah.

Oakland and the adjacent town of Mahwah can claim one very influential resident—Les Paul and his then wife, Mary Ford. Les Paul invented the solid-body electric guitar that made the sound of rock 'n' roll possible. He is the only person to be both inducted in the Rock & Roll Hall of Fame and the National Inventors Hall of Fame. In the 1990s Paul McCartney

Beatles (U.S.A.) Limited

P. O. BOX 505, RADIO CITY STATION, NEW YORK, NEW YORK 10019

BEATLES FAN CLUB
OFFICIAL HEADQUARTERS

August 12, 1964

Miss Debbie Gendler
34 Dacotah Avenue
Oakland,
New Jersey 07436

"AN EVENING WITH THE BEATLES"
141 East 40th Street, New York 16, N.Y. • MO 1-0900

Please enter my reservation for "AN EVENING WITH THE BEATLES" on Sunday evening, September 20th, 1964, 8:30 P.M., New York Paramount Theatre, as follows:

Orchestra:

.... Seats @ $100.*
.... Seats @ $ 50.*
.... Seats @ $ 25.
*Includes Champagne Supper

Balcony:

.... Seats @ $25.
.... Seats @ $15.
.... Seats @ $10.
.... Seats @ $ 5.

Enclosed is my check for $...........................

☐ I cannot attend, but enclose my contribution for $...........................

NAME ....ZONE...........STATE...........

ADDRESS...

CITY...........

Please make your check payable to UNITED CEREBRAL PALSY
(Your contribution is income tax deductible)

.... have as much success with her.

By the way, we have given your name to Mr. Norman Kimbell
of the United Cerebral Palsy Associations, and he will
probably be contacting you in reference to the Beatles'
Charity Show which is planned for September 20. I am
sure that you will give him your whole-hearted cooperation
.... I am not sure precisely what it is that he wants
but as I understand it, it is little more that helping to

Here's a letter from Bernice Young at Fan Club Headquarters notifying me to expect a phone call
from Norman Kimball of United Cerebral Palsy to assist with the Beatles fundraiser scheduled
for September at the Paramount Theater in New York. It seemed like an opportunity to do good.
Instead, it was a major disaster and a learning experience that has stayed with me forever.
AUTHOR'S COLLECTION

visited Les Paul at his home studio right on the Oakland/Mahwah border just off Ramapo Valley Road. It was also around this time that the Short Line Bus Company established a regular route to Port Authority Bus Terminal in New York; that opened Oakland to becoming the borough it is today with much easier accessibility to New York City.

It was getting close to Scott Muni's estimated arrival time, and the band kept telling the kids he would be here at any moment. I had given Scottso very detailed driving instructions, and I got nervous that the kids and their parents complained. It was already past curfew for many. Without cell phones, we didn't know where Scott Muni was. My dad had an idea. He would take a police car to look for the missing Scottso.

At about 11:30 p.m., accompanied by police car sirens and flashing lights, Scott Muni drove right up to the stage area to 150 cheering fans. Many had already left. He had gotten caught in the Labor Day traffic escaping the city. Immediately Scott took to the stage and introduced the band individually, handed out his signature "Muni Money," signed autographs, and related a fun story about WABeatleC and the Beatles.

Then there was a short break, and Scott Muni disappeared.

Sharon and I searched all over, only to find him cornered by the VFW downstairs at the bar drinking beer. What? We had waited all night, only to have him join the VFW after twenty minutes.

I marched downstairs and took him kindly by the hand, smirking at the VFW men. How could they? Even today, sixty years later, I harbor a deep sense of hostility toward the Oakland VFW.

Scott returned to the stage for another hour. We gave him the biggest scream when he said he would be interviewing the Beatles on television on September 18. He posed for pictures with those who had had the stamina to remain. It was nearly 1 a.m. when Scott pulled away in his white Pontiac, heading back to New York City.

FANS HELP OTHERS TO SOMETIMES HELP THEMSELVES

PART 2—THE DONATION

Late Saturday morning the club members met at my house and counted the proceeds from the dance. After a few expenses, we had an amazing $275 to be donated to United Cerebral Palsy. The fundraiser was a huge success, and we were on our way to hand a check directly to the Beatles and get our hugs. Mr. Kimball had promised.

The charity show was just two weeks off, and we were confident that we'd be there. I phoned Mr. Kimball to let him know about the dance's success. He seemed very pleased and told me he'd let me know in a few days about the arrangements to present the check to the Beatles as promised. As entering high school freshmen, we gathered in our new school cafeteria at lunchtime chatting about the Beatles and waiting for Mr. Kimball's instructions. Other classmates who didn't participate in the fan club chapter regarded us as strange as we walked around nodding to each other in a secret code of anticipation of the big day.

When I didn't hear from Mr. Kimball, I called again. This time the secretary did not put me through. Mr. Kimball was busy. I called back again and was told the same thing. Now, we were just a few days away from the event. I phoned again. This time Mr. Kimball got on the phone. Sternly, unlike his previous friendly tone, Mr. Kimball let me know that Jane Pickens Langley had decided that we would not be permitted to give the Beatles the check. She simply didn't "fancy" the idea.

"You told me on the phone, Mr. Kimball, that if we raised the money, we could personally hand it over to the Beatles. You promised!"

Mr. Kimball barely spoke.

"But at least we would be able to go to the show and just give someone there the donation," I pleaded.

"No, sorry. Put the check in the mail, and I will get it to the right place," was Mr. Kimball's reply. "And the tickets are sold out," he added.

"What? That really can't be! We worked so hard to raise the money."

All my reasoning proved futile. I hung up the phone not knowing how to tell my friends. The following day at lunch I shared the disappointing news, and we all ate in total silence, unable to even look at each other. At just fourteen, this was for many the first crushing blow received from the adult world. For me personally, it was simply the beginning.

Two days before the concert, I was listening to WABeatleC radio. The station was sponsoring a giveaway for two $100 tickets to the benefit. My breathing stopped as I heard a familiar voice. It was Scott Muni, and he had someone on the phone.

"Cheryl Goodman of Laurelton, Queens, is that you?" he asked.

A meek voice on the other end said, "Yes."

"You're the winner of the two $100 tickets to attend the United Cerebral Palsy benefit and not only that, but you get to go to the champagne party after the concert, and you get to meet the Beatles!"

My heart sank with sadness and disappointment. We did all the work, raised money, and none other than our own Scott Muni gave it all away. It was a hard lesson to learn: things aren't always fair.

You can hear Scott Muni make that phone call at http://www.music radio77.com/images/winnerscottso.mp3.

And the money we raised? Jane Pickens Langley, so sorry; I sent the check to our regional Cerebral Palsy Center of Bergen County, which sincerely appreciated the fan club's dedication and effort to help others and not themselves.

MEET THE PARENTS

TEDDY AND MERA

Just a few years ago, my cousin Sue, with whom I haven't had a close relationship until recently, commented that I was very spoiled, and my parents never said no to anything. At first, I was annoyed by her comment and thought she was wrong. In time, though, I do agree that my parents, Teddy and Mera, rarely said no. But was this a big negative, as Sue implied? I don't believe so.

Agreed: my Beatles exploits were indulged and wholeheartedly supported by my parents; without them, this would be a very brief story. The Beatles adventures had to be helped along at the outset; I was too young to drive, had no money, and depended on my parents—as everyone does—if they're lucky enough to have two great parents. They figure prominently in this story, albeit in the background, but I owe it all to them and never dismiss their contribution. The most frequent question people ask about my exploits with the Beatles is what about your parents? How were you able to do all these things? How did you get them to let you be so free at such an early age? Are they referring to wild schemes such as sleeping overnight on the streets of New York waiting for a movie premiere or walking through the East Village at age sixteen at night? How *could* they allow me to do all this?

A few of my Beatles Fan Club members couldn't even have their club membership cards sent to their house for fear of their parents' anger. When we graduated from eighth grade, many of the girls received sparkling necklaces to mark the milestone. I received a Concord reel-to-reel sixteen-track tape recorder that I desperately wanted, along with Rolling Stones tickets. By positioning my shortwave radio in front of the microphones, that device enabled me to tape the BBC's *Top of the Pops* radio show. Listening to the latest music and pop culture news out of England afforded me the edge to keep ahead of the pack. Without my parents' love, support, and understanding, none of this could have happened.

My dad, Teddy, was born and grew up in New York's Lower East Side, the son of Russian immigrants, and found that he had a talent for dance and ultra-left-wing politics. In 1938, my dad was among the first men Martha Graham welcomed into her all-female dance troupe. He performed with Martha Graham while attending CCNY until World War II came calling. He became a tech sergeant in an army radar unit stationed in France and Germany, lighting the runway for nighttime aircraft raids.

When my dad returned, he finished his education. Much to his dislike, he was relegated to working in my mom's family clothing manufacturing business. He had a showman's personality that made him always the center of attention when he walked into a room. Burgeoning Broadway talent such as Betty Comden and Adolph Green were his pals; they would frequently visit and share their latest compositions such as "Singin' in the Rain" or "Just in Time." The actor John "Julie" Garfield (he died when I was only two) was a friend from the Lower East Side and later the Bronx.

When I fell in love with the Beatles, it brought show biz and music back to his everyday existence. He appreciated their raw talent, humor, and energy. My dad understood the undying love that I had for the band. Not everyone could be open to uncharted territory.

My dad took the most abuse because of the Beatles. Every day, and I mean every day, my dad arrived home with newspapers, teen magazines, paperbacks, Beatles trinkets from W. T. Grant (a store like Woolworth's), all to support my interest in the Beatles.

His pals would chide and mock him; why are you spending money on this junk? What is wrong with you? These guys are worthless, just an overnight fad, and here you are buying four plastic dolls with instruments to please your daughter, items she will throw away. He would share with my mom and me the comments he received, with friends even calling the Beatles anarchists and worse. These acquaintances in New Jersey had no clue about his politics in the thirties. This was not anarchy. They didn't get it, living in their small-minded parochial environment. My dad would laugh back in a knowing way, but their reaction never deterred him from bringing home nightly surprises.

My mom and dad generally would take turns driving me (many times with friends) to fan meetings, concerts, interviews, television shows, waiting hours sometimes in the bitter cold or sweltering summer all with good-natured unequivocal support. How they enthusiastically drove through dense fog to Alexander's on Route 4 in Paramus because Beatles hairspray had arrived—that was beyond the cause.

I never took the opportunity to ask why they felt it so vital to support my Beatles interest. One night, though, I overheard my mom explaining to someone over the phone: she was happy that I was focused and reading newspapers, show business trade papers, and books, no matter what the subject. They encouraged my devotion to all things British and supported my voluminous and expensive, for the time, correspondence with worldwide pen pals and fan club members across the country. I was also respectful and did not lie or deceive them about my exploits to get out of the house, as some did with their parents. I learned to have utmost regard for my parents as people, not solely authority figures who set the rules.

As I evaluate my parents' actions, I believe their objective was to give me direction, support, and independence to shape my future, however that appeared to the outside world. As I got more involved in the fan club, learning how organizations function, businesses grow, and the entertainment industry operates, I wanted to learn even more. I began to delve into subjects my parents didn't understand, and I enjoyed being with them and their inquisitive friends, sharing the details of what I had absorbed.

I started to speak a different lingo—box office grosses and ratings, audience shares, viewer demographics, publicity campaigns, and to succeed I had to keep up with the necessary tools of the industry. . . a subscription to *Variety* (my bible), *The Village Voice*, and *Billboard*. Attending *The Ed Sullivan Show* or *Hullabaloo* was not any longer just to scream or watch Lada Edmunds Jr. go-go dance in the cage on set, but to observe the mechanics of how a television show comes together. I believe hidden in this is the only logical answer. They respected my interests, nurtured them, and provided me the foundation and tools upon which I could build a rewarding career and a life. They were being *parents*.

My dad didn't live to see me graduate from college, be hired at CBS, get married, become a parent, or appreciate the Beatles' impact still going strong sixty years later. He had no inkling how precious those twenty-five-cent magazines would become or see my family hanging with Mike McCartney and family. Life has its subtle way of working things out and giving meaning to what we can't always explain.

I think he had the last laugh.

NOTHING IS REAL

Using alternative names to protect the innocent was standard procedure in the Beatles Empire and Brian's other talents. I'm not sure who first decided that pseudonyms were needed for nearly everyone working around the Beatles, sometimes even the Beatles themselves, but alternative names were often assigned. I've read that PR guru Tony Barrow thought it a good idea to protect the people who were doing the work from fans and other nuisances.

Anne Collingham, the official Beatles Fan Club secretary in London and the teen everyone wanted to be, was a fictitious person, as I discovered. I spent two years writing letters to Anne. In London there were so many names that no one knew who was legit—along with Anne, there were Bettina Rose, Mary Cockram (who posed as Anne), Yvonne Sainsbury, Monica Stringer, Maureen Donaldson, Val Sumpter, and the lone male fan clubber, Michael Crowther-Smith. As at Beatles (U.S.A.) Ltd., where Bernice Young functioned under multiple names, the British Club under Tony Barrow's direction seemed to do the same. What best represents this craziness was *The Beatles Monthly* magazine. This official British Beatles Fan Club publication was distributed from December 1963 through June 1968. It was a small magazine that could easily be carried inside one's three-ring school notebook, hidden from teachers and parents. I loved receiving every issue in the mail. In-depth interviews about the Beatles and others associated with their organization were aimed at a fifteen-year-old reading level. The monthly had great insider photographs, whether from the set of *Help!* or a Beatle enjoying a cup of tea at home. Each issue had printed lyrics to a Beatles song and articles that would keep us up to date on upcoming important tours, personal appearances, vacations, and studio recording sessions.

Most fun for me was the listing of people from around the world wanting to meet fellow fans. It was difficult to add your name to the pen pals list. Finally, after many attempts I found my name in print. It was exciting. Requests came from fans in Tokyo (Shinichi Sato), Rotterdam (Wilem ver Dietz), and San Sebastian (Rosa Velez). I shared these new pen pals with members of Beatles Fan Club #28, and we would spend afternoons writing messages to our far-off friends about the latest in Beatles news. Shinichi was especially communicative and would send us packages of photos, postcards, and other fun items celebrating the 1964 Tokyo Olympics.

Like the nonexistent Anne Collingham and Lynn Hargrave, *The Beatles Monthly* had its share of fictional characters.

First publisher Sean O'Mahony of Beat Publications, who published the magazine, used the name Johnny Dean. Tony Barrow, the Beatles' PR manager who worked with the media for years, used the name Frederick James. I later learned that they were his middle names.

What proved most disturbing was that the Beatles' roadie, Neil Aspinall, used the name Billy Shepherd. I never understood the need for this, but I'm guessing that due to the vast number of invasive and inquiring fans, privacy proved important to the entire management team. These were the insiders whose insights I devoured each month; to find out that they didn't exist was devastating.

In mid-1976, publisher Sean O'Mahony revived the magazine and reissued the complete set of seventy-seven original monthlies between 1976 and 1982. With the Beatles' popularity still going strong, he decided that he would publish new editions for a few years. That lasted until early 2003. Even though I look back now with no bad feeling for Johnny Dean, the insightful information these "people" gave us was indispensable.

Even Paul McCartney used different names, some considered artistic license—Bernard Webb, Paul Ramon, Percy "Thrills" Thrillington, Billy Martin, A. Smith, Clint Harrigan, Sam Browne, among others. Ringo, John, George also went by other names—Apollo C. Vermouth, Richie Monaco, Carl Harrison (after Carl Perkins I am sure), Mel Torment, Ognir Rats, and Johnny Silver. Today I continue to have questions about many names, not knowing who was real.

SID BERNSTEIN HERE

The last time I saw Sid Bernstein he was strolling leisurely down Fifth Avenue flanked by two of his children, arm in arm. It was a mild day, and the sidewalk was crowded. I was in New York for a meeting with A&E television executive Kris Slava for the upcoming television special *Heroes for the Planet with Charlotte Church* that Weller/Grossman was producing for the network. I was ahead of schedule, so when I spotted Sid, I had to stop.

Sid looked much older than when I had last seen him, easily thirty years before, but that was to be expected. But in my mind, time was frozen when it came to the Beatles. Still, Sid was so very recognizable and had a great smile. He didn't remember who I was when I walked up to him and his two children, reintroducing myself. I repeated my name and reminded him of his many kindnesses to me on numerable occasions years before. It was OK. Just standing there for an instant felt special.

To a Beatles fan, Sid Bernstein was an icon in the most pristine terms. He identified the Beatles' talent long before anyone else and persuaded Brian Epstein to bring them to the States. Sid was so secure in their prospects for superstardom that he would put his name, money, and reputation on the line trying to convince Brian Epstein in early 1963 to bring them across the pond. From my reading, not from what Sid told me, he was taking a class at the New School for Social Research and was assigned to read British newspapers. Because he was involved in music promotion and management, articles on the Beatles and the sensation they were causing across the United Kingdom and Europe piqued his interest. Sid tracked down Brian Epstein at his parents' home in Liverpool in early 1963, and a complicated business relationship took off.

Brian's reluctance to commit to concert dates in New York frustrated Sid but did not deter him from his goal. That determination is what made Sid Bernstein a risk-taking showman. Sid was undying in his resolve about the Beatles' eventual success. He kept after Brian until his New York visit to secure *The Ed Sullivan Show* for the Beatles in early November

1963. It was during this same visit that Sid offered the Beatles $6,500 for two shows at Carnegie Hall. Brian accepted. Sid felt that with their Sullivan appearance just days before, he was assured of a complete sellout. The two shows on February 12, 1964, were a huge success; even Happy Rockefeller, the wife of then New York governor Nelson Rockefeller, was in attendance.

After the Beatles performed at Carnegie Hall, Sid himself became a celebrity. Articles in my scrapbook feature Sid being interviewed by all the top New York City press outlets. Sid eventually became famous not just for organizing Beatles performances: he booked all the major British bands such as the Kinks and the Rolling Stones, the Animals, the Moody Blues, Manfred Mann, The Zombies, and American bands such as the Blues Project and Blood, Sweat & Tears. Sid's best venue was the Academy of Music on Fourteenth Street and Third Avenue in Manhattan. Built as a movie theater in 1927, it was a great place to see groups. With just around three thousand seats, it was intimate but old and dumpy; the springs popped out of the seats. Who cared? This venue is where I first met Sid Bernstein.

I had purchased four tickets to see Herman's Hermits on a Saturday afternoon in June at the Academy of Music. The order was for three of the most expensive tickets at $4 each; what arrived were four $3 tickets. I was upset because I wanted to sit in the best seats. I was spoiled, wanting to be right in front. My mom called Sid Bernstein at his office the following day and explained the mix-up. He said he would take care of my friends and me when we got to the theater.

Upon our arrival, Sid was there to show us to our seats. I was so excited to meet "Mr. Bernstein" because I had read a lot about his accomplishments and all the other artists with whom he had worked—Judy Garland, Tony Bennett, and his involvement in the upcoming Beatles' Shea Stadium concert that had just been announced for the summer. As we walked down the center aisle, I couldn't believe that we were getting closer and closer to the stage. At that moment, when we could walk no farther, Mr. Bernstein showed us to three seats . . . front row.

He left us to attend to other business, and a man in his twenties came over and asked if everything was OK. He was curious why we were sitting in the best seats in the house. He was convinced that I was Mr. Bernstein's daughter because who else would be receiving such special treatment.

I had great times at the Academy of Music seeing so many British groups there; it felt like home. I had as good a seat as I did that first time, and I enjoyed some of the most exciting and live best music of the decade. Eventually it was renamed the Palladium in the 1970s and then demolished. Today in its place stands a New York University dorm.

In addition to booking talent, Sid Bernstein started managing bands. His first group was the (Young) Rascals. The band came from Garfield, New Jersey, and I got to know Felix Cavaliere and Eddie Brigati, two of the band members. It was pure coincidence that one evening I spotted Sid at a concert in Passaic, New Jersey. I couldn't believe my good fortune. It wasn't long after I had met Sid at the Academy of Music, and he remembered our meeting.

From that point on, I frequently would drop in to see Sid in his office when I visited the Beatles Fan Club. Sid's temporary office had moved from his home on West Twelfth Street and Sixth Avenue to 565 Fifth Avenue to 119 West Fifty-Seventh Street, practically next door to fan club headquarters at the time. Sid was a busy entrepreneur, but he would always spend a few minutes talking about what shows were planned, the latest with the Beatles, and their upcoming concert schedules. Sid was a wealth of insider knowledge. All this while, he was drinking a chocolate egg cream supplied by an office assistant. In fact, nearly every time I stopped by his office, he was drinking an egg cream or had just finished an egg cream. He never abandoned his Bronx roots.

When tickets to the Beatles at Shea Stadium went on sale shortly after meeting him, I really didn't know what to do. Members of the fan club were asking for my guidance on how to get tickets. It was my responsibility to help obtain them. I wasn't sure if I should ask Mr. Bernstein outright because that might seem way too pushy. As the promoter for the Shea Stadium concert, Sid Bernstein would select the people to attend the Beatles' press conference when they arrived from England to kick off their tour. I discovered this bit of news when I stopped in one afternoon at the fan club. Mr. Bernstein had a lot of influence. Bernice Young at the fan club had put my name on the list for his consideration to attend the press conference, and above all else, I could not put that in jeopardy. After having been burned regarding tickets before, to be safe, I did what every fan did and ordered the maximum four tickets through the mail.

Feeling nervous that this plan to attend the press conference wasn't happening, I wrote Bernice Young. In a return letter, she recommended that I contact Sid. I followed up that day.

Bernice's suggestion worked—what arrived were four VIP tickets to see the Beatles at the sold-out Shea Stadium concert. So did the four tickets I ordered through the mail. The extra tickets made four fan club members very happy.

To demonstrate the never-ending pursuit of the Beatles by Sid, on September 19, 1976, he placed a full-page ad addressed to George, John, Paul, and Ringo in the *New York Times*. He asked the Beatles to reunite for $1 million for a worldwide charitable concert of their choosing, anywhere from Bethlehem to Liverpool on either New Year's Day or Easter 1977. He outlined how the revenue from this event would be distributed among deserving charities around the globe. Always a visionary, Sid created this mega-charitable event years before the big money-raising rock concerts. Only George Harrison's Concert for Bangladesh preceded him in 1971. Sadly, the Beatles didn't respond to Sid's well-meaning ad.

Never deterred, Sid kept moving forward with more concerts and more opportunities. He made substantial sums of money and lost them many times over. Sid Bernstein passed away in August 2013, at age ninety-five. I never felt like Sid was in it solely for the money, unlike so many others who congregated around the Beatles and their management. Last year I spoke with Sid's son, Dylan Bernstein, and we both agreed that for Sid, it was always more about the thrill of finding that special talent he could introduce to the world.

GLASGOW? I'M A LIVER BIRD

In March 1965, I received a call at home one afternoon from Peter Eden, who said he got my phone number from Bernice Young at the Beatles Fan Club. I rationalized that if Bernice gave this man my phone number, he must be OK. Mr. Eden proceeded to tell me he needed a fan club organizer for his latest talent, who had signed with Hickory Records in Nashville. His name was Donovan Leitch, although in the United Kingdom he was known simply as Donovan. He said that Bernice told him I could do a "bang-up" job running the club for this new talent, who sounded a lot like Bob Dylan.

I innocently asked why if he was from the United Kingdom had he signed with a country music label in Nashville. Simple; his record company abroad, Pye Records, has strong ties with Hickory. Mr. Eden shared some information on Donovan: he was born in Glasgow, Scotland, and then his family made their way to England. Now, that sounded better. I was a Liverpool gal and didn't have time to start learning about Glasgow. He asked me questions about what was needed to get started: a good headshot to be made into 8 x 10 handouts, a biography about Donovan, a membership card, an address where membership fees and correspondence could be sent, and a fact sheet. Then a list of DJs and press people to contact is top of the list. Mr. Eden said he had staff at Hickory who could put it all together.

"Will you do it?" he asked.

Well . . . if Bernice referred me, "Of course."

It seemed easy enough until a black-and-white negative arrived in the mail. That was the headshot? I needed copies. The biography, with words misspelled, came a few days later. I sent the headshot negative to a photo duplicating place by mail as that was the cheapest. Then it dawned on me: Who is paying for all of this? Me? It seemed like it, as there was no talk of any payment.

I phoned Mr. Eden. Bernice had told him that the Beatles Fan Club didn't pay me for my help, so why should he? The Beatles were different: this was Donovan, a little-known folk singer from Glasgow.

Costs were accumulating, and cooperation from the record company dwindled. I couldn't handle Donovan any longer, and I let the people at Hickory Records know that my time was up. Not long after my departure, he left Hickory for the Epic label, Clive Davis and the legendary Mickie Most as his producer. It is said that Paul McCartney whispered in the background of Donovan's hit, "Mellow Yellow." The two became friends, with Donovan traveling to India to study with the Maharishi Mahesh Yogi at the same time the Beatles were there. Of course, I followed Donovan and still do from afar. He is an amazing talent, and I feel proud that I was around at the beginning.

MEMORABILIA MADNESS

Collecting memorabilia played a big part in the Beatles experience. Beatles dolls, wigs, board games, magazines, hairspray, talcum powder, bubble-gum trading cards, posters, bracelets, scarves, pins, record players, wallets, and purses—the list goes on and on. Without all the merchandise, being a Beatles fan would never have been as much fun as it was. At school I would wear my Beatles sweatshirt plastered with Beatles pins and badges screaming "I Love the Beatles," along with a precious charm bracelet and necklace proudly displaying their images. After school I would play with friends' the board game "Flip Your Wig" with Beatles music blasting from my Beatles record player. At night, while resting my head on a red, white, and blue Beatles throw pillow, I admired the bedroom walls covered with photos and posters of the Beatles. My favorite was of all four Beatles standing in front of the door at the London Palladium. The poster still hangs in my house today. On my dressing table was a can of Beatles hairspray; beside it, a can of Beatles talcum powder. These playful items that we begged our parents to buy proved valuable investments if one's mom didn't throw them out. Fortunately, my mom kept it all.

Looking at the vast amount of memorabilia quickly manufactured as early as February 1964 to meet the demand by Beatles fans, you would think the group made their money not from music but from licensing their name and likeness. Unfortunately, they made virtually nothing from merchandise in the early years.

Before the Beatles' first trip to the States, Brian Epstein was interested in hiring a manager who would run the merchandising opportunities, which proved so time-consuming and overshadowed his other responsibilities. Brian wanted to devote himself to managing the careers of his groups and viewed the merchandise as nonsense. The only items Brian personally licensed were an official fan club sweater and Beatles pin—to a London-based manufacturer who happened to be his cousin. Brian was so removed from the artifacts that he approached his lawyer to hire a responsible person to take charge.

David Jacobs, Brian's solicitor in London, immediately began to look for someone to run the operation both in England and the States. One evening at a party David ran into someone he had casually met before and hearing that he was unemployed, asked if he was interested in the Beatles job. That was Nicky Byrne. David Jacobs was a noted London lawyer representing many Hollywood names including Judy Garland, Zsa Zsa Gabor, Sir Laurence Olivier, and Liberace, having helped him strategize his mega libel case against the *Daily Mirror* newspaper that he famously won. Brian Epstein and David Jacobs had much in common. Their fathers were both in the furniture business; they were Jewish, stylish, and gay. It was at David Jacobs's country home in Sussex where Ringo and Maureen Cox spent their honeymoon in 1965, hidden from the media.

According to David Jacobs, Nicky Byrne had no experience in merchandising. He had been a race car driver and managed a club for a while, but David thought he had strong qualifications to do an excellent job and relieve Brian of the responsibilities that licensing Beatles-endorsed products would demand. Prior to the advent of the Beatles, the only real merchandising and licensing was by Disney. At the time no one realized the monumental potential in the Beatles name.

With Brian's approval, David Jacobs put Nicky Byrne in charge of the entire merchandising business, where he would pay Brian's company, NEMS, a commission for each license agreement. Nicky must have been a sharp businessman or David Jacobs an outright fool because they agreed to Nicky receiving 90 percent of the monies, paying NEMS 10 percent commission that then had to be split with all four Beatles. Brian, hearing the deal from David Jacobs, thought it was fair enough, never imagining the huge potential in the goods. When asked about the deal, David reported back to Brian that "10 percent is better than nothing." Brian agreed.

The company Nicky set up in the States was called Seltaeb—Beatles spelled backwards. Seltaeb products were the best. I remember going to stores looking at all the Beatles memorabilia, wanting to be sure it had Seltaeb on the label or product. I didn't hesitate to buy unlicensed merchandise but always preferred the Seltaeb items. It wasn't disclosed until lawsuits several years later that income from licensed Beatles merchandise wasn't going to the four guys but to Nicky Byrne, supporting the grand style he was enjoying, living in a fancy New York hotel with twenty-four-hour chauffeur service.

However, by late summer 1964, there was a newly renegotiated split. Approximately 48 percent now went to NEMS and the Beatles, with Seltaeb maintaining a controlling interest in all merchandising with 52 percent. NEMS continued to face considerable financial losses and added new problems. Seltaeb was duplicating licenses in the States for product already granted to British companies prior to the deal set forth with Nicky Byrne. NEMS sued Seltaeb for misappropriation of funds and improper accounting practices. Byrne chose to countersue, alleging that NEMS was prohibiting Seltaeb from moving forward with what he had been hired to do—procure merchandising deals for the Beatles.

Walter Hofer in New York handled the court matter. Brian was called to appear, but mysteriously chose not to fly to New York. The court found in Seltaeb's favor, awarding a judgment against NEMS and the Beatles for $5 million.

Learning of the catastrophic courtroom loss, Brian immediately flew to New York and, in consultation with his other New York attorney, Nat Weiss, hired famed lawyer Louis Nizer to represent him in the aftermath of the judgment. Nizer's retainer was $50,000. Brian assumed full responsibility for the entire debacle and paid the retainer out of his own personal funds. It wasn't until early in 1967 that the case was permanently resolved.

All the sources I have read about this issue agree that Brian realized early on that he had made a gigantic error. Until the end of his life, Brian believed that the Beatles never knew about the first deal with Nicky Byrne. The fear that Brian lived with, that the Beatles would not renew their contract with him in the fall of 1967 due to the loss of millions of pounds in connection with licensing deals, is attributed by many as the cause of the apparent overdose of drugs/alcohol that led to his untimely death. The Beatles have all weighed in on the matter, coming up with different excuses for Brian's lack of business sense. Many people associated with Brian look to David Jacobs as the source of the problem. Because he was the solicitor, it was incumbent upon him to vet Byrne's abilities and to have done the right deal for Brian and the Beatles. It is calculated that this licensing mistake cost the Beatles more than $100 million in 1965 dollars.

Even as the legal wars raged, they didn't deter sales. Remco Toys, based in New Jersey in early 1965, reported the sale of more than 750,000 sets of small rubber Beatles dolls. According to the Peter Brown and Steven Gaines 1983 iconic *The Love You Make: An Insider's Story of the Beatles*, the Lowell Toy Company was producing Beatles wigs at the rate of thirty-five thousand per day.

Car license frames that say "he with the most toys win" surely is speaking about Beatles fans. The rush to own as much as possible was the way to show off to your friends and to assert your preeminent love for the group. The competition was fierce, and I didn't hold back. Nearly every cent I could put together went to build my Beatles collection.

Woolworth's in Ridgewood or W. T. Grant in Wyckoff were my favorite places to shop close to home for Beatles memorabilia. Visiting my grandmother in New York City provided endless opportunities for acquiring memorabilia at stores with bigger inventory. Alexanders on Route 4 in Paramus sold Beatles talcum powder, nylons, and sweatshirts now worth hundreds. I wish I had bought boxes. Most major publishers were printing Beatles books and magazines to distribute to newsstands as quickly as possible, all illustrated with the same Dezo Hoffmann photos. Researchers and writers were hired to put together stories on the Beatles and their lives.

Other popular teen heartthrob singers such as Pat Boone wanted to get in on the action. Under Boone-Lyon Enterprises, Boone produced Beatles color portraits that sold for $1 for the group and $1.70 for a pack of four individual portraits. Everyone wanted a piece of the Beatles.

I kept every piece of fan literature and all doodles from fan club headquarters. Everything was sacred and worth treasuring. I started notebooks filled with newspaper clippings. The first articles I saved were Dr. Joyce Brothers's series of front-page interviews with the Beatles conducted at the Plaza that appeared in the *New York Journal-American* during their first 1964 trip. The series is a lot of fun to reread, especially where Dr. Brothers struggles to psychoanalyze the group and search for insightful meaning to their uniqueness and massive influence on teens spanning the country.

The national Beatles Fan Club tried its best to provide chapter presidents special insider treats. Being put on the Capitol Records distribution list to receive upcoming Beatles album releases was the best. We also were sent special Beatles Christmas records we lovingly called "flexies." Flexies were the size of a 45rpm record but flexible like Mylar. These holiday messages recorded by the Beatles each year were only provided to fan club members and are highly collectible today.

I haven't substantially added to the collection except for my scrapbooks/notebooks that number forty-nine volumes. Since the advent of the internet, keeping a scrapbook is obsolete; however, I still add articles of personal interest when they come along. My collection is my own. Unlike many collectors, I've not spent thousands of dollars to purchase items. It started in December 1963 and came to an official end in the early 1970s. The additions have been only when I was involved in a project or interviewed, so everything has personal value and meaning.

The pins, sweatshirts, drinking cups, pillows, jewelry, hats, notebooks, clocks, record players, and lunchboxes are just a few of the items I will always cherish. Memorabilia was a way we could outwardly celebrate and share with everyone our love for the Beatles. Even today my assembled items are meaningful treasures.

BRIAN'S "FAVOURITE" GAL

CILLA BLACK

It was mid-January 1965, and I left school early because I went with my mom to collect something for my grandmother. Instead of doing the errand, I asked if I could drop by fan club headquarters. This wasn't a planned visit, so I did not anticipate what might happen. I was shocked to see Brian Epstein outside of Walter Hofer's office. At first, I didn't want to enter, but I was spotted so I slowly stepped in and said hello to everyone. Brian smiled and seemed very welcoming. What good fortune.

Brian was in New York to set dates for the Beatles' upcoming summer tour and promote visits for Cilla Black and Gerry and the Pacemakers. Just when I entered the office a phone call came in for Brian, and I could overhear the discussion about Cilla Black and the Persian Room at the Plaza hotel. Cilla was headed to New York.

Cilla, whose real name was Priscilla White, was the lunchtime hatcheck girl at the Cavern Club in Liverpool. She worked during the day as a typist; at noon she went to the Cavern lunchtime shows and at night hung out at clubs with the local bands. Cilla got to be friends with all the musicians, especially Ringo, and one night they handed her the microphone to sing. Bill Harry in his music paper *Merseybeat* reported on Cilla's great singing, and her career took off. Everyone remembered that her last name was a color, but never remembered which color, so they referred to her as Cilla Black. When she met Brian Epstein after the Beatles told him about the talented Cilla, and he learned her real name, he said, "Keep it Cilla Black."

Cilla was the only female in Brian's stable of talent. Her first recording was the Lennon/McCartney song "Love of the Loved." It proved a huge hit in Britain; by 1964, she had #1 hits appearing on the same bill with the Beatles and Gerry and the Pacemakers. Cilla even performed before the Queen in the 1964 Royal Variety Performance. As big a star as she had become in the United Kingdom, Cilla never became a cross-Atlantic success like Dusty Springfield or Petula Clark. Brian tried every means to get Cilla recognized for her talent in the States, but she never became a household name.

Through the door I could overhear Brian getting testy with whoever was on the other end of that phone call. It sounded like Brian was in control, but at the same time fair and honest in his dealings. The gist of the conversation was that if they still wanted to work with the Beatles, then they had to book Cilla. That was the deal. Brian would not take no for an answer; when he hung up the phone, he looked secure in his resolve. I don't know the details, but Cilla was booked for a three-week stint at the Persian Room in the Plaza hotel starting in late July 1965, ending when the Beatles arrived in New York City to play Shea Stadium.

Before I left that afternoon, I also heard that Brian was arranging for Cilla to appear on *The Ed Sullivan Show* during another trip in the spring. Brian's plan was that if America saw Cilla on the popular show, it would help record and ticket sales at the Persian Room during the summer.

Before I left, Brian asked me how my fan club activities were going.

"Great."

I also mentioned the dance proceeds for United Cerebral Palsy and that Scott Muni came to host. He called it "very admirable." Brian's acknowledgment of the club's work was worth all the trouble. He didn't need to know that we were misled and treated poorly, because the proceeds made it to the overall organization anyway.

As hungry as Brian was for Cilla's success in the States, that was how desperately I needed to know the dates for Cilla's Sullivan appearance. During the next few days, I phoned CBS a few times, eventually finding out that she was booked for Sunday, April 4.

So, in mid-March I wrote a letter to Brian Epstein at his office in London asking if I could see Cilla when she visited New York. I felt like I knew Brian well enough to ask him outright. Upon receipt of my letter, Wendy Hanson responded, instructing me to contact her at the Plaza on April 1 to make plans about a meeting with Cilla, provided that it could take place at CBS.

As instructed, I phoned Wendy. We arranged to meet in the lobby at *The Ed Sullivan Show* at 7 p.m. that Sunday. Although she was always reserved, I got the sense that Wendy was pleased that this was working out. By 6:30 p.m., I was outside Studio 50. I had no ticket, just the letter from Wendy setting the phone call. No one would let me in, so I stood in front watching the audience line grow as I had all too frequently experienced in the past. This was getting to be standard operating procedure. Then I saw Wendy heading to the entrance. The doors opened, and I was whisked inside, leaving the line behind.

As we were ushered to the two best seats in the house, Wendy told me that at the show's conclusion, I would join them in Cilla's dressing room. I was nearly as excited as when I saw the Beatles for the first time at the same television studio only fourteen months earlier. This time a meeting

NEMS ENTERPRISES LTD

DIRECTORS: B. AND C. J. EPSTEIN

SUTHERLAND HOUSE, 5/6 ARGYLL STREET, LONDON, W.1
TELEPHONE: REGENT 3261
CABLES: NEMPEROR LONDON W1

22nd March, 1965.

Miss Debbie Gendler,
34, Dacotah Avenue,
Oakland, N.J.
U.S.A.

Dear Miss Gendler,

Mr. Epstein has asked me to reply to your letter of March 17th regarding the possibility of your meeting Miss Cilla Black when she appears on the Ed Sullivan show on April 4th.

I will be happy to arrange such a meeting for you, provided it is possible through CBS. May I suggest, that you telephone me at the Plaza Hotel on April 1st when I will do my best to set up this meeting for you.

With all good wishes.

Yours sincerely,

Wendy Hanson
Personal Assistant to Brian Epstein

WH/JN

Plaza 9-8000

OFFERS CONTAINED IN THIS LETTER DO NOT CONSTITUTE CONTRACTS LICENSED ANNUALLY BY THE LONDON COUNTY COUNCIL

I had asked Brian Epstein on a few occasions about the possibility of meeting Cilla Black. I was very excited to receive this invitation.
AUTHOR'S COLLECTION

was assured. Cilla sang her first song, "Dancin' in the Streets," to the audience's delight and big applause. Next up was a handsome French singer, very popular, Jean-Paul Vignon, who had a few exuberant fans in the audience. For Cilla's final song, she belted out "You're My World." As Cilla sang, I noticed Brian Epstein leaning against the stage's black curtains with arms folded, watching intently. I didn't know he would be there.

This glimpse is the Brian Epstein image I will always cherish. He was dressed in a dark suit with impressive solid gold cuff links that sparkled in the light, just as I had remembered from our first meeting in November 1963. I couldn't take my eyes off Brian. He looked so proud, so focused on her singing. Brian didn't move; he just stood transfixed in a classic stance with arms folded until she finished the song and took her bow with Ed Sullivan. With the audience applause tapering off, a man motioned to me. I walked to the side of the stage and up steps. There was Brian, still leaning against the stage curtains. I gave him a huge smile of eternal thanks; he nodded with pleasure, acknowledging my excitement as I was escorted to Cilla's dressing room.

Turning the corner, my escort and I got into a very unstable elevator. There were stairs, but I was taken to the fourth floor the special way reserved for the show's stars. Vince Calandra, who worked on the Sullivan show, recently reminded me that Sullivan's dressing room was on the second floor, makeup on the third, and dressing rooms on the fourth floor. I was wishing we had walked up the stairs. The PA and I stepped out of the elevator. A door swung open, and there sat Cilla, wrapped in a cozy pink chenille robe, removing her excess makeup. Wendy Hanson stepped into the room and introduced us as Cilla stood to greet me with a smile and handshake. Cilla asked how I liked the show. I was too intimidated to say much. I remember feeling like I had walked in on an intimate gathering already in progress—they had done this so many times before.

Chiming in was Bobby Willis, who eventually became Cilla's husband and manager for more than thirty years until his untimely passing in 1999. Bobby was very proud of Cilla's performance, and he hoped that this would make her a big star in America. I agreed with Bobby, who most certainly nodded his head in my direction. Bobby seemed protective of Cilla, but when Brian joined us in the dressing room, Bobby respectfully moved to the side.

Brian started organizing dinner plans. He wanted to take Cilla to Malkin's. I didn't know Malkin's but learned that evening that Brian loved the place and went there frequently. It was located on East Seventy-Ninth Street between First and Second Avenues. The owner, Mike Malkin, was a nonpracticing lawyer and was gay, so it was through their mutual friends that Brian came to feel comfortable and welcome there. The place was located on the ground floor of a small apartment house. The interior was dark with a long bar, narrow dining room toward the back, and a jukebox. Dress was always jackets, dress shirts, and ties for the guys, and trendy fashions for the gals. It wasn't just for the music crowd either. Limousines were usually parked out front, and the Rockefellers were known to drop in. Seems like both John and Paul also enjoyed Malkin's. Even after Brian's death in 1967, I discovered a photograph of both Beatles (in jackets and ties) taken in May 1968, when they visited NYC to announce the formation of Apple Corps., with Mike Malkin enjoying the scene at his place.

In 1984, Mike Malkin met a tragic death just around the corner from his former restaurant. He was found shot to death in the entrance to his apartment on East Eightieth Street. His maid discovered him slumped in the doorway; he had been shot with a small-caliber handgun. Police ultimately concluded that he was killed by someone he knew—most likely a hit, as nothing from his apartment had been stolen, although valuable paintings and antiques were displayed prominently. He was another associate of Brian's who met an early tragic end; he was only fifty years old.

As Brian placed a call to Malkin's, Cilla signed a postcard-size photo of herself, and I thanked them all for such a memorable evening, sharing hugs and handshakes. I don't remember the exact words, but they just didn't come out right, and I felt awkward as usual. It was about 9:45 p.m., and I had to get home. I had school the next day, and my parents were waiting for me at the stage door on Fifty-Third Street. Before I left, Cilla and Bobby made sure that I knew she would be singing at the Plaza during the summer and hoped I'd be able to make it there as Brian simultaneously nodded in the background.

"Of course, I will be there! Would never miss it," I added. No one realized that I was underage.

On the way out of the studio, you had to pass an alcove just inside the stage door to exit. There stood comedian Alan King, who had been a guest on Sullivan that evening. I quickly pulled out my autograph book, which he signed. How inappropriate it must have seemed. At fifteen it sometimes was difficult to contain my excitement when I saw celebrities.

A few weeks later I asked my mom if we could go shopping to buy Wendy and Cilla a "thank-you" gift for their kindness. It took several days to decide what would be appropriate—purse-sized lipstick cases with mirrors, which we promptly sent off in the mail.

In the end, *The Ed Sullivan Show* appearance was a disappointment for Cilla and Bobby, but for Brian it was devastating. He couldn't understand why Cilla wasn't catching on in America. Brian, who had a reputation for being controlling, brought together some friends to discuss the challenge of getting Cilla noticed. It was agreed that to become a big name in the States, Cilla must remain here for an extended time touring across the country. But she couldn't arrange the time away from England. The best hope they had was the three-week engagement at the Plaza's Persian Room.

Brian engineered the ideal situation. Cilla would begin her stint at the Persian Room the end of July, and her three weeks would culminate with the Beatles' arrival in New York City to kick off their 1965 cross-country summer tour at Shea Stadium. Together Cilla and the Beatles would also appear for a pretape at Studio 50, for *The Ed Sullivan Show* on Saturday, August 14, not to be broadcast until Sunday, September 12. Brian strategized that placing Cilla on the same stage with the Beatles would expose her talent to a huge impressionable audience that would appreciate her personal connection to the Beatles.

It was now the end of July. For Cilla's debut at the Plaza, Brian Epstein and Wendy Hanson flew to New York City to attend the big event. I had a gift to deliver to Wendy in care of Brian, who was staying at his usual place, the Waldorf Towers. Wendy was entrenched at the Delmonico again. I went up to Brian's room, and instead of Wendy he opened the door. He seemed different—nervous, distracted, and somewhat rude; not the well-mannered, dignified person I had met on other occasions. Brian grabbed the package and shut the door. Unable to understand what had just occurred, I walked onto Park Avenue bewildered, lost.

Before I went to the hotel, I had arranged to see a movie that afternoon with Sherri Katz, a fan club member from Long Island, whose grandmother lived in an apartment on West Fifty-Eighth Street right near the Plaza. I hoped not to seem upset when I saw Sherri, because I could not share what happened with anyone but my parents. We walked to the Paris movie theater, showing recent but not first-run movies, to see the Jack Lemmon film *How to Murder Your Wife*. It wasn't of interest to two fifteen-year-old girls, but it served as a perfect distraction.

Right around this time I was also nervously waiting to see if I would be chosen to "Meet the Beatles." According to a letter I received from Bernice Young, Sid Bernstein, the concert promoter for Shea Stadium, was to select two Beatles Fan Club chapter presidents to "Welcome the Beatles Back to America." Brian had said during his NYC visit in April that I would be invited to do the welcoming, but after what happened at the Waldorf Towers, I wasn't confident.

Also, I had wanted to see Cilla's Persian Room cabaret show with my parents, but they decided it was best to stay home. I felt awful as I had told Cilla and Bobby just a few months earlier that I would be there. This was only topped by the fan club gossip that Brian had shown some strange behavior at Cilla's Persian Room opening, not wanting to attend with Wendy. I knew that Brian preferred men, I wasn't that unaware, but

Minutes before the historic show, Ed shares a few words with the Beatles.
PICTURELUX/ALAMY STOCK PHOTO

Taking a brief respite from Beatlemania with my mom and dog, Lollipop, in March 1964.
AUTHOR'S COLLECTION

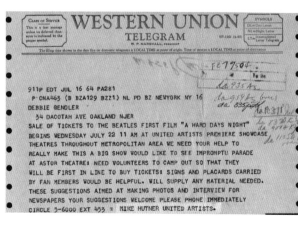

The fans were always needed for publicity, but this was over the top. We were asked to sleep overnight on the street to stage a photo op for the sale of tickets to the opening of *A Hard Day's Night*. Never one to say no to any Beatles stunt, there I was on the Great White Way. Here's the telegram I received with the call to action.
AUTHOR'S COLLECTION

I couldn't wait a moment longer to attend the preview screenings of *A Hard Day's Night*. I watched the film twice, back to back. It may have been a hot July day outside, but it was even hotter inside. Here are two tickets to the preview screenings.
AUTHOR'S COLLECTION

It was brutally hot standing across the street from the Delmonico Hotel on August 29, 1964, trying to catch a glimpse of our heroes. I was part of that crowd.
MIRRORPIX/ALAMY STOCK PHOTO

George Harrison's mother, Louise, and I corresponded for five years. In nearly every letter, she included a snippet of George's clothing. Here's a piece of his sock.
AUTHOR'S COLLECTION

Pictured with me is WABC DJ Scott Muni, who hosted my ill-fated Beatles Fan Club charity dance for United Cerebral Palsy.

©*THE RIDGEWOOD HERALD-NEWS—USA TODAY* NETWORK

At Brian Epstein's invitation, I joined him and Cilla Black backstage at *The Ed Sullivan Show* on April 4, 1965. Brian was at her side, trying to ensure her success in America.

AUTHOR'S COLLECTION

I finally made it to the Beatles press conference on August 13, 1965, at the Warwick in New York City. Here I am pictured standing on the side. When I reviewed the photo, I spotted Andy Warhol in the same shot.

AUTHOR'S COLLECTION

WABC DJ Cousin Brucie Morrow was a thorn in my side throughout the entire Beatles press conference at the Warwick. He brightened up when I asked him for his autograph.
AUTHOR'S COLLECTION

When the Beatles took their seats on the dais, I immediately pulled out my Kodak Instamatic, and in the first five minutes used up the entire cartridge of twelve exposures. Here is one of the cherished photographs that I shot that afternoon.
AUTHOR'S COLLECTION

Here's one taken moments later.
AUTHOR'S COLLECTION

When the press conference ended, The Beatles were taken to their suite on the thirty-third floor. I was told to wait until the room emptied out, and I would be escorted up to meet them. With no one else around, I eyed the items that they had touched and decided they'd be great additions to my memorabilia collection. Here is Ringo's cigarette package with the duty-free sticker still attached.
AUTHOR'S COLLECTION

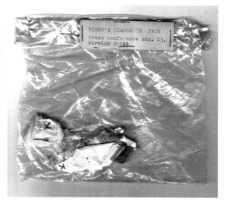

After an unimaginable day, here I am back home clutching John Lennon's latest book, *Spaniard in the Works*, which road manager Neil Aspinall handed me, and the press kit for the movie *Help!* given to the journalists in attendance.
AUTHOR'S COLLECTION

For many, the Beatles were a threat to our nation. Even I received hate mail when my picture and story appeared in a local newspaper after I met the Beatles. Nothing was wrong with our American guys, but I loved these Brits more.
©*THE RIDGEWOOD HERALD-NEWS*—
USA TODAY NETWORK

DATEBOOK

71 washington place, new york 11, new york

PRESS

This is to certify that Debbie Gendler
is accredited editorial correspondent No. 3171
for Young World Press, Inc.

Signature *Debbie Gendler*

Authorized by _____ Expires 1/1/66

I was a stringer for *Datebook* magazine when the Lennon "more popular than Jesus" comment blew up. The original quote in Datebook left me in a quandary about being associated with the publication. Fan club members were upset. In the end, six members ripped up their membership cards.
AUTHOR'S COLLECTION

Mikal standing in front of Ed Sullivan's residence on the eleventh Floor of the Delmonico Hotel on Park Avenue. She is holding a sign to identify the suite as Ed's home.
AUTHOR'S COLLECTION

Wendy Hanson was always business first, even when surrounded by her world-famous colleagues.
© BEATLES BOOK PHOTO LIBRARY. ALL RIGHTS RESERVED.

Knowing I was traveling to England, I contacted the editor of my favorite British pop weekly, *Fabulous 208*. I spent an afternoon at their London office. Pictured here on the right is Anne Wilson, editor, and assistant Sue. Fabulous 208 was my bible, with drop-dead centerfolds of all the latest groups, suitable for your bedroom wall. AUTHOR'S COLLECTION

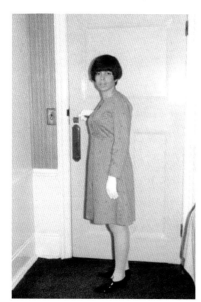

As editor of the high school newspaper, I tried to inform and enlighten the students with new and sometimes radical concepts. Taking a classmate along, we visited with Allen Ginsberg at his Lower East Side apartment. The interview received the Columbia University Second Place Award in 1968 for Best High School Journalism. Here's Ginsberg in a photograph I took that day.
AUTHOR'S COLLECTION

This photo was snapped while I was leaving the Piccadilly Hotel in London, off to the Bag 'O Nails. My clothes are as "mod" as an American could purchase that day at Miss Selfridge.
PHOTO BY MERA GENDLER

On December 1, 1981, I hosted a book signing party at my home for Michael McCartney. Here is the invite. In attendance were Joan Collins, Graham Nash, Spencer Davis, and Joey Molland; Little Richard showed up late.

AUTHOR'S COLLECTION

Debbie Gendler
&
Stephanie Bennett & Jeannie Sakol
of Delilah Books
invite you to a party for
Mike McCartney
in honor of his new book
THE MACS

Tuesday, December 1, 1981
Place: 442 South Clark Drive
Beverly Hills
Time: 6:30 to 9 p.m.
RSVP: (213) 852-2442

Please bring this invitation.

Mike McCartney at the book signing party pictured with my mom, my husband, and me.
PHOTO BY JILL JARRETT

Spencer Davis and his girlfriend dropped by at the Michael McCartney signing at my house. Spencer's best known song, "Gimme Some Lovin,'" was sung by Steve Winwood.
PHOTO BY JILL JARRETT

Beatles (U.S.A.) Limited

P. O. BOX 505, RADIO CITY STATION, NEW YORK, NEW YORK 10019

BEATLES FAN CLUB
OFFICIAL HEADQUARTERS

July 13, 1965

Miss Debbie Gendler
34 Dacotah Avenue
Oakland,
New Jersey 07436

Dear Debbie:

We have obtained permission from the organizers of the Beatles' tour to have two chapter presidents of BEATLES (U.S.A.) LIMITED attend each of the press conferences for the Beatles. Final decision as to which ones will be admitted will be made by the promoter of each concert, as it will be the promoter in each city who will set up the press conference in his city.

As a result, I am passing on your request to the promoter for the New York concert with the hope that you will be able to attend.

Good luck and best wishes to you.

Sincerely,

BEATLES (U.S.A.) LIMITED

Bernice Young
Director

BY:s

Fan club national headquarters let me know that there was a chance I would be invited to the Beatles press conference in August. My fingers were crossed.

AUTHOR'S COLLECTION

I heard through sources that Brian felt compelled to be with Wendy that evening and was visibly angry in her presence about the situation. Gossip was that he would much rather have shared the night with a young man he had met. My dreamy, idealistic Beatles world started to unravel as real life got in the way.

As I was finishing this chapter, I was checking out Mike McCartney's Twitter account. I hadn't logged onto his account before, but Mike was planning a photographic exhibit at St. George's Hall in Liverpool, and I wanted specifics. I logged on and was startled to see a photograph posted just the day before of Mike standing next to Tom Jones at Cilla's funeral service in Liverpool.

Just two weeks earlier, at her home in Spain, Cilla had suffered a stroke, had fallen, and it all came to an end at age seventy-two. I immediately phoned Mike, who told me that she had received a true Liverpool send-off. How sad this loss is for everyone who followed and appreciated Cilla's phenomenal fifty-year plus career. I am happy to have made Cilla Black's acquaintance, even though her star never rose in the States. She wasn't just Brian's "favourite" gal—the United Kingdom loved her, too.

A TOUCH OF CLASS

WENDY HANSON

I can't remember exactly when or where I first met Wendy Hanson. It could have been at the fan club office or at *The Ed Sullivan Show*. Wherever it was, in my opinion, Wendy had the most enviable position: personal assistant to Brian Epstein. As much as I loved the Beatles, I was fascinated by Brian Epstein's work. The business of managing bands struck a chord, and I vowed to learn as much as I could despite my young age.

Back in 1963, when I met Brian Epstein, Wendy hadn't been hired yet. The story goes like this: when Brian was in New York City with the Beatles for the first time, it was pure chaos. Brian's primary focus was the Beatles; however, he was besieged with phone calls, requests for meetings, and business proposals coming in from all over the country. Most were legitimate; however, there were the fast-talking schemers with various deals. Capitol Records quickly noted that Brian needed someone to field his calls and guard the door. They turned to a young, well-respected English woman, Wendy Hanson.

The Capitol executives knew Wendy because she lived and worked among prominent music talents in New York City. Wendy hailed from the West Yorkshire town of Huddersfield, born into a well-to-do family. She was educated, spoke three languages, and was attractive, tall, slim, and blonde. Upon Wendy's arrival in the States in 1953, she took a job as personal assistant to Leopold Stokowski, the famous NBC orchestra conductor. Wendy's working environment provided her opportunities to establish friendships with influential artists such as Rudolf Nureyev.

Wendy's years with Stokowski uniquely prepared her for the time she spent working for Brian Epstein. Stokowski had some very strange phobias; he refused to be photographed informally because some have said that he was paranoid about his looks and age. And, although it was out of fashion, Stokowski would wear formal cutaways with an ascot tied in a distinctive knot that even when asked how to tie the ascot, he refused to divulge his technique. Wendy was accustomed to being at his command 24/7.

Wendy, when she chose, was very welcoming to people involved in the arts and would try to help their careers. Conductor Anthony Morss relates in an interview from the late 1990s that it was Wendy Hanson who helped him become an associate conductor to Stokowski back in the day. She also served as the personal assistant to Italian American Pulitzer Prize-winning composer Gian Carlo Menotti and worked with the Israeli Philharmonic under Zubin Mehta. I've read that Wendy was a presidential campaign secretary to John F. Kennedy after she left working for Stokowski, but I never heard that mentioned during the years I knew Wendy.

With a stellar reference from Capitol Records and the prominent people she previously had worked for, Brian hired Wendy on the spot even though her musical tastes were firmly classical. From her first day on the job, she was in the eye of the hurricane of Beatlemania and found herself headed to Miami for the Beatles second Sullivan show appearance. At the end of this first American trip, Wendy returned to England to work for Brian at his London office. She found a lovely place to live—61 Eaton Square in Belgravia, close to her boss and elegant to suit her style. Wendy had refined, exquisite taste. That was essential if one were to work directly for Brian Epstein.

I saw Wendy several times in New York City and was always ecstatic that she remembered my name. I would write letters to her, and she would answer promptly herself or via her personal assistant, Joanne, or later, Jody. During a trip she and Brian Epstein made in 1966 to New York, I spotted Wendy peering into a glass display cabinet on the ground floor at Bonwit Teller and went up to greet her. It was such a thrill because she seemed pleased to see me. Bonwit Teller was an upscale department store housed in a historic building that in 1980, without any concern for iconic architecture, was demolished by Donald Trump to make way for his palatial Trump Tower.

I was on my way to Steuben farther up on Fifth Avenue to buy my parents a gift for their upcoming twenty-fifth wedding anniversary. At age sixteen I had saved some of my allowance to buy my parents an appreciative gift for all their patience and not just spend cash on Beatles items. Looking back, though, the financial investment would have been wiser if I had bought my parents a can of Beatles hairspray.

Wendy decided she would join me for the short walk to Steuben. We spoke about living in London and how I hoped that one day I could visit the city that encompassed so many dreams. She smiled graciously as we said goodbye, agreeing to see each other again. I stood at the door of Steuben watching Wendy continue up Fifth Avenue toward Central Park feeling so happy I could bust.

I stepped into Steuben, which was darkly lit with glass display shelves covered in black velvet and illuminated by back lighting. From a pouch I pulled out the $135 I had saved and asked to see what that would buy, but the woman behind the counter was distracted and uninterested in making a sale. I stood there patiently waiting for attention. Because my mom had always wanted a piece of Steuben glass; for the never-ending support for all my Beatles-related activities, this anniversary gift had to be extra special.

There was a lot of commotion in the store. When I asked, they pointed to an adjoining room where a dignitary from the United Nations was selecting a wedding gift for then President Johnson's daughter Lucy, who was to be married to Air National Guardsman Patrick Nugent. Arriving at Steuben accompanied by Wendy Hanson impressed me far more than the president's daughter. I made my selection and handed my savings to the salesperson. The gift would be shipped close to their wedding date in October. It wasn't until I arrived back in New Jersey that I realized they hadn't given me a receipt for the purchase. I worried for three months until just days before the anniversary. The gift arrived in perfect order. Steuben was quite the place.

Brian regularly assigned Wendy many responsibilities in additional to her standard routine. During one Christmas season she had to arrange for Harrod's to stay open after closing so the Beatles could shop. As the arbiter of fine taste, Wendy was also in charge of buying the staff gifts for Brian. She would spend hours in Asprey's on Bond Street selecting just the proper tasteful item.

One task, though, put her over the edge. Brian asked Wendy to help get legal clearances from everybody pictured on the Sgt. Pepper album cover within one week. Neil Aspinall had been on the task as well, but he was not making enough progress due to looming deadlines, so Brian brought Wendy in. Wendy feverishly spent days on the phone trying to contact the people depicted or their representatives. The record label and Brian didn't really like Peter Blake's cover, but I've read that Paul thought it was creative. At the outset Wendy was able to reach Mae West directly. At first, she didn't want to be on the cover; she let Wendy know that she did not need to be in a lonely hearts club band. At least half of the people couldn't be contacted, and Brian was fearful of lawsuits. He would have much preferred brown paper bags be used for the album. *The White Album* would have been more Brian's style.

At Mike McCartney's seventieth birthday party, I met Sir Peter Blake, the artistic genius who designed and staged the Sgt. Pepper album cover. He shared some facts about it with me that evening. The collage took two weeks to build, and the Beatles only spent three hours at the

DIRECTORS: B. AND C. J. EPSTEIN

SUTHERLAND HOUSE, 5/6 ARGYLL STREET, LONDON, W.1
TELEPHONE: REGent 3261
CABLES: NEMPEROR LONDON W1

17th May, 1965

Miss Debbie Gendler,
34, Dacotah Avenue,
Oakland, New York,
U.S.A

Dear Debbie,

I arrived back from a short holiday to find your parcel.
How sweet of you to send me the lovely lipstick case.
I shall use it often and cannot thank you enough.

I sent the other box, by hand, to Cilla this afternoon.

Again, thank you very, very much.

Yours sincerely,

Wendy Hanson
Personal Assistant to Brian Epstein

WH/JN

OFFERS CONTAINED IN THIS LETTER DO NOT CONSTITUTE CONTRACTS.   LICENSED ANNUALLY BY THE LONDON COUNTY COUNCIL

Thank-you letter from Wendy Hanson, personal secretary to Brian Epstein, thanking me for the gift I had sent to her and Cilla Black.
AUTHOR'S COLLECTION

photographer's studio posing for their photos. The plants at the edge of the cover photo, according to Sir Peter, are not marijuana, putting that urban legend to rest. Trivia lovers also know that the original name for the album was Dr. Pepper, at least until someone remembered soda.

In December 1966, shortly after Wendy cleared the images, she decided the time had come to leave Brian's employ. I don't know the intimate details of her leaving, but I can guess. Brian's personal status had become very difficult to deal with—drugs, disappearances for days on end. Wendy, always the very self-assured professional, had begun to lose her footing as well. More on this later.

Wendy returned to the States, where she worked with many musical entities and in 1970, married wealthy American financier Byron Moger. I would read about her from time to time in the *New York Times* society columns, at a concert premiere, or see her elegantly dressed for an evening at the Met.

In January 1991, at home in Arezzo, Italy, she fell down some steps, the impact proving fatal. Wendy was fifty-six years old. I admired Wendy Hanson even if there was sometimes a crack in her perfect Eaton Square image. When I think of those frantic fun-filled Beatles years, Wendy is among my most cherished memories. She treated me with utmost concern and respect.

I SAW THEM STANDING THERE (AGAIN)

I sneer when teens say they have worked hard their entire life to achieve a goal. Entire life? When they are only fifteen years old? Maybe I should be more tolerant about such comments because that is how I felt on Friday, August 13, 1965, as I waited for the Beatles to arrive at the Warwick Hotel. They were on their way into Manhattan from JFK airport—the first stop on their groundbreaking tour across America.

My friends at Beatles Fan Club headquarters had let me know about four weeks earlier that the local promoter, Sid Bernstein, for the Shea Stadium show would make the final selection of who would welcome the Beatles to America, attend the first press conference, and have a private meeting with them. I had let everyone know that I desperately wanted to be that person—including Brian Epstein, who had led me to believe I would be chosen.

I had great faith that if Sid Bernstein saw my name as a possible attendee, he would select me to be the greeter. Nervously, I awaited the mail delivery. My memory is somewhat blank on how I was notified, but it was only a few days prior to the press conference that I was selected. Big hug for Sid Bernstein! This would be an amazing experience to finally meet the Beatles.

I had little time to prepare. I had a cute English-looking cotton floral dress, and my mom gave me a locket of hers to wear around my neck. I had spent the night before feverishly writing on slips of paper questions I would ask the Beatles when it was my turn at the press conference. The most important thing, though, was my camera. Because I would attend a press conference, I felt very comfortable bringing along my new Instamatic 300. I made sure I had film and plenty of the small Sylvania peanut-sized flashbulbs. Twelve photos were on each drop-in film cartridge, and the small flashbulbs were a pain to use because they had to be changed for each picture.

Some of the specifics leading up to my arrival at the Warwick Hotel are lost to time. There was a scattered rain shower on our way to the city, although I don't remember it being overly hot or humid. My mom came with me. Again, that was a good thing, because I was stopped by the police and private security surrounding the hotel. I had to flash the printed letter I had many times to prove that I was permitted inside the hotel.

In addition to Sixth Avenue, the side streets were barricaded with fans shrieking at every person who entered the hotel. We made our way through the front revolving doors and just stood in place. On the immediate left was a dark, intimate-looking bar full of people. It was just around 1:30 on a Friday afternoon. Beyond the revolving doors were a few steps down to the lobby and reception desk with the elevators at the back. We didn't know where to go. Finally, someone approached us and told us to either stand or take a seat in an area with a few seats. It wasn't a big lobby. We positioned ourselves close to the revolving door: my mom knew I wanted to be right in front.

As we stood between the door and the bar, a woman in the bar motion to my mom. She and I exchanged glances: we recognized her as WCBS-TV, Channel 2, news reporter Jeanne Parr. I thought she was even more attractive in person than on television. She offered to buy us a drink, which mom uncharacteristically accepted, and I had a Coke. My mom continued to talk with Jeanne, explaining that I was there to meet the Beatles.

Ms. Parr was there to cover the story. She was upset because a young female reporter from WCBS-TV news would be asking the questions and moderating the press conference with the Beatles' publicity manager, Tony Barrow. When I look back, I understand why she was so upset. Reporter Joan Murray had been hired in April 1965 by WCBS-TV to cover local news. She was the first African American female to break into news in a major market and seemed to be the up-and-comer getting this sought-after assignment.

I wasn't really interested in Ms. Parr's story. I left my mom in the bar and went to wait by the front door. Jeanne Parr's suspicions did prove justified because she gradually faded from the New York television scene. I later went to work in television, so I have thought of her and the careers of many hardworking, viable, and creative women in this industry, easily disposable as they are constantly upstaged by youth, nepotism, and insecurity. Writing this book has given me the opportunity to research some of the interesting people I've encountered along the way, bringing surprises. Especially with Ms. Jeanne Parr. Living in Los Angeles you run into people from time to time, having seen them on TV, with little fanfare. It was a pleasant surprise to learn that actor Chris Noth, from *The Good Wife* and Mr. "Big" is the son of Jeanne Parr. I have seen Chris many times—at Peet's Coffee on Sunset Boulevard, at the Ralph's market on Doheny Drive, at a party at the Four Seasons Hotel. My daughter has seen him even more times, once on an American Airlines flight from JFK to Los Angeles. I wonder if he knows his mother was there to cover the Beatles.

When I overheard that the Beatles had landed and would arrive in about forty-five minutes, I went back into the bar and pulled my mom out to wait at the door. An event organizer told us that the press conference would take place immediately upon their arrival. We were instructed to stand back from the door when the Beatles arrived so they could get in safely, go up the elevator to their rooms, and head to the mezzanine level for the press conference where I would be taken along with all the reporters who now packed the lobby.

As I shoved my notes with the questions for the Beatles into my purse, I heard loud screams from the street, and police officers right outside the door formed a ring around the entranceway. Traffic on the street had stopped. I looked to see if their cars were coming. Nothing yet.

Because the traffic on West Fifty-Fourth Street headed east, no one realized that the limousine driving the Beatles from JFK would come along Fifty-Fourth in the opposite direction. New York City's finest had become skilled at confusing the thousands of fans waiting outside the hotel. My mom and I were standing at the bottom of the steps extending down from the revolving door that the Beatles must pass through to enter the hotel lobby. I had dreamed about this moment forever.

Then a black limousine halted abruptly, and the revolving door swirled in anticipation of the arriving guests. In a flash, each Beatle whirled by. I can't remember precisely who came through the door first; I think it was John, followed by George, Ringo, and Paul, but due to the fast motion of the door, Paul stumbled on the nearby inside lobby steps, knocking right into my mom. I couldn't believe how lucky she was—to have been touched by a Beatle. They were whisked past reporters and photographers packing the lobby and were handily maneuvered to the bank of elevators directly opposite the entrance. Their arrival seemed over before it even started. I turned around to watch the elevator rise to the thirty-third floor and stop.

Everyone moved toward the carpeted staircase leading to the mezzanine, where the press conference would take place. At the top of the second flight of stairs was another smaller lobby filled with people smoking and drinking. To my right was the Warwick Room, where the press conference was to be held. I was led into the room. It was filled with banquet chairs arranged in rows, floodlights, and in front a long table covered with a tablecloth, set with a few glasses with a pitcher at one end, ashtrays, and microphones.

I placed my bag on the floor and took out the Instamatic camera, flash-bulbs, pad, and pen to take notes. I also had handy my list of questions if I got the off chance to question the Beatles. The room gradually filled up. Although I was seated in the second row, about six men with gigantic cameras and lights filled the floor right in front, making it more difficult to see the table where the Beatles would sit. The men kept darting around, and I was getting nervous that they would block my view entirely.

But coming right toward me was someone recognizable—Cousin Brucie Morrow from WABeatleC. He was taking the seat to my right! I was excited to see him and immediately felt part of the commotion. After all, he was Scott Muni's colleague at WABC, and there was a connection. He seemed to vaguely remember the Beatles Fan Club dance that Scott Muni hosted after I explained who I was and why I had been invited to the press conference. Now looking back, he didn't know what I was talking about or care.

I handed him my autograph book. He took interest in seeing my autographs of Cilla Black, Duke Ellington, Ella Fitzgerald, Tom Jones—others who had been guests on *The Ed Sullivan Show* when I attended the live broadcasts. He signed it willingly—it made him feel important in this room packed with his competition for the Beatles' attention. Cousin Brucie then took out his microphone from a box and plugged something in and jabbered away about each detail as the press conference unfolded. The room grew tense as everyone jostled for a better position.

Faster than I can describe, the Beatles entered from a side door and headed to the front table. Cousin Brucie, who I had thought was my friend, began pushing and jabbing me with his left elbow. He was so aggressive that I felt forceful pressure against my ribs. What was this all about? The Beatles were finally coming into the room, and I had to deal with this pushy man?

Many years later, when I was working at Weller/Grossman Productions in Los Angeles, a segment producer was hired: Paige Morrow. That night I told my husband I thought she was Cousin Brucie's daughter. There was a slight resemblance, and a few other details about her growing up made the connection viable. After a few days, I worked up the courage to ask her. Paige seemed startled that anyone in Los Angeles would know who he was, having spent his entire career on New York area radio. I shared with Paige my run-in with her dad at the Warwick press conference and his killer instinct and elbow. Instead of trying to defend her dad's actions, Paige laughed in agreement: "You really met my father!"

Leaning into the seat in front of me, I would not let Cousin Brucie or anyone get in my way. Here they came—first Ringo, then John, Paul, and last, George. I stood up to see over the heads of the reporters who blocked my view. The four moved to the end of the table, where they posed for photos, and then they took their seats. From left to right, there was Ringo, John, George, and Paul. Behind them stood Brian Epstein, wearing his signature sunglasses; and Beatles press representative Tony Barrow, holding a microphone and trying to keep the press orderly and appropriate. Mal Evans stood in the background with Neil Aspinall.

To Tony's left was WCBS's latest star reporter, Joan Murray. The questions started, and I took notes the best I could. I knew that everyone would want to know all the details. Reporters asked John why he was chewing gum. what Ringo would name his yet unborn baby. There were the usual questions: how it feels to be back in the USA, and if their popularity was fading. The press, always interested in the Beatles' romantic lives, noted that the two married guys sat together and the two single Beatles together. John blurted out that they were "queer," and the entire room laughed inappropriately. I didn't get the humor.

Vietnam was mentioned, followed by questions about their just-released movie *Help!* In between I managed to take photos. The camera was a challenge. I had to change flashbulbs for each shot. Things kept dropping—the pen, then my pad, and then two exposed sharp wires at the bottom of the flashbulb cut my index finger, and I began to bleed. What next? I couldn't take notes during the Q&A, and Cousin Brucie never let up. I took a few more pictures, and in a flash the press conference was over, somewhere between 5:30 and 6 p.m.

The Beatles were led out of the room in single file.

Just two weeks prior to the Beatles' arrival in the States, their second feature film, *Help!*, premiered. Like the year before, I attended two preview screenings. It was a fun film, but I liked *A Hard Day's Night* much better. John singing "You Gotta Hide Your Love Away" in the bathtub was amazing, even though the film's premise was inane and, in my opinion, forced. The plot centers around Ringo, who came upon a valuable ring that made him a target of many scheming people to get it back. The movie took the Beatles from the slopes of Austria to the beaches of the Bahamas. United Artists had to be sure to recoup their investment and lost no time in realizing this with the assembled press. To promote the film, those attending the press conference also received the press kit to the movie. It was packed with 8 x 10 photos from the film along with printed materials. I loved the handout. It would be a great addition to my growing Beatles memorabilia collection. Also, I was very surprised to see that Ringo was wearing the same ski shirt he had worn in *Help!* Amazing that with all his fame and fortune, Ringo chose to wear wardrobe from the film.

With the press conference over, the reporters collected their handouts and headed out to file their stories. Sid Bernstein's assistant told me to remain in my seat, and someone would return to escort me up to the Beatles suite. I asked if she could let my mother, who waiting in the hotel lobby, know that I was OK. She said, "Of course."

I sat in the Warwick Room forever. I felt forgotten. Attending the press conference would be as close as I would get to the Beatles. I thought that was OK because that was a once-in-a-lifetime event. The only disappointment was that I was supposed to meet the Beatles. I knew my mom was waiting in the hotel lobby, and I thought I should go down and get her, but what if someone came at that minute and thought I had already left? It was smart to sit in the now silenced room all alone.

I seized the opportunity to inspect the room closely. I looked around to be sure no one was there. Did I dare grab Ringo's emptied pack of cigarettes just tossed on the table? Or could I touch the ashtray full of Beatles' cigarette butts? The folded starched white napkin that George used during the press conference was just sitting there. And . . . the glass of water that Paul sipped from sat there with some water in it. Did I want those items for my Beatles collection?

This was my one and only chance. If I didn't move now, I would regret it for the rest of my life. Wouldn't that pushy Cousin Brucie do this if he had the chance? Keeping a lookout over my shoulder, trying to appear casual, I cautiously approached the table with my handbag hanging from the crook of my left arm. The bag had room. I was out of film, having taken all twelve photos on the cartridge, so I wasn't worried about that. My notepad was barely legible and stained from the cut.

I held my breath. Without hesitation, I reached for Ringo's cigarette pack and dropped it in the bag. Oh, my God—I had it! Next the napkin just slid in, followed by the ashtray full of ashes and butts. I coughed, and some of the ashes flew away—well, I couldn't be bothered with that. Now came the challenge—the glass of water that Paul had been drinking from. There was nowhere to empty the water remaining in the glass, and I desperately needed it in my collection. At that precise moment, the side door opened. Oh, well, there wasn't much water in the glass anyway. I just casually dropped it into my purse, unnoticed. A female assistant walked me to my chair and said, "Let's go upstairs."

I picked up the *Help!* press materials and was ushered into a freight elevator and up to the Governor's Suite on the thirty-third floor. It got that name because then Governor Nelson Rockefeller had an office across the street and had stayed at the Warwick. If you ever go to the Warwick, don't let them tell you the Beatles stayed on the twenty-seventh floor. Hotel management tried to do that with me. I was there—it's the thirty-third.

I closed my eyes—the moment had arrived.

The Beatles had taken over the entire floor. As I stepped off the elevator, to the immediate right were large swinging wooden doors that were open, down a short hallway and to the right were Brian Epstein with Tony Barrow and Neil Aspinall standing in front of the suite's entrance door. They nodded hello and welcome but didn't seem to stop what they were doing. I expected to see the Beatles. Instead, all attention was focused on the window that led to the fire escape.

On the other side of the window was a girl just about my age, shouting for the Beatles. First hotel security, then New York City police closely trailing behind, rushed into the suite, prying open the side window to bring the girl inside. Others were rushing around to apprehend the fan. I couldn't believe what I was seeing. She had climbed all thirty-three floors on the outside fire escape just to see the Beatles. Concerned by this unanticipated breach, security had the fan stand in an inner area, looking back at the window, where she began to cry.

After nearly two years of dreaming about this moment, I had always envisioned the Beatles lined up, greeting me in an orderly way in a formal setting. My vision was half correct. At that crucial moment, George entered the room. His first words were, "Let her stay." George told Tony Barrow to tell the police that after all she risked, they could at least let her in. Paul came into the room next, followed by Ringo and John. Jeez, here I was right next to the Beatles, part of the same crisis. I silently moved to the side, watching, hoping that I wasn't mistakenly viewed as part of this scheme, and then was asked to step out into the narrow hallway.

Together the Beatles all agreed that the fan should be allowed to enter, but the New York City cops took Tony Barrow aside. The Beatles had been overruled. If word got down to the street that all one needed to do was climb the fire escape to the thirty-third floor to meet the Beatles, the Warwick would be overrun with fans risking it all no matter how dangerous.

All four Beatles obligingly moved aside, and the fan was led out of the suite not knowing that the guys had seen her from the other side. She would have been so happy. Maybe she will read this account of what happened and finally learn sixty years later that they thought her brave accomplishment deserved a meet-and-greet.

With the immediate crisis resolved, I cautiously moved to the center of the room where all four Beatles were just as I had always envisioned, in a single line, meeting other invited guests. One of Brian Epstein's press assistants brought me over for the proper introduction as #1 fan club secretary. Shaking each of their hands, first I said hi to George. He already had seen me during the crisis and acted like we were old friends, giving him the liberty to be dismissive. Then Paul, who seemed like he was having a great time just being in New York looking around the room. Next was John.

I stood before John with my hand outstretched. His demeanor was so different than I had expected. He stared at me oddly, and for a moment I was frightened. How could this be happening? John looked down at me and pointed to my purse hanging on my left arm. "What's that coming out of that bag?" Paul and George both looked around and leaned over. Ringo, who I had yet to meet, came around the side to stare. Out of the corner of my bag, water blackened with ash was leaking onto the carpeting.

Oh, no. The water from the glass! How could I possibly explain this? I had been found out. I wanted to run away, find my mother downstairs, and never come back. My Beatles life was finished.

John pushed the point again and started to make fun of me and the situation. How could he do this? John leaned over and said, "OK . . . let me see what is going on in there." I had no choice but to open my bag so he could peer in. George thought it was funny and broke the tension. Paul remarked about being back in New York, and this was part of the craziness of America. Piece by piece, John made me play show 'n' tell—the napkin, the twisted cigarette pack, the ashtray, and the glass that now was empty.

"Do you like rubbish?" John asked. I meekly replied," No, just this garbage. It is for my collection." I pointed to the *Help!* press materials as if to show that I was always looking for memorabilia to supplement the collection. Nothing helped. He just tore into me more, repeating that he would remember me from New York as the "rubbish girl." When John realized that I was about to break down in tears, he motioned over a few other people in the room to look at my treasures. John Lennon, who I revered, was making fun of me before everyone in the hotel suite.

I never was introduced to Ringo; it was too late. John moved away, still shaking his head, and Paul thought it was to be expected. George just stood next to Ringo, not sure what to do or say. Having no intention of leaving my new treasures behind, I made sure that I collected all my belongings and shoved them back into the wet bag. They were now more precious than ever and were going home with me, even though my days of being a fan were over for sure. What would I tell my mom or my friends back home? That I was caught by the Beatles having wrongly taken their garbage? This was the most important moment of my life, and I had ruined it.

I looked around, and food from the Stage Deli had arrived for everyone to enjoy. Huge sandwiches were served from catering trays, and I remember extra Russian dressing being slapped onto each Beatle's work of art on rye. They devoured the meal, agreeing, "There's nothing like food in

America." I was invited to have a sandwich, and I politely accepted, trying to prove John wrong in his opinion of my motives. The water stain on the carpet began to dry.

With the feast over, the Beatles moved into an adjacent room, where I could overhear the voice of Cousin Brucie broadcasting live from the hotel. I had had my fill of *him* for the day. 1010 WINS's Murray the K, the true Fifth Beatle, was more my style anyway.

I sensed that it was time to leave. Meekly, I waved goodbye to all the Beatles in the other room, including Cousin Brucie. Brucie nodded to show how popular he was and commented to the Beatles who were gathered around him, "She's a doll," pointing in my direction. They seemed as bewildered as I was about the remark. I thanked Brian Epstein, Tony Barrow, the press assistants, and a man standing with them—Andy Warhol.

Regulations required everyone to be escorted to the freight elevator, and I was instructed to wait in the vestibule leading to the hallway. Neil Aspinall, Beatles road manager, saw me down with a hotel security guard. When we reached the ground floor, Neil pulled something out of his jacket pocket—it was a copy of *Spaniard in the Works*, John Lennon's new book.

"It's from us," Neil said, "for your collection."

THE *REALLY* BIG SHOW

SHEA STADIUM

I was still reeling from meeting the Beatles just two days before when it was time to head to Shea Stadium. The glow hadn't worn off, and I was spinning with joy. I distinctly remember planning my outfit to wear to the concert. Bell-bottoms were the latest rage, and I went to Franklin Simon on Thirty-Fourth Street in Manhattan to purchase a denim pair and a matching blue and white striped T-shirt. Franklin Simon was a favorite store; I also bought my avocado-colored suede go-go boots there and a madras button-down-the-front dress that I wore on several *Clay Cole Show* appearances.

The day tickets went on sale for the Shea Stadium concert, I had wasted no time and bought four through the mail just like everyone else. But with the help of fan club headquarters and the kindness of the show's promoter, Sid Bernstein, I received four VIP tickets. So now, with eight tickets, I was able to share them with friends.

I gave the purchased four tickets to fan club members and asked three other friends to come with me to the concert. Two of the girls, Eileen O'Neill and Eileen Tierney, didn't live in Oakland. I think they lived in Franklin Lakes or Wyckoff. The other friend who came along was Roz Sax.

Roz was a friend I had met in Atlantic City while visiting my grandmother, who would spend her summers staying at the Breakers, a kosher hotel on the Boardwalk. Roz was an Atlantic City native whose mom worked at the Breakers. I enjoyed going there for visits because I had local friends in Roz and her best friend, Joanne Saracini, and could meet the groups that played the famed Steel Pier, known for the diving horse.

Earlier that summer, 1965, I was introduced to marijuana. It was a scary prospect. I had gone to see the Byrds play on the Steel Pier, and afterward, along with Roz and her friend Joanne, I got invited back to their hotel for a party. As we walked into the hotel room, there stood David Crosby handing out joints to everyone. The air was thick with a heavy smell. Reluctantly, I accepted a joint and tried it. Not sure if I inhaled, but I couldn't understand what all the fuss was about.

Joanne is a lovely person as I remember her during our teen years, along with her younger brother, Victor. Each summer I would join Roz, Joanne, and sometimes Victor on Atlantic City's boardwalk to play Skee-Ball or just walk around in the evening. It was with deep, deep sadness that I learned from Roz that Victor was the pilot in command flying United Airlines Flight 175 on September 11, 2001, from Boston to Los Angeles. Victor was stabbed by the hijackers while trying to control the plane. It remains difficult to fathom Victor confronted by these attackers. When in New York, I have gone downtown to see his name Victor Saracini etched in the granite memorial, the first name listed under UA Flight 175.

Some of the performers and groups I saw on the Steel Pier that summer with Roz and Joanne were Peter and Gordon, Herman's Hermits, and Gary Lewis and the Playboys. Gary Lewis, oldest son of superstar comic Jerry Lewis, was surprisingly very normal for having been raised in Hollywood. I had an invitation to join the band and their girlfriends for a get-together after the show. I went to their motel, and I remember talking with Gary Lewis's girlfriend, Norma. Just two years ago, I had email correspondence with Gary Lewis. I emailed him copies of the autographs I got that day, and he emailed back. It's always fun to catch up. Until I looked at the autographs, I hadn't realized that I had one from Tommy Tripplehorn, one of the Playboys. Tom, it turns out, is the father of Emmy-nominated actress Jeanne Tripplehorn, known as the lead wife in HBO's *Big Love*, along with other roles.

You can get a sense of how exciting it was to be going to Shea Stadium from an episode of *Mad Men* when Don Draper phones his daughter Sally to tell her she is going to see the Beatles at Shea. Sally starts to scream hysterically. Matthew Weiner got it right.

It was finally time to leave for Shea Stadium. Roz, the two Eileens, and I left for Port Authority Bus Terminal in Manhattan, where we connected with the subway and train to the stadium. It was exciting to be experiencing this with others. So many Beatles activities I did alone, so sharing the excitement with friends made it especially fun. This would be the concert of the century. In retrospect, history has proven that correct.

When we got to the stadium, we couldn't believe our great luck with seats right in front center. Sid Bernstein had really come through with the best seats. As we got ready for the *really big shew*, we started talking with the girls sitting next to us. They were from Queens and Long Island. One of the girls was the younger sister of singer Brian Hyland. Brian had two big hits that I recognized—"Itsy Bitsy Teenie Weenie Yellow Polka Dot Bikini" and "Sealed with a Kiss" a 45rpm I owned. I always liked that song pre-Beatles.

As I had come to expect at Beatles concerts, having attended two the previous summer, the audience had to sit through a slew of other performers. I only remember three, although I have sufficiently blotted two other acts out of my memory. First was what I thought was singer Brenda Holloway; I never heard of her before or after her performance. King Curtis followed. I only recollect the immense saxophone that King Curtis played. His music was not appealing at the time.

Sitting through these other acts was, again, a lesson in patience. Sounds Incorporated played; even though the group was also managed by Brian Epstein, it wasn't great. Murray the K was there. So was Cousin Brucie Morrow, who had told me at the Warwick hotel press conference that he would be the announcer. He hadn't exaggerated; he was onstage announcing Shea.

The more than fifty-five thousand seats were filled with screaming fans when we heard an approaching helicopter close to the site of the 1964–1965 World's Fair in Flushing Meadow, Queens. Next, we were told that a Wells Fargo armored van would drive the Beatles directly into the stadium. I can't remember whether I saw the van. The image sticks in my mind, but I'm not sure whether I witnessed it or remember it from published photos of the Beatles' arrival onto the field.

And then Cousin Brucie announced that the Beatles were in the house.

Ed Sullivan walked across the stage, right in the middle of the field at second base, picked up the microphone, and in an instant introduced the Beatles. They raced across the field onto center stage. The roar that went up was so loud that many police officers, stadium security, and even fans covered their ears.

Only thirty-five minutes and twelve songs later, the concert was over almost before it started. We barely heard a note, even sitting in great seats. I also remember one girl who managed to make it over a fence and go for the Beatles in the middle of the field. Police took off running after the fan, capturing her before she got close to the stage. If there was one specific memorable moment during the concert I still have, it is of John Lennon running his elbow up and down the keyboard as the Beatles sang. I think they realized that there was so much screaming that it made no difference whether they played and sang. No one could hear anything.

It seemed crazy that just two days before I had been in a hotel suite where the Beatles were standing right before me: surreal. Now fifty-five thousand people were going mad over them.

The significance of this evening at Shea Stadium was not lost on the media present or any of the fans. Even at our young age, we all sensed that this marked a new era for concerts and for the Beatles. They had become super idols, far apart from us, in the center of a huge, open field, where access to them was completely denied. As exciting as the night was, it made me long for the concert intimacy of Forest Hills Tennis Stadium, where we had each felt that our favorite Beatle was there playing for us. The challenge of performing, touring, and putting on a *really* big show was here to stay.

HATE MAIL

It had been an amazing month, one that I would cherish always. Without question, meeting the Beatles was the highlight of my entire life, all fifteen years. A newspaper reporter phoned for an interview about having welcomed the Beatles to America. The article proposed would be a fun human-interest story with a definite local angle. The best part is that they would be sending a photographer to illustrate the article.

The photographer took a photo where I am dreamingly looking at an 8 x 10 glossy photo of Ringo from the *Help!* movie press kit handed out at the Beatles' press conference just days before. After the article appeared, my parents and I received congratulations from friends and neighbors. Many of the comments centered on how a fifteen-year-old girl from a blue-collar town in northwest Bergen County pulled off this amazing feat. A few friends proved not to be real friends; they were jealous. Some refused to believe that I had gotten to meet the Beatles. Others found ways to discredit me, saying I just used them as fan club members for self-promotion. Fortunately, a few friends remained happy for me.

Despite all of this, I was enjoying the rest of the summer anticipating the start of my sophomore year in high school, going to concerts, visiting fan club headquarters, and connecting with other fans. Then it all came to a scary halt.

I had just picked up the mail. Mail was my lifeline to the world, and I anxiously waited for it every afternoon. But on this day, there was an odd letter with my name scribbled on the envelope. The writing looked bizarre. When I opened the envelope, the newspaper article and photo of me were folded inside. I thought it was sweet that someone was sending me another copy. When I unfolded the piece of paper, handwritten over the photograph was the message "You're Nuts!!!! What's wrong with our American boys???"

This was my first piece of hate mail. Notoriety wasn't all fun. I understood that the Beatles weren't loved or even tolerated by all. My dad was consistently ridiculed over my Beatles antics. As I said earlier, a few school friends weren't permitted to join the fan club because their parents felt the Beatles were a bad influence. One mom even went so far as to tell my mom that the Beatles were demons destroying our way of life. There were all sorts of comments, but to receive mail like this frightened me and alarmed my parents.

On my next visit to see Pam and Sue at fan club headquarters, I took along the hate letter. They thought it bold, but then pulled out a mailbag containing hate letters they had received. We all had a good laugh and decided I was in good company.

This wasn't the last time I received critical mail, and in a strange way I relished the controversy that the Beatles engendered. Nothing was wrong with our American boys, but for now, I loved these British imports more.

CRISIS MANAGEMENT

The Beatles' popularity kept pace with their record releases and the ever-growing influence of British groups on American bands such as the Turtles, the Byrds, Paul Revere and the Raiders, and the Grass Roots among many others. But internally, the Beatles camp was beginning to show signs of wear. Brian Epstein spent much of the year in crisis management mode, which began to take its toll on his physical well-being and mental state.

In March 1966, the Beatles held a photo shoot with one of their favorite photographers, Robert Whitaker. He had been working with them since 1964 when the group toured Australia. Brian Epstein took a liking to Robert Whitaker's work and made him an official Beatles photographer. The photographs from this shoot were to be used for the upcoming Beatles album, *Yesterday and Today*. Until 1967, Beatles albums in the United Kingdom and the United States did not contain the same songs. England always was ahead of us, and I depended upon my overseas pen pals to send me the latest British releases prior to their American debut.

Being a creative, forward-thinking individual, Robert Whitaker came up with a controversial album cover concept: posing the Beatles in white butcher coats with chunks of raw meat and decapitated dolls with their mutilated body parts positioned on the Beatles shoulders and laps. Radio stations, on receiving advance copies of the album, went into an uproar over the disturbing photograph, which became known as "the butcher cover." People protested the gruesome photograph, especially because its intended target was teens. The day before the album was to be officially released in June 1966, the head of EMI/Capitol Records ordered all copies recalled immediately.

National Beatles Fan Club had an arrangement with EMI/Capitol Records that fan club chapter presidents be sent review copies of all upcoming Beatles' record releases. It wasn't any different with the "butcher cover." When the uproar started and with the massive recall underway, I saw no need to return the album. I hadn't been contacted to

102

do so, and today the pristine album remains one of the centerpieces of my memorabilia collection.

Robert Whitaker took full responsibility for the tasteless photograph. Urban legend has so many versions about the reasoning for the cover. Some say it had to do with how Beatles music was "cut up" by the record label. Mr. Whitaker said he came up with the idea to show the fans that the Beatles were real people. Whatever the reason, it sent Brian into a tailspin. He had to defend the Beatles to their fans and, essentially, their parents. The album cover was immediately replaced with another photograph Mr. Whitaker took of the Beatles, with the band grouped inside around an upright steamer trunk. Many of the returned butcher cover albums had the new cover slick pasted over the recalled version. Fans have toiled trying to artfully remove the slick from the original cover. Although not nearly as valuable as the mint cover, over the years the peeled copies have grown in desirability.

In 1991, I was working on a daily morning ABC TV show, and Robert Whitaker was on a tour promoting the publication of a book of photographs, including some of the Beatles. Of course, I had him booked on the show and spent quality time with him in the Green Room. My butcher cover album had never been opened, the plastic seal intact. I knew I was in the presence of an amazing photographer, and it would be my only opportunity to get his autograph on his most iconic work. I carefully opened the outer plastic and gave him a pen. He signed his name on the back of the album cover and dated the signature. I've kept the script from that show together with the signed album. As Mr. Whitaker stood up to go into the studio, he turned to me and said, "That's the first one I ever signed. I don't even own a copy."

Also, in March 1966, Maureen Cleave, a newspaper reporter who had always been on intimate terms with the Beatles, published a series of four interviews, one with each Beatle, on "How Does a Beatle Live?" Maureen was considered such a fine resource that Brian Epstein kept her home address and phone number at 12 Randolph Crescent W.9 readily available in his address book. During her interview with John Lennon, he said that in his opinion the Beatles were "more popular than Jesus now." The series went virtually unnoticed until Tony Barrow, the Beatles' press representative, gave the teen magazine *Datebook* the rights to publish the interviews, and America went crazy. Not only did I have to deal with fan club members dropping out of the club, but I was coincidentally a stringer for *Datebook*. It was difficult to reconcile my magazine connection with the harm the publication brought upon the Beatles. A few parents demanded that their daughters resign from my fan club chapter.

As the storm was beginning to brew in the States, the Beatles began their summer tour in Japan. There, the conservative government protested their appearance at the revered Budokan Theater in Tokyo, known only for martial arts spectaculars. Among the best vintage film pieces in color of the Beatles are the Budokan performances. In contrast to screaming fans in the rest of the world, these Japanese teens are sitting in their seats, totally composed, not saying a word, politely clapping between songs. It is awesome! The scene in Tokyo seems organized, but Brian had his hands full. The Beatles were held hostage the entire time in the Tokyo hotel due to their immense popularity, leaving Brian to manage governmental pressures placed upon their appearances. It is said that John managed to sneak out briefly, but when he was recognized, he dashed right back to the hotel.

Tokyo proved inconsequential compared with what awaited the group in the Philippines. Imelda Marcos, the wife of the president (later was known for her collection of more than three thousand pairs of shoes), had sent an invitation to Brian Epstein for the Beatles to join her at a breakfast reception at the palace while in Manila. Brian politely declined, saying that it wasn't their policy while on tour to attend official events. Brian had also turned down an invite from President Lyndon Johnson to visit the White House during a tour. Imelda was furious at their rebuke of her invitation and immediately ordered the end to all security around the Beatles. The snub was broadcast on television. Brian then went on TV to apologize to the nation, but the power was cut off when he began to talk. The hotel was under siege from local fans and police; and without security, the Beatles immediately headed for the airport.

When they arrived at the airport, demonstrators upset with the Beatles' snub of their beloved first lady began to physically attack the group. Police carrying raised guns circled the Beatles, and their road manager, Mal Evans, was physically beaten. They took refuge with other travelers as locals tried to hit them with strange objects. The Beatles and staff barely made it onto the plane. As they breathed a sigh of relief, along came the airport police with guards marching down the aisle of the plane toward their seats. Brian and Mal Evans were taken off the plane, and Brian was ordered to pay back to the government a huge sum of the proceeds from their Manila concerts. The plane was delayed until the government was confident that the payment was secured. Brian and Mal were let back onto the aircraft, and it finally took off. When the aircraft was fully airborne, John Lennon commented that he would never fly over that place again.

That concluded the tour in the Far East, and the Beatles happily prepped for their 1966 summer return to America, where things were so much more civil—or so they thought. Brian had underestimated the impact of the Maureen Cleave article. Upon arrival in the United States, the Beatles found another storm brewing, even possibly more dangerous than the mess in the Philippines.

A radio station in Birmingham, Alabama, announced that because of John's comments about the Beatles being more popular than Jesus, they were organizing a bonfire to burn Beatles albums. Across the country other stations jumped on the bandwagon, and before long Brian had a major crisis to handle. In New York City in early August 1966, shortly before the tour launch, Brian desperately tried to explain what John meant. The American public wasn't buying it, especially from a Jewish guy. When the tour started in Chicago a few days after Brian's impassioned plea, John decided it was his turn. At a press conference, he desperately tried to clear up the misunderstanding, but his words dug an even deeper hole, overshadowing the entire tour that, sadly, would be their last.

My fan club members were really upset. So were Bernice, Pam, and Sue at national headquarters. I stopped by the office one afternoon and read through letters that had arrived. Members were quitting the club, saying terrible things about John and the Beatles. It reminded me of the hate mail I had received after the article appeared in the newspaper about me meeting the Beatles. Was this comment going to prove those hateful individuals right? It was an awful time for those of us who were loyal to the Beatles at any cost.

Sensing that trouble might be brewing for the second Shea Stadium concert scheduled for August 23, 1966, I was concerned for the Beatles' legacy. I felt helpless knowing there was nothing that could be done. My parents and I were spending a few days in Rockland, Maine, visiting an artist friend of my dad's, when I read in the *Boston Globe* that the Beatles would be performing at Suffolk Downs, a famous Boston racetrack. Begging my parents to take me to the concert, I promised I would do anything to see the group again. My indulgent parents relented without much fuss. I think my dad was curious to see the Beatles. This would be the fifth time I had seen the Beatles as a group perform live, and the last. We purchased two tickets from a man selling them on the street approaching the racetrack for about $27 each, if I remember correctly—a lot of money in 1966. The face value was $5.75. The seats weren't that great, but I didn't care—all I needed were the Beatles.

Suffolk Downs was an awful place for a concert. Although much smaller than Shea Stadium, the stage was set back far from the fans, and the track served as a barrier between the seats and the stage where the Beatles would be performing. The concert started at 8:30 p.m., and East Boston was hot and humid. First, the obligatory opening acts. This time they were not that bad: The Ronettes, whom I enjoyed; Bobby Hebb, who sang his hit, "Sunny," for what seemed like an eternity; and Brian Epstein's American band, the Cyrkle, who performed their hit "Red Rubber Ball."

Anticipation for the Beatles began to swell. Four limousines drove onto the racetrack, some of them decoys, but out of one came the Beatles heading for the stage. The screaming was louder than ever, and no one could hear any music. The sound system was awful, but listening to the Beatles performing wasn't why we came here anyway. This concert seemed even shorter than the previous year's Shea Stadium concert, easily under thirty minutes. I remember several girls fainting. One guy charged the stage and made it right up to the Beatles, defying tight security. The audience makeup seemed different from New York fans—guys our age, seemingly, were now into the group.

After the album *Rubber Soul* was released at the end of 1965, boys my age were beginning to listen to the Beatles' music. They didn't possess the fan fervor of the girls, but appreciation for the Beatles' talents was beginning to be acknowledged by progressive young men. Everyone was a Beatles fan!

TWO EMPTY SEATS

Returning home from Maine, it was now New York's chance to welcome the Beatles back to Shea Stadium. Again, Ed Sullivan was introducing the Beatles. I know because I had planned to stay overnight at the Delmonico Hotel with a gal pal, Mikal Gilson, on August 23, 1966, to attend the concert. I wrote Wendy Hanson about possibly seeing her. She said I should be close and suggested that the Delmonico would be the only location to stay if the opportunity came about. She would give me a call. With fingers crossed that concert tickets would materialize, I didn't buy any. The previous year for Shea Stadium, I ended up with eight tickets; now I had none.

As always, I was looking forward to seeing Wendy again, although she couldn't promise that a meeting could be arranged. About a month before the concert, I received another letter from her wanting confirmation that the reservation at the Delmonico under my name was completed. I wrote back: everything was set to checking in August 23 and out the next day. How exciting! Two summers before, after the concert at Forest Hills, I stood for hours across the street from this landmark location, dreaming of catching a glimpse of the Beatles inside. Now I would be a guest! Looking back, I can't imagine that reception would welcome two sixteen-year-old girls and let them check in without any questions asked. At the time, this seemed standard procedure. The room cost $165 for the night, expensive in 1966 dollars, and I saw the room charge was marked paid in advance. I was too excited to think anything of it.

Our eleventh-floor room, overlooking Park Avenue, had a large closet, marbled bathroom, lounge chair, two double beds—and an impressive view. A friend who lived in Manhattan, Judith Rudnick, came to visit, and we had lots of fun, gossiping the afternoon away. It was about 5 p.m., and Judith left for home. Mikal and I went to soak up the posh atmosphere and the hotel's amenities. As we waited for the elevator, a shiny black door opening to our right caught our attention. Out came Ed Sullivan and his elegant wife, Sylvia. They joined us to wait for the elevator. The room we had been given was on the same floor where Ed Sullivan lived.

Mr. Sullivan, who would be introducing the Beatles again at Shea Stadium, asked, "Are you going to see THE BEAT-TLES?"

"No," we both replied in unison, dumbstruck in the awkward situation.

Mr. Sullivan looked at us strangely. Did I seem familiar? I had met him a few times at his Sunday show, but I was completely out of context in this setting. I nervously pointed to our room down the hall where we were staying, letting him know we were guests. They looked perplexed, questioning my response, which clearly didn't seem proper.

The elevator door opened, we stepped back, and they entered, bewildered why we chose not to get in the elevator. I think there were still elevator operators, and he was holding the door for us. Needing to come up with some excuse fast, I said that we had forgotten something back in our room. They jointly wished us a good evening as the elevator doors gracefully closed. Mikal and I raced back to our room, slammed the door, and screamed!

I needed to stay close to a phone in case Wendy called. After another hour passed, we decided she was busy tending to Brian's needs, and we were hungry for dinner. Mikal suggested a restaurant her uncle frequented in Chinatown, BoBo's. We took the subway there, ordered lobster rolls, and hastily returned to the Delmonico.

Wendy's phone call was the primary reason we rushed back, but also the city was dangerous. A year earlier I had met up with a fan club member from Long Island to attend an afternoon concert featuring The Kinks and Moody Blues at the Academy of Music on Fourteenth Street. It was about 5 p.m., when it ended, and I headed to Port Authority Bus Terminal to catch a bus home. The bus terminal was disgusting, and the floors so grungy that the soles of your shoes stuck to the accumulated filth. I was on the escalator up to the second floor when I sensed something behind me. I took a quick look, and there was a flasher in the stereotypical tan raincoat, completely open. I started to run up the escalator stairs but before I did, I took a second peek just to be sure. It was terrifying but not scary enough for me to tell my mom. That would have been the end of going to New York City alone. I shared the incident with Mikal.

Riding the subway back from Chinatown to the Delmonico at 7:30 p.m., even with a friend, made me nervous. Mikal and I spent the rest of the evening watching television and waiting for news reports out of Shea Stadium. Not being there was heartbreaking, and I fell asleep with tears running down my cheeks. We never heard from Wendy. The next morning, we packed our overnight bags and headed for New Jersey. I desperately tried to keep a brave face for the fan club members who curiously showed up, anxious for a new installment of my Beatles adventure.

One month later Wendy, back in London, wrote a letter asking why she hadn't heard my thoughts about the concert at Shea Stadium. For

Wendy, with whom I had always been super polite and grateful, not receiving some form of communication from me was unusual. I always followed up with small gifts or notes. Wendy's letter closed with the message that she hoped my friend and I enjoyed the concert—and the special treatment afforded me by the staff and Mr. Sullivan. Now it all made sense—Ed Sullivan's strange reaction to us in the hallway; why we never received a phone call from Wendy coupled with her insistence that we stay at the Delmonico, for which Brian Epstein's company paid. Ed Sullivan had been clued into the plan. We were intentionally given a room on the eleventh floor where he lived, because he was asked to watch after us. Tickets to the Shea Stadium concert were being held at the front desk, marked with my name, but we were never notified to pick them up, nor did a staff member deliver the tickets to our room. The front desk, no matter how five-star the place was, royally messed up! I saw Mikal at our fiftieth high-school reunion, and the first thing we said to each other was . . . remember Ed Sullivan!

In the shadow of all the Beatles controversy, the 1966 Shea Stadium concert didn't sell out, resulting in eleven thousand seats unfilled. Two of them were ours.

PLAYING BRIAN EPSTEIN

I had paid close attention to the business details within the music industry, so I thought it was finally time to find a local band and build an empire, just like Brian Epstein. From what I picked up during fan club visits along with reading *Variety* obsessively, observing record executives and concert promoters like Sid Bernstein, and meeting DJs, I believed I had what it takes to be a successful talent manager.

It wasn't long before I came upon a local band of four guys called US. I approached my best pal, Beverly Don, who was there to help execute a business plan. Fortunately, one of the band members, Brian Grauerholtz, was in our high-school class. During lunch in the school cafeteria Beverly and I struck up a conversation with Brian, asking him about the band's interest in being managed. He thought it was a great idea and told us to come over to his drummer's house in Wyckoff to meet the rest of the band during their next rehearsal.

Ken Turner, guitarist; John Sesnick, drummer; and Steve (I don't remember his last name), with Brian on guitar, comprised the band. They played local outlets with little fan following, but I had confidence that I could make them famous like all the groups arriving from England. Their signature song was a cover of "Gloria." Beverly and I would shout out the song's lyrics throughout the school corridors. Both Beverly and I thought John Sesnick was the cutest of the bunch. We would hang on every word he said and giggle, but before long John's older brother, Steve, seemed even more interesting.

Steve lived in New York City and managed music talent for Andy Warhol. In less than one year from when I met him, Steve became the official manager of the Velvet Underground. Over several months of working with US, I got to know John's mother well, and one day Steve was home in Wyckoff. He was curious who would ever consider managing his brother's band. Immediately upon meeting Steve, he and I got into conversation, eventually moving from the kitchen to the backyard, enjoying a warm day with a cold Tab in hand. Even though Steve was so much older and wiser about the music industry and was working with Andy Warhol, he had no interest in his brother's band. During our conversation I told him about my Beatle experiences; he added that he had met Brian Epstein casually. Unconvinced of the band's potential and doubting my credentials, Steve suggested that I come to the Plastic Exploding Inevitable on St. Mark's Place to experience the Velvet Underground and Nico one day. He would get me in, even though I was underage.

That was a great idea: learning from Steve how to manage a band. This presented one of the only times I had to make a case for my parents to let me go to New York City. St. Mark's Place was adjacent to Alphabet City, and the area had too many drug dealers and prostitutes, both male and female. They were very reluctant to give me permission, but having briefly met his parents, they finally gave in to my repeated requests. I had to promise to take a taxi back to my grandmother's apartment right after the show.

Indeed, the area was dangerous, yet it also held intriguing opportunities. Not long after my parental battle was won, I wrote a letter to poet Allen Ginsberg requesting an interview for *Drumbeats*, the high school newspaper where I was editor. Before I knew it, Ginsberg agreed to be interviewed, and along with a fellow reporter, Andy Wirkmaa, we found ourselves at his Avenue B walkup close to St. Mark's Place.

While there we observed Mr. Ginsberg along with his live-in partner, Peter Orlovsky, engaged in their daily routines and famed beat poet Gregory Corso, who spent the entire time we were there lounging on a mattress on the floor, reading. Mr. Ginsberg gave us an in-depth lesson on Frodoland while Peter left to do grocery shopping. Upon Peter's return he began to sweep the floor and tidy up the apartment.

The danger wasn't the Alphabet City neighborhood but the community-wide controversy that ensued when the interview was ready for print. Mr. Ginsberg reserved the right to approve the article. When he saw that the four-letter words he insisted on using were not included in our final draft, he threatened to demonstrate for freedom of the press at our school. He was familiar with Oakland, having grown up in nearby Paterson. We were under siege from all sides. Andy went to bat against the school bureaucracy fueled by Ginsberg's hostility to the establishment, but we lost. As editor, I decided to risk it and hoped Mr. Ginsberg didn't see *Drumbeats*. I decided to stay away from Alphabet City.

No one had issues after the published article received accolades from faculty, townspeople, and students for innovative reporting. *Drumbeats* even won Columbia University's second-place award for journalism that year, which I accepted on behalf of the paper at a luncheon at the famed Waldorf-Astoria.

And what happened with the band US? I am surprised that you don't recognize them as a '60s singing sensation. I contacted people I thought might help. I made unsolicited phone calls to key music industry executives, most of whom I had only read about in the pages of *Variety*. No one suspected that I was only sixteen years old. Finally, after days of rejection, I was able to arrange a day of meetings with the only two entities who agreed to see us—a late-morning meet-and-greet with Jerry Wexler, vice president at Atlantic Records, and an afternoon meeting at Ashley-Famous Talent Agency for representation.

At that time Mr. Wexler was producing Ray Charles, Wilson Pickett, the Coasters, and the Drifters. It wasn't the right fit for a British-style group. I wanted to see the executives at the Beatles label, Capitol, but they never responded to my calls. Failing other opportunities, Jerry Wexler was willing to meet, so why not? I had the band assemble a reel-to-reel tape of their original songs and covers and created bios for each band member. After a few weeks of dedicated preparation and anxious anticipation, we were ready.

As I was just about to leave to meet up with the band for the meetings, the phone rang. It was Mrs. Grauerholtz and Mrs. Turner, saying that they wouldn't let their sons go to the meetings.

"What?" My screams even startled my dog.

Their excuse was that New York is dangerous, and with John Sesnick driving, they feared we would get lost or be in an accident. I told them I knew the way, having gone from Oakland to New York City nearly every weekend my entire life. Desperate to save the meeting I added that my parents and I had been among the first people to drive across the George Washington Bridge when the lower level opened four years earlier.

All my efforts to make these four guys a worldwide sensation were squelched because two moms would not allow them to go to New York City. Agreed, danger did lurk, and indiscriminate crime was rampant, but we would be together in daylight. I was devastated. Beverly tried to console me when I told her what had happened. I had put so much hope, time, and effort into this band. Did Brian Epstein have to deal with the Beatles' parents or Gerry and the Pacemakers family's paranoia? What would he do? I was being Brian Epstein.

I telephoned both offices to cancel the meetings and thanked them for their interest, trying to keep the invitation alive should the parents alter their decision. I hurt inside more than anything else. It wasn't a matter of pride because I did my best to manage the band and to score these meetings. It was just sadness; we were so close to something big.

For years I followed Jerry Wexler's meteoric career, signing Dusty Springfield, Aretha Franklin, Otis Redding, Led Zeppelin, Bob Dylan,

Carlos Santana, and later Dire Straits and George Michael. Mr. Wexler was among the first music executives to be inducted into the Rock & Roll Hall of Fame in 1987. Ashley-Famous Agency became mega-talent agency ICM, and after a 2022 acquisition, CAA, with a list of music clients that is the who's who of the industry. Could US have made it? We'll never know.

The Velvet Underground show was an amazing evening; and truthfully, I was too young to attend, but it was an experience. Andy Warhol was holding court along with several of his film regulars that I recognized—Holly Woodlawn, Joe Dallesandro, and feminist writer Valerie Solanas.

Jumping forward two years to 1968, right around high-school graduation, I was home watching the 6 o'clock news when a story came on about Valerie Solanas. Valerie believed that Andy Warhol had stolen her play and was going to quietly produce it without Valerie being properly credited and compensated. Angered, she bought a gun, and the previous evening had fired it at Warhol three times, missing him twice. The third shot wounded him. Shot? I had met this deranged woman: my parents' concern was right. Valerie, charged with attempted murder, served three years in prison. The '60s, when we struggled for peace and love, were turning ugly and dangerous.

The day after the Velvet Underground show I phoned Steve to thank him for the evening. Instead of listening to my rambling—thank you, it seemed, wasn't cool—he interrupted, "I'm surprised you're not up at New York Hospital."

"Why?" I asked.

"Brian Epstein's been admitted suffering from hepatitis."

COOKIES FOR BRIAN

I didn't know what hepatitis was or how one contracted the disease, but hearing that Brian Epstein was at New York Hospital signaled that I had to pay him a visit pronto. My parents were visibly concerned when I shared the news that Steve Sesnick confidentially divulged Brian's hospitalization. I telephoned the hospital, but no one was listed under his name. I guessed his New York lawyer Nat Weiss took care of that. Fake names seemed to be the norm anyway.

I begged my parents to take me to see him. My dad knew the hospital well, having been stuck there in an elevator. In November 1965, the infamous Northeast blackout thrust thirty million people into total darkness at approximately 5:20 p.m. for up to thirteen hours. The blackout was blamed on human error during routine maintenance of a safety relay on an electric transmission line in Canada. At that exact time my dad was leaving New York Hospital after visiting his cousin when the elevator came to a sudden halt, in complete darkness. Fortunately, he only had to wait about thirty minutes until the doors opened because the hospital had backup generators. Without streetlights, he slowly made his way back to New Jersey through the surreal darkness of Manhattan.

Reluctantly, my dad said he would drive me into the city so I could take Brian cookies. I loved to bake, and still do, so I went through my mom's recipe file and decided to make him snickerdoodles. I selected this recipe because one ingredient was currants. Scones sometimes had currants, so the cookies would be a familiar taste of home. I also decided to bake enough to drop off some snickerdoodles at fan club headquarters, too.

New York Hospital was at Sixty-Eighth Street and York Avenue. It catered to the exclusive and private. When I conducted research on the hospital, I couldn't find a list of who was born there but one of people who died there: Andy Warhol, Richard Nixon, Malcolm X, and Jim Henson. When my dad and I arrived, we talked to the attendant at the visitors' desk. At first, she would not confirm that Brian Epstein was a patient. I showed her the tin of cookies I had baked; she said she would be right back. After waiting for about fifteen minutes, she returned with someone who escorted me up to his room. Nat Weiss was standing outside the room and said that because someone else was there, he would head home to his place at Sixty-Third Street and Second Avenue.

From a distance behind a glass partition, Brian looked tired. His skin was sallow, and he seemed to have no energy or his usual vibrancy. Joanne Newfield, Brian's secretary, even remarked in a 1967 interview that about ten months prior to his death that Brian looked "awfully jaundiced." From afar I said hello and handed the nurse the tin of cookies. I think he tilted his head in acknowledgment. Brian seemed surprised that someone outside of his closest circle could find him. We spoke briefly about England and his heading home in a day or two. I told him I had always wanted to see England. He said England was especially lovely in April. Why didn't I plan a visit then?

I smiled at him and said enjoy the cookies, "I baked them!"

Brian really didn't respond, but as the door closed behind me, I thought, *I'm going to England.*

Here's the recipe for Brian's Snickerdoodles:
3¼ cups sifted all-purpose flour
½ teaspoon salt
1 teaspoon baking soda
1 teaspoon cinnamon
1 cup butter
1½ cups sugar
3 room-temperature eggs, well beaten
1 cup walnuts, chopped
½ cups currants
½ cup chopped raisins

Sift together flour, salt, baking soda, and cinnamon. Mix butter until soft and add the sugar gradually until smooth. Beat in the eggs. Stir in the flour mixture, walnuts, currants, and raisins. Drop them from a teaspoon onto a greased cookie sheet and bake in a preheated 350° oven for twelve minutes. Makes four dozen cookies. Store in airtight container.

LONDON BOUND

From the moment I first talked about visiting London, I began to plan. I bought travel books and detailed street maps. I wanted to be sure that from the moment I set foot on English soil, I would be set to go. I studied maps for hours learning how to get from place to place. *London A to Z* was my teacher. At holiday time all I wanted was spending money for the upcoming trip. Brian Epstein said April was the month to go, so April it was.

I looked at airlines. After discussing this with my parents, BOAC was the only airline: it was how the Beatles traveled. My mom and I would do this trip together, leaving my dad at home. When I visited Beatles headquarters, everyone was so helpful, sharing advice and suggesting people and places to visit.

I had my own agenda, too. I had pen pals to meet and scheduled a stopover at the fan club. All was running smoothly until mid-December when a letter came from Wendy Hanson, Brian Epstein's personal assistant. Wendy was setting up the more important stops for the trip—to see Brian Epstein, hopefully see the Beatles or possibly other groups that Brian managed, and attend a play on the West End. But the letter sent my visit into a tailspin.

Wendy was resigning her post with Brian at the end of the year. The news was shocking. Wendy was very apologetic about the circumstances that had left her no choice but to resign. She suggested I stay in contact with Jody Haines, her personal secretary, who also worked at Brian's office. Jody would pick up where she left off. Jody included a note with Wendy's letter, assuring me that she would carry on with Wendy's itinerary, and I should contact her directly when I arrived. With Wendy gone, it would not be the same.

I contacted Jody immediately, and she seemed very enthusiastic about the trip. She told me to write closer to the time. Sensing that I would now have to make my own way, I started to write letters after the New Year. Putting together a list, I wanted to see the offices of *The Beatles Monthly* and its editor, Johnny Dean, along with the people at *Fabulous 208* magazine. I wanted to attend a show at the London Palladium; see EMI (Abbey Road) Studios; visit the fan club on Monmouth Street; check out Paul's new house on Cavendish Avenue; explore Harrod's and Fortnum & Mason; and shop the mod stores on King's Road and Carnaby Street and stop at Anello and Davide, workshop for the famous Beatles boots. I had hoped to go to Liverpool following up on a suggestion from Mrs. Harrison, George's mom, visit a trendy nightclub, and walk across the Thames. George's mom was encouraging me to take this trip as we had been corresponding through the mail for nearly three years at this point.

First, though, we needed to select a hotel. I remembered Wendy Hanson saying that the Piccadilly Hotel at Piccadilly Circus would be a central place to stay. She also mentioned that my mother would enjoy shopping at Simpson's right across from the hotel. Martin Moss, a friend, was the managing director of Simpsons Piccadilly and would look after us. His wife, photographer Jane Brown, had also photographed the Beatles. Harrod's was only a short taxi ride away, and the trendy shops at Carnaby Street were off Regent Street and Oxford Street, easily within walking distance from the hotel. A map told me that Wendy was correct, so my mom made a reservation via phone with the Piccadilly Hotel.

Based on my correspondence with Mrs. Harrison, two weeks would be a perfect length of time. I would have just turned seventeen. We chose to leave in the evening on Friday, April 21, and return on Thursday, May 4. On Saturday, May 6, I had to take the SATs. We never considered that I might have jet lag, which could affect my test taking. In those days, the SATs didn't carry the stress and undue pressure they carry today.

I could barely contain myself during school the day I left. I remember sitting in Nick Acocella's English class, raising my hand, and saying that I was leaving for London that evening. I invited my friends Beverly Don, Linda Guldemann, and Michele de Medici to come to JFK airport to see us off. With bags packed and my BOAC shoulder bag ready with my personal items, we left right after school, knowing there could be a lot of traffic driving from New Jersey to the airport. Beverly recently reminded me how excited I was and that on the way back home, my dad took my friends to Jahn's Ice Cream Parlor on Route 4 in Paramus/Fair Lawn to share the legendary Kitchen Sink (assorted ice cream flavors in a huge, silver-plated bowl, enough to serve twelve people).

The flight was smooth, but my mom and I couldn't sleep because we were both so excited. This was my first long plane flight. The only other times I had flown were from LaGuardia to Boston during the summer on the way to camp in Maine. The plane landed in the early morning hours only to find it rainy and bleak—not the swinging London of my imagination. We took a taxi to the Piccadilly Hotel, and the adventure began.

NEMS ENTERPRISES LTD

DIRECTORS:

B. EPSTEIN · C.J. EPSTEIN · G. ELLIS · B. LEE · V. LEWIS

SUTHERLAND HOUSE, 5/6 ARGYLL STREET, LONDON, W.1

TELEPHONE: REGENT 3261

CABLES: NEMPEROR LONDON W1

13th December, 1966.

Miss Debbie Gendler,
34 Dacotah Avenue,
Oakland,
N.J. 07436,
U.S.A.

Dear Debbie,

Unfortunately, my plans have changed since I last wrote to you and I am leaving this job at Christmas. Therefore, I shall not be in London when you arrive in April.

However, do get in touch with Jody Haines who is my secretary.

I do hope you have a very happy Christmas.

With all best wishes.

Yours sincerely,

Wendy Hanson
Personal Assistant to Brian Epstein

WH/jmh

Wendy Hanson, Brian's personal secretary, was an amazing person; she could juggle five things at once with ease and sophistication. Wendy helped plan my visit to England in 1967, and I was shattered to receive this letter that she was leaving her job before my trip.

AUTHOR'S COLLECTION

NEMS ENTERPRISES LTD

DIRECTORS:
B. EPSTEIN · C.J. EPSTEIN · G. ELLIS · B. LEE · V. LEWIS

SUTHERLAND HOUSE, 5/6 ARGYLL STREET, LONDON, W.1

TELEPHONE: REGent 3261
CABLES: NEMPEROR LONDON W 1

Dear Debbie,

     As Miss Hanson says in her letter I am her secretary. I do hope you will keep in touch and let me know if your plans change.

     At the moment, I would suggest that you phone me on the above number when you arrive and perhaps we can work something out then.

     I look forward very much to seeing you.

Jody Haines

When I got to London, Jody gave me perhaps the biggest tip: the boys were back in the studio. Get in touch with George Martin at EMI.
AUTHOR'S COLLECTION

After a short nap, we began to explore. We got to the corner and forgot to look right; with oncoming traffic, we both jumped backward onto the sidewalk. This close call unsettled our nerves, so we went looking for a cup of tea. A lovely tea shop caught our eye, and we popped in for our first cup of steaming hot tea with milk and sugar and some tasty biscuits. It was surreal to be in London. The place I had dreamed about for three years had become a reality; a reality that I believed I had worked hard to achieve.

With rain now coming down fiercely, I wrote in my trip diary that coming to London at this time of year wasn't such a good idea. We went back to the Piccadilly and tried to watch TV, but the picture was all snowy, and we were battling terrible jet lag. Mom and I were already missing my dad, wishing he had come along. Dinnertime came quickly, and with few options we found ourselves in a chain restaurant called "Fortes" right in Piccadilly Circus, with flashing lights luring tourists into the dry indoors. We ordered what we heard was the national dish, steak and kidney pie, already knowing from my mom's friends that it was awful, but hey, we would sample it. After just one taste my mom and I looked down at our plates, pushed them aside, paid, and left. The food was all that English food's reputation had prepared us for—terrible. We hoped that the next day would be better.

We woke to bright sun and a sumptuous English breakfast in the down-stairs dining room: eggs, sausage, beans, mushrooms, grilled tomatoes, and bacon that looked like ham. I was introduced to my first croissant with thick strawberry preserves set on exquisite china with silver-plated utensils placed on freshly starched white linens. This was the England I had expected.

FAB FOR *FABULOUS 208*

One of the best ways to keep on top of all the emerging British groups and latest news was subscribing to *Fabulous*, later renamed *Fabulous 208* magazine after a 1966 merger with Radio Luxembourg; *208* was their broadcast wavelength. Australian Beatles photographer Robert Whitaker of "butcher cover" fame began his career at the magazine. The States had many teen magazines but none like *Fabulous 208*. Primarily in full color, with a center pinup suitable for a bedroom wall, it was published weekly, and I arranged for a subscription. I discovered the pop magazine from an English pen friend, who sent me a centerfold of the Beatles for my school locker. The photographs were truly fabulous, deserving of this magazine, and I treasured every issue.

Not only did I keep up with the British beat through *Fabulous 208*, but it had articles and photos on the latest fashion trends from Mary Quant, Twiggy, Carnaby Street, to the happenings at London's hippest clubs and the top television shows. It was from the pages of *Fabulous 208* that I virtually met Cathy McGowan, my idol, of *Ready, Steady, Go!* Cathy, who became known as "Queen of the Mods," was a trendsetter. Cathy had long straight brown hair, with fringe (translation, bangs) cut across the forehead grazing her eyes that were outlined in dark exotic eyeliner and lips strictly Yardley of London. She wore the cutest clothes with white stockings, all purchased from King's Road shops. I have heard from multiple sources that Cathy was the inspiration for a scene in *A Hard Day's Night*. It goes as follows: when George Harrison mentioned to a television producer that the girl passing by them is the "TV girl" who gets everything wrong, the producer replies, "She's a trendsetter."

Beside insider features on the groups, *Fabulous 208* also shot photo spreads in stars' homes, giving us all a peek into the band's real lives. The writers also shared a look at their own *Fabulous 208* offices. They were on Farringdon Street in London's Fleet Street, where many musicians and actors of the day would stop by for an impromptu visit. The magazine office was a place for pop stars to hang out.

When I confirmed the dates for travel to London, the *Fabulous 208* office was one place I had to see during the trip. I wrote the editor assistant, Anne Wilson, whose name I saw listed in the masthead. I included in the letter that I was the editor of my high school newspaper, *Drumbeats*, and was thinking about a career in journalism. I wanted it known that I had a professional interest in visiting besides being a fan of the publication.

Writer Jon Savage in an article in London's *The Observer* dated Saturday, September 5, 2009, wrote about *Fabulous* and the few other teen pop music publications:

> It's the nearest you'll get to experiencing the 60s as they happened, which should be mandatory for any pop obsessive . . . the 60s pop mags help to reassert an alternative canon; one where women have equal status; one where enthusiasm and sharpness win out over pomposity every time.

Anne replied quickly. She invited me to visit the offices while in London. When I called the first Monday after we arrived, Anne deemed the next day was perfect. I had arranged to spend Tuesday with my pen pal, Vivien Carter, and my mom, touring some sights. My mom, though, encouraged me to keep the date with Vivien, and they would do something together while I visited *Fabulous 208*.

As I expected, it was raining when I headed for the office, but my excitement could not be dampened. Vivien and my mom dropped me off in front of the building, and they continued in the black taxi. An old elevator took me up a few flights to the entrance. Issues of *Fabulous 208* were tacked on the walls. Anne was there, her secretary, and several others. I also remember a very cheery young man with red cheeks named Cliff who was working on an upcoming issue. They walked me through the entire process from conception to distribution of the magazine. I was very impressed and tried to listen closely, even though my excitement prohibited me from fully concentrating. My memorabilia collection includes at least forty issues of *Fabulous 208* intact.

In addition to publishing their standard issue, editors were engrossed in planning a special insert to cover the upcoming "14-Hour Technicolor Dream Concert" to be held that Saturday, April 29, in the Alexandra Palace (Ally Pally) just north of Central London. The event was sponsored by the underground newspaper the *International Times*. Years later, I learned that my friend Jim Haynes was one of the primary promoters of the event and booked Pink Floyd to perform at dawn. Cliff, a staffer at *Fabulous 208*, was curious whether I was going. "I don't think so," I replied. Being so singularly focused on the Beatles, if they weren't performing, why would I go? Was that a shortsighted mistake!

One of the artists featured was performance artist Yoko Ono. John Lennon went to Ally Pally with his friend John Dunbar (married to Marianne

Faithfull at the time) from his Indica Gallery. It was a last-minute decision; he had only met Yoko six months earlier at the Indica, where Yoko was exhibiting her work, "Unfinished Paintings and Objects." A BBC show called *Man Alive* shows John Lennon in the crowd enjoying the action. Too bad.

It was Anne who suggested that my mom and I must walk over to the Indica Gallery after hearing that I was staying at the Piccadilly Hotel. The Indica at the time was still underground, known only to select artsy circles, which seemed to include Anne. Unbeknownst to me at the time, the Indica would figure prominently in the Beatles story, both for Paul McCartney and John Lennon.

The thought of finding my way back to the hotel via the Underground to join Vivien and my mom was somewhat daunting as it was nearly 5 p.m. One of the friendly secretaries at *Fabulous 208* volunteered to take me along on her way home and point me in the right direction for the Piccadilly Circus Underground stop. Her name was Susan, and we exchanged a few letters when I returned home as we discovered we were both the same age. Susan and I had little in common except our love for music and groups. At seventeen I was preparing for college the following year; my new friend was already working full-time. Back home, at age seventeen we really weren't taken seriously—we were just "kids." In England by age seventeen, most "kids" were working adults, many on their own. England, I was experiencing, moved to a very different beat.

MAKE MINE "MOD"

I would be remiss not to include something on the mod fashions and makeup of the time that seemed to be at their height when I visited Swinging London in 1967. Fashion trendsetter Mary Quant was at the pinnacle of her popularity with the introduction of the miniskirt in 1964, soon to be followed by her move into makeup and fashion accessories. Wearing tights, patterned or light colored, was the fashion. The same year the trendy mod sticklike model Twiggy became the face of Yardley, and we all wanted to wear their quintessential English lavender fragrances.

Supermodels such as Jean Shrimpton and George Harrison's wife, Pattie Boyd, led the influencers with go-go boots, pale soft makeup with dark eyeliner and heavy mascara, sporting either the short Vidal Sassoon boy haircuts or long straight hair with thick fringe.

Carnaby Street reigned supreme as a fashion mecca, as did Chelsea's Kings Road. One of the shops on Kings Road was on my must-see list—Granny Takes a Trip. Known as the first psychedelic clothing shop in London, it was opened by three colleagues in early 1966: Sheila Cohen, who collected vintage clothing; Sheila's boyfriend, Nigel Waymouth, a journalist/graphic designer known for iconic '60s psychedelic posters; and talented John Pearse, who had amazing tailoring skills learned while working in posh Savile Row. The store serviced its famous clientele with one-of-a-kind fashions; the customer list was a who's who—Jane Asher, Noel Redding, John Lennon, George Harrison, the Stones, Jimi Hendrix, Dennis Hopper, and, later, Eric Clapton, David Bowie, Miles Davis, Paul McCartney, Robert Plant, and even Salman Rushdie. The Beatles sported Granny Takes a Trip–designed shirts in the photo for the inner sleeve of the *Revolver* album.

I first learned about Granny Takes a Trip from *Time* magazine when it devoted an issue to the Swinging Sixties. One of my first stops upon arrival in London was Kings Road, but I was disappointed. The street didn't have the excitement I had expected—it was run-down, devoid of swinging anything—until I reached Granny Takes a Trip. Entry to the shop was through the beaded curtain. Inside it was a happening place with clothes of unusual fabrics, lace, and crazy colors hanging all around the shop. Music was blasting. It was small, just two small rooms, which reeked of incense (or what I thought was incense). The view from the street was very deceptive, except for one important feature—the front of the building. Known for its pop art Warhol-inspired rotating facades, when I visited the front was a huge painting of the 1930s actress and sex symbol Jean Harlow.

Relationships among the owners deteriorated. John Pearse left, and Nigel and Sheila signed over 51 percent ownership to their store manager and local fashion businessman, Freddie Hornik. Freddie was known from another clothing shop, Dandie Fashions, on Kings Road. Interestingly, Dandie became for a short time the Beatles' Apple Tailoring shop with Neil Aspinall working as a director of the company. In addition, the store's basement also housed the Apple-financed hair salon where Leslie Cavendish, the Beatles' hairstylist, worked.

After Dandie's decline, Freddie Hornick brought in two New York fashion entrepreneurs to assist at Granny. They changed much of the merchandise, but rock royalty still flocked to the trendy shop. In 1970, they opened a boutique in New York and, eventually, Los Angeles in 1972, at 468 North Doheny Drive on the border of Beverly Hills and West Hollywood. It was not far from where Peter Asher would later open his talent management company. In 1974, under new management, Granny Takes a Trip moved to 8000 Sunset Boulevard and stayed in business for six years.

Nigel Waymouth lived in Los Angeles for more than a decade. Now he is back in London, where he continues occasionally as a graphic artist. Tom Hanks and Eric Idle own pieces of his artwork. Nigel's son Louis was a writer on *The Late Late Show with James Corden* and was among the show's regular performers. John Pearse will always be known as a tailoring stylist for the most discerning in London. Freddie Hornick died at age sixty-five in London in 2009, and I don't know what happened to Sheila Cohen. By now she could be a granny herself.

Also involved in Dandie as an investor was a close McCartney and Lennon friend, socialite Tara Browne. Tara was the heir to the Guinness fortune and was the poster child for rock royalty who attempted to cut through class boundaries via music and wealth. It was reported that Tara also was an investor in the popular London discotheque Sibylla's along with George Harrison. Evidence that George owned a small fraction of the disco is scant; rumor was that they made him a part owner to ensure the club's success with the mod crowd.

Tara's friendship with the McCartney brothers is not what made him the enduring icon he has become but his untimely death at age twenty-one. He was said to be immortalized in the Lennon/McCartney song "A Day in the Life." I understand that all the Beatles were taken with Tara, and his passing was a powerful wake-up call that despite tremendous wealth and influence, people are not invincible.

WITH A LOT OF LUCK

I had already been in London a few days and wasn't yet in contact with anyone at Brian Epstein's office or the fan club. After finishing breakfast in the elegant hotel dining room, I phoned Brian's office and was told I could visit in late morning. Wanting to plan the day, I also phoned the fan club; a fellow there said Wednesday was a good day to stop in even though things were in chaos. Even without Wendy Hanson's organization, appointments were falling into place.

During the nearly three years I had corresponded with Wendy, I wrote her at Sutherland House on Argyll Street, but my phone contact told me to go to 24 Chapel Street in Belgravia. Chapel Street was a short taxi ride from the hotel. Passing Hyde Park, I got my bearings, because my mom and I had walked leisurely through the park to Buckingham Palace on our first full day in London. People were now randomly sprawled out on blankets or reclining in lawn chairs, trying to catch the rays of sun finally breaking through the cloudy London skies.

When the taxi announced that we had arrived, I fumbled through the shilling notes and coins, holding out my hand with the money so the cabbie could help himself to the fare. I had the hardest time with British currency—tuppence, quid, halfpenny, bob notes, and shillings until decimalization of the currency took place in 1971.

The building we stopped at looked odd, more like a person's home on a residential street. I took a deep breath, walked up the front steps, and rang the bell. I was ushered into a beautifully designed entry by what seemed like a butler right out of a movie. Jody Haines, Wendy Hanson's former personal secretary, greeted me; and we talked about Wendy and how sad I was that she wasn't working there any longer. Jody smiled, agreeing that she missed Wendy as well. Joanne Newfield would be down shortly. Jody was a major Beatles fan and got the job by bringing attention to herself at Beatles concerts by always taking carnations for the group. In fact, Jody brought so many carnations that she and a friend became known as the "Carnation Girls." Brian and staff noticed and thought she would be a loyal addition to the team.

Wendy frequently spoke of Joanne Newfield, and her initials appeared beneath Wendy's signature on our correspondence. In 1965, a twenty-year old Joanne met George and Ringo at a London Club. George suggested she ring up Brian Epstein, who needed more office help. Joanne was a fan one day and a staffer the next, working with Wendy Hanson. After Wendy left, Joanne became Brian's personal assistant working out of his home on Chapel Street. They had a close relationship, both having come from middle-class Jewish families, and they connected on many levels. It was Joanne with Brian's butler and housekeeper, who found Brian lying motionless in his bed in August 1967.

For a short time, Brian formed a partnership with Robert Stigwood, best known for the Bee Gees' management, and in late 1967, after Brian's death, Joanne went to work for Stiggy. The following year Joanne married Bee Gees drummer Colin Petersen, and they moved to Australia. I've heard that Brian brought in Stiggy to prove to the Beatles that business remained in high gear, specifically in view of Allen Klein's growing interest in the band.

Looking around, I sensed that this wasn't an office; it was Brian's home. The fireplace had ornate carvings and marble insert and brass andirons in what seemed to be the living room. Above the fireplace was a large, gilded mirror with items placed on the mantel, candles, and a large sofa with coordinating chairs and a very used velvet chair positioned close to big windows. I also spotted photographs of children: one looked like Julian Lennon; another was of a bit younger boy and of a young girl. Much later I learned she was Joanne, Brian's niece. The floors were polished hardwood and covered with Persian rugs that looked very expensive, the windows with heavy patterned drapery. Bookshelves were filled with leather-bound volumes and a few statues. Everything had the feeling of prized European antiques that one would find in a wealthy grandmother's apartment or museum. A large painting looked like it had been created during the time of George Washington.

I waited nearly ten minutes for Joanne, who introduced herself with caution and formality. Wendy was not the gushiest individual, but Joanne looked at me with reserve. I had hoped that Wendy let Joanne know who I was, but apparently that hadn't happened. Joanne had to know something about my history because she regularly typed Wendy's correspondence to me. Brian was in, I was told, but had little time to spare because he was off to see Dr. Flood. Quite a strange name. I asked if I could at least say a quick hello.

Joanne motioned for me to remain seated in the chair. I spotted something I had never seen in a house—an intercom. I sat patiently until a man opened the door cautiously; Brian trailed behind. He didn't look well. The other man had been arranging flowers in a vase before he was asked to bring Brian to the drawing room. Brian then introduced me to his butler; he had the traditional butler's name, James.

Brian seemed tired, depleted. He was dressed casually, not with the elegant gold cuff links I had seen him regularly sport in New York City. He asked how I was enjoying my trip. I told him I was headed to Liverpool and would be seeing Mr. and Mrs. Harrison; I had come to know them well through letters. Brian said I would like it up north where the people were like those in New York. Louise Harrison would be a fine host. He wished me an enjoyable stay and said to call the office if I needed anything.

It was the last time I saw Brian. I later learned from the New York fan club gals that I was fortunate to catch Brian. He was home for a short stay as part of his rehab at the Priory Clinic in London's section called Putney. Indeed, it has proved to be a forever memory of a person I truly loved and respected.

Joanne and Jody escorted me to the front door, this time with a sense of careful understanding. It was almost like I had been let in on a secret. They asked what else I had planned, and I told them I would try to visit the fan club the following day. If Wendy had still been working for Brian, the plan was for me to spend the entire day at the office. They said I would enjoy meeting the girls there, namely Bettina Rose(?) or Maureen Donaldson or Val Sumpter. Freda Kelly was up north. The office was in the midst of moving, Joanne explained, as she inched back into the hallway.

Jody sensing my disappointment, coming this far for so little, whispered that I should follow up with George Martin because "the boys" were back in the studio.

"In the studio?" I repeated.

Jody quickly jotted down a phone number to call later that afternoon. "That should be all you need," she explained.

Would I be going to EMI Studios? Jody really came through! The visit had lasted less than twenty-five minutes. I rushed back to the hotel clutching the phone number with a renewed spirit and energy. In London, everything was possible.

When I got back to the hotel room, I shared this amazing news with my mother and I decided to phone George Martin immediately, not wait as instructed. After three attempts I talked to a person named Colin, who was vague about details. "Yes, some members of the Beatles were expected that evening" is all I had to hear, not caring about anything else.

"Could I stop by?" was all I could think to ask.

Colin didn't say yes, but he didn't say no. "Tomorrow would be best." They had just started, and everyone was still arriving. "Around 4 . . . till tomorrow then." I let Colin know that I had corresponded with George

Martin, hoping that it would validate the connection when I showed up the next day.

I had originally wanted to visit the fan club, but that would have to wait. When I called to say I wouldn't be visiting as planned, no one seemed to care. I detected chaos in the background. I was still wondering who was at the fan club . . . Maureen Donaldson, Bettina Rose, Val Sumpter, or Mary Cockram, whose name wasn't even mentioned.

I had no promise that I would even get to see the Beatles as they recorded late at night. At least George Martin would be there, which was more than I had hoped.

We passed the early part of the next day visiting the Tate Gallery. My mom was quite tired, but when it was time to head to EMI, she chose to come along. I hadn't been formally invited to visit, so having her along was a smart idea as evidenced by her actions with the police in front of the Sullivan theater years earlier. By now she was also curious to know some of the people I had been talking about for so long.

We took the red double-decker bus to EMI. I don't remember why we chose the bus, but I guess we wanted to see more of London than just the tourist areas accessible from the hotel, and my mom's feet were tired from the Tate. Fortunately, I still have the diary of my trip with all the details. The bus route was #139; I don't know if it still runs today. We got off the bus and walked down one street toward Abbey Road, according to my *London A to Z*, but found ourselves in the other direction instead, in front of a Jewish-style delicatessen called Panzer's. We went in and bought a few things to take back to the hotel. Panzer's is still open for business.

We finally arrived at the front entrance to EMI Studios. A man standing at the top of the stairs opened the door for us. No reception person was in sight. We felt awkward but kept walking. Then a King's Road–style girl around my age stopped to ask if we needed help to find our way. The hallway was quiet because I think we arrived too early. I told the girl, whose name I wrote down as Jackie, that I had spoken with Colin the day before about visiting.

"Yes, you then want Studio 2," she said and led us to the door.

Not knowing what to expect, we opened the door carefully. Two men were standing in a cavernous room, their arms folded. Another gentleman was descending a narrow flight of stairs against the wall. One of them was George Martin—I recognized him immediately. I didn't know the other two people, although I came to learn that the man on the stairs was Geoff Emerick, the studio audio engineer on most Beatles recordings. Geoff was already working at EMI well before the Beatles first arrival to record.

Geoff temporarily left working with the band a little over a year later. He attributed this to being unable to work with the Beatles and all the infighting during the recording of *The Beatles White Album*. Geoff ultimately returned to work on the *Abbey Road* album, for which he received a Grammy, and later worked with Paul on his solo and Wings albums. It's common knowledge that Geoff always favored Paul.

Years later, I met Geoff again when Mike McCartney introduced us before Paul's concert at the Los Angeles Forum on Thanksgiving 1989. Geoff sat right behind us for the show. Geoff wrote a great book about the Beatles titled *Here, There and Everywhere—My Life Recording the Music of the Beatles*. A must-read. Sadly, he passed away in 2018.

As we entered the studio, Mr. Martin came right over and kindly introduced himself. I explained how I came to be there, and he seemed fine with that explanation. I told him we had exchanged letters back in 1964, and 1965, writing about the song "Things We Said Today." Whether or not he remembered, he nodded his head.

The studio was smaller than I had imagined. A grand piano was off to one side, and there were microphones, chairs, two small tables, and standing light fixtures under a high ceiling. The floors were covered with well-worn patterned rugs. At the top of the stairs was a big glass window overlooking the space where we stood. That was the control room, which was dark, and I remember a small clock positioned high on the wall that I stared at nervously, not knowing where to look.

Mr. Martin told us we could take a seat on the red chairs against the wall. He also asked if I had met any of the Beatles before. I related the incident of the meeting at the Warwick after their press conference. For some unfathomable reason, I explained how I stuffed their trash into my purse, and how, while shaking John Lennon's hand, cigarette ash and water leaked through the bag's side seam. All three men laughed. One commented that they'd be checking my bag before I left the room.

The Beatles would not be recording that evening, but Paul, and perhaps Ringo, was due to stop by. "Would we care to wait?"

"Sure," I responded, trying desperately to remain composed even though I was ready to collapse.

Mr. Martin added that the song in the process of being recorded was "Magical Mystery Tour" for a new album they had just begun the night before. We remained seated on cushy red seats, silently observing the three men going up and down the stairs—when in came Ringo. A few minutes later, Paul followed. It was startling, and my mom and I remained seated, trying to blend into the wall. Looking back, I think our lack of emotion stood out more than if I had rushed in their direction. It was around 4 p.m. They weren't there to work but had just stopped by on their way to somewhere else. I couldn't discern the exact nature of any of this. Paul, I overheard, had recorded late the night before and had no interest in putting in time this evening. It was beginning to feel awkward because there was no purpose to our presence in the studio.

George Martin motioned that our visit was about over. He mentioned to Ringo and Paul that these two Americans had stopped by and asked if they remembered me . . . the fan club gal with the leaky rubbish. They both nodded, with little reaction or interest. I tried desperately to get their attention, mentioning that I would be going to Liverpool to see Mrs. Harrison and, hopefully, Jim and Angela McCartney. I stressed that I had written them letters, and they had invited me.

Paul ignored my comment but countered, saying, "So . . . you're over here from America—have you been around touring and to any of clubs . . . the Bag O' Nails?"

I responded, "No, I don't know anyone in London who goes to clubs," and added, "The only club I had ever heard of was the Marquee Club."

That really wasn't true. a few other clubs were on my list, but I was too stunned to remember the names. Luckily, the Marquee Club got a reaction because Paul nodded like he thought it was acceptable. He suggested that I go that night to the Bag O' Nails.

"It's a good place to go," he said as mom and I rapidly left the studio, clutching our Panzer's goodies.

The minute my mom heard there was a possibility that I might go to a club she decided, "We need to go shopping." My clothes weren't suitable. Trendy was the word!

There wasn't time for a bus back to Piccadilly. We headed by taxi to Kings Road and Mary Quant's shop, Bazaar. I didn't find anything appropriate: everything was geared to a Twiggy-like figure, and that wasn't me! However, the salesgirl, Linda, convinced me to have my hair cut like all the London mod girls. She made an appointment for me at 7 p.m. At least my hair would be perfect! Linda said Barry Kibble's place was all the rage with insiders, whereas Vidal Sassoon received the publicity and attention.

Barry Kibble was in today's terms a "hairdresser to the stars," as reported in his 2006 obituary. "Although not quite Vidal Sassoon," his son commented, "he was a top London hairdresser in his day . . . part of the '60s fashion scene," he added.

With my hair appointment set, my mom suggested that we go to Selfridge's on Oxford Street—a big department store. When we inquired at the information desk where best to look for a dress, we were directed to a new boutique within the store called Miss Selfridge. After trying on a few things, my mom spotted an outfit—lime green empire-waisted polka dot dress with a matching coat. Perfect for an April evening at a club. With no time for tailoring or shortening, it fit perfectly, so we bought it. We also purchased white hose—very Pattie Boyd Harrison inspired—that would work well with new British ghillies (patent leather tie shoes) I had purchased the day before on Regent Street.

We arrived at Barry Kibble's salon right on time. The place was packed with women having their hair styled. Barry owned the shop with his mom, Doris. I sat down in Barry's chair, and we discussed what type of cut I wanted. I explained that I didn't want my bangs cut. The entire shop full of clients and Barry laughed. What had I said?

Barry explained that in England they hadn't been called "bangs" in years—very old-fashioned. In London bangs were called fringe. How long did I want my fringe? Long!

I walked out of the salon barely recognizing myself with this stylish mod cut. I wondered how this cut, which many would say looked like a boy, would go over back in New Jersey. But, hey, this was 1967 London, and how fortunate I was to be here. With a new dress and haircut, I was ready for the Bag O' Nails!

Prior to George Martin and Paul mentioning Bag O' Nails, I hadn't heard of the club. There were other clubs, though, that I was very curious about. The Marquee Club on Wardour Street topped my list. I first heard about the Marquee Club from New York publicist Connie de Nave, who worked for the Rolling Stones and Herman's Hermits among others. Connie was at a Herman's Hermits concert that Sid Bernstein promoted, and she mentioned in conversation that the Marquee was the place where the Stones played live for the first time. I noted that one day I would like to visit this amazing place. Every prominent English group played there—the Kinks, the Spencer Davis Group, Manfred Mann, the Animals, the Yardbirds, Cream, Pink Floyd, and later the Police, the Cure, and David Bowie. From what I learned, this was the single most important venue for emerging bands, and I thought it would be interesting to experience it firsthand.

The other two clubs were The Scotch of St. James and the Ad-Lib Club owned by Oscar Lerman. The Scotch of St. James became known for its upscale clientele and pop royalty, who would go there from the Indica Gallery next door in Mason's Yard. The Beatles frequented the Ad-Lib Club. In 1964, I bought an album called *Live at the Ad-Lib Club—music by The Aztecs*. I bought the album because the cover bore a picture of the Beatles and their signatures, endorsing the club as their favorite. The Aztecs as a band were unknown, but if the place was good enoughfor the Beatles, it was good enough to include on my must-see list. When I arrived in London, I discovered that it had burned down a few years earlier. I was lucky that I hadn't mentioned the Ad-Lib to Paul when he asked if I knew about London clubs. It would have been very uncool to think the place was still around.

A few years ago, I learned some Beatles trivia about the Ad-Lib. Owner Oscar Lerman married Jackie Collins, and they had a daughter, Tiffany. Both Jackie Collins and Tiffany Lerman were guests on the television

E.M.I. RECORDS LTD

Controlled by Electric & Musical Industries Ltd—the greatest recording organisation in the World

E.M.I. HOUSE · 20 MANCHESTER SQUARE · LONDON W.1

Tel: HUNter 4488 · Telex No. 22043 · Inland Telegrams: EMIRECORD, LONDON TELEX · Cables: EMIRECORD, LONDON, W.1

C/S9/JLS.

August 5th. 1964.

Miss Debbie Gendler,
34, Dacotah Avenue,
Oakland.
N.J.
U.S.A.

Dear Debbie,

Thank you for your recent letter which was passed on to me by the T.V. producer Paul Noble.

I appreciate your kind remarks very much and I am very glad that you like the Beatles' new records. 'The Things we Said Today' is one of my favourites too.

With best wishes,
Yours sincerely,

George Martin

G.H. Martin.
Artists & Repertoire Manager.

STATESIDE · M-G-M · MERCURY · TOP RANK · LIBERTY · UNITED ARTISTS · VERVE RECORDS
AND OF COURSE—E.M.I. TAPE RECORDS AND EMITEX

I saw George Martin interviewed on New York's WNEW-TV in 1964. I wrote him in care of the show's producer, Paul Noble, who forwarded my letter to Mr. Martin about the song "Things We Said Today." This is Mr. Martin's response. This letter exchange turned out to be critical when I arrived at EMI Studios (Abbey Road) in 1967.

AUTHOR'S COLLECTION

show where I worked. When in studio, I mentioned that I had met Oscar Lerman once in London. Tiffany immediately questioned, "At Tramp?" Tramp was his very popular 1970s London and Los Angeles clubs. I said, "No . . . from the Ad-Lib!" I think I dated myself terribly because she looked at me somewhat doubtful that I was that old. It was also at the Ad-Lib, Tiffany added, where John and Cynthia and George and Pattie had visited the night they were first given LSD. I had planned to ask Jackie Collins about that the next time I booked her on the show, but shortly after her appearance she passed away.

CLUBBING SWINGING LONDON STYLE

It was after 9 p.m., with a hint of daylight lingering above the gray clouds. I was ready to leave for Bag O' Nails. My mom saw me down to the hotel lobby, and I decided to walk because it was just a short distance to the club, and it would pass some time. Cutting behind the buildings from Piccadilly rounding Swallow Street, I passed another popular disco, Sibylla's, a fixture of the London club scene. I had heard that George Harrison had an ownership in Sibylla's; supposedly, Guinness heir Tara Browne had been an investor, too. If club owners could get rock royalty engaged in any type of ownership, usually it translated into success for the club, and Sibylla's was no different. For this evening, Sibylla's was just another club among many; it was all about Bag O' Nails. I reached Regent Street and walked toward Oxford Circus.

I arrived at the Bag O' Nails without a map, proud of that accomplishment. Kingly Street, where the club was located, was adjacent to Carnaby Street. I later read in a magazine that Neil Aspinall once recounted that while walking on Kingly Street, he and Paul McCartney worked on details about the Sgt. Pepper album. I just remember feeling so at home on those streets that evening.

I wasn't confident how I would get into the club. Many London clubs were by membership only. But the doorman, looking me over, heard my American or Canadian accent (he wasn't sure), and I was in. Being American was helpful. Back in 1967, Americans weren't standard fixtures in London yet. We stood out from the crowd, and many Brits hadn't met anyone from the United States. That worked to my advantage because the first person I met that evening talked about the States, curious why I was in London and what I thought about his city.

The nightclub was so dimly lit I barely could find my way. In the basement room, where the activity was going on, the band was playing on a stage at the far end. Booths were on both sides, at varying levels, where people were seated. At the opposite end of the room were also raised seats. I could tell that it was difficult to have any conversation because the live music was blasting, and people were dancing in the center of the room on the long, narrow dance floor. Maybe that was a good thing. I wished I had a friend to enjoy the club with for the evening.

I walked over to a table and sat down next to a group who motioned for me to join them. One of the guys introduced himself as one of the New Animals. I knew who Eric Burdon and the Animals were and liked them a lot but didn't know the New Animals. A year earlier I had even gone to JFK Airport to see the Animals and Dusty Springfield arrive on the same TWA flight. Welcoming groups to New York was always fun when there was nothing else special to do in town. Carey Transport from Manhattan to JFK was my standard mode of transport, and in the earliest trips friends Sharon and sometimes Roz, visiting from Atlantic City, would join in the fun.

Not feeling secure in my knowledge of the Animals, I played along, pretending I knew just who he was. The conversation primarily centered on music, clubs, drug references, and the "14-Hour Technicolor Dream Concert" that everyone was discussing. They were curious who was the most popular in America now and wanted to know if I had ever seen Bob Dylan (no, I hadn't). I responded the best I could over the loud music. I told them that Donovan was a favorite. Not knowing I had any knowledge of Brian Epstein, they asked if I had been to see Donovan appearing at the Saville Theatre, which Brian owned. *Donovan*, I thought to myself. *I should never have given up the unpaid job running his fan club!* Until that moment, I hadn't thought of visiting the Saville. One in the group added that they had heard all the Beatles had attended opening night just a few evenings before. Did I blow it with Donovan!

I didn't want to seem too interested in Donovan or the Beatles, so I made a mental note to ask the hotel concierge about getting tickets the next day and just let the topic fade into the music. A girl in the group mentioned the name Spanish Tony Sanchez and that she was gobsmacked about something he pulled off. They used strange words in London. I could see that the name caused everyone to pay immediate attention. I asked if he was a musician. Everyone laughed because I hadn't heard of him. Many British artists didn't make it in America, and it sounded like he was a guitar player. Over the din the woman quickly explained that he was the person you could go to buy special items. I just let Spanish Tony Sanchez drop.

Someone by the name of Carl Douglas was spotted entering the club, and the entire group started to talk about him and check him out. I hadn't heard of him either but quickly learned that he was a regular performer at Bag O' Nails. Tonight, it seemed, he was just dropping by, and everyone made a big deal of it. It wasn't until 1974, seven years later, when I heard the name Carl Douglas mentioned again, this time in connection with his one-hit-wonder "Kung Fu Fighting."

I was underage, but that didn't seem to bother anyone. I freely joined in with a round of rum and Coke followed by some scotch. I was beginning to feel sick. For the next round, I pulled out a £50 note. Drinks were on me. It was an easy way to make friends. Fortunately, I didn't need to make change and trusted the server to be honest.

It was after 11 p.m. when Paul, with Beatles roadie Mal Evans and a man I didn't recognize, entered the club. It was a relief to see Mal. I was curious about what had happened at the airport in Manila, and this was the perfect time to ask him how he was doing after the beating. I hadn't yet learned that some things you simply don't bring up.

From first impressions, the man with Paul and Mal was not part of the Beatles world I knew. He was walking with a very confident gait. I should have paid more attention: I learned that he was Prince Stanislaus Klossowski de Rola, better known as "Stash." Stash was a semipermanent houseguest at Paul McCartney's home on Cavendish Avenue.

Mal Evans was, for me, by far the more interesting person. He was a former Cavern Club bouncer and Liverpool telephone engineer who Brian Epstein hired to work as a road manager for the Beatles. Together with Neil Aspinall the two men would drive the Beatles van and set up their equipment at gigs. He was a big guy, serving as a Beatles bodyguard and deterrent to groping fans. Mal accompanied the Beatles on all their tours and many personal trips. Mal also appeared in their films and eventually wrote and produced music for Badfinger and Joey Molland, who showed up at Mike McCartney's book signing party at my house in Los Angeles years later.

As close as Mal was to the Beatles, his pay and status never reflected his abilities, contributions, and loyalty. Neil Aspinall was moved into increasingly responsible positions, but Mal always hovered over the band. In time, financial problems plagued Mal and, in turn, his relationship with his wife and son suffered. He traveled to India with the Beatles, attended Paul's marriage to Linda, and helped compose music, lyrics. and the concept for the Sgt. Pepper album, receiving no royalty payments or acknowledgment of his contributions. Later in his career, Mal worked with Keith Moon and Apple recording artist and George Harrison's friend Jackie Lomax, but otherwise he had a difficult time of it.

In the early 1970s, Mal separated from his wife and moved to Los Angeles, primarily influenced by John Lennon's move west when he left Yoko temporarily for his "lost weekend" adventure with May Pang. Mal was working on a book of Beatles' memoirs and living with a girlfriend when severe depression overshadowed his life. On January 5, 1976, Mal's girlfriend became increasingly frightened that he was playing with an air rifle and seemed ultra-depressed. She first called Mal's book collaborator, who tried to help. With little luck, she then called the police, telling them Mal had taken an unknown amount of Valium. The police went to the house to investigate. Upon arrival, they went directly up to Mal's bedroom, where he refused to put down the air rifle. The police didn't know it was an air rifle, and Mal ignored their demands. Belligerent toward the officers and refusing to put down the gun, Mal aimed at the police. In self-defense, the officers fired their guns, killing Mal instantly. At only age forty this was an incomprehensible ending for a trusted friend and colleague who had given his all to the Beatles but received few rewards in return. Mal's son Gary, along with trusted Beatles historian Ken Womack, wrote a book based on Mal's extensive diaries, which was to be published in 2023. I hope this part of Mal's life will finally be sorted out.

By now Bag O' Nails was packed. Everyone kept their eyes glued on Paul, sending him drinks in return for his acknowledgment of their existence. It was apparent that Paul had his regular table. At my new friends' urging, I went over to Mal, Paul, and Stash. Paul seemed surprised to see me, even though he had told me about the club. Nervously, I signaled my new pals to come over and told Paul and Mal they were asking me about living in New York. It was perfect timing, because both Paul and Mal talked about their trip to the States from which they had just returned.

Paul spoke about visiting Jane Asher in Denver, and I tried to tell him that I had chosen Colorado for a fifth-grade school project. He asked me if I liked it there. I told him I'd never been. Paul looked at me like I was a very strange sort. The New Animal knew Paul, and they talked separately. Everyone ordered more drinks, and Paul, Mal, and Stash ordered food—steak, chips, and peas. This was way beyond my comfort level, but here I was at the Bag O' Nails, listening to live music with a bunch of famous people. Life could never be better than this moment. How could I ever explain this to my friends back home?

Even with Mal Evans there, I said little because I was frightened to speak, and the music was blasting. Drinking and observing was how I spent the rest of the night. Discussing the incidents in Manila didn't seem appropriate at midnight. I overheard Paul and Mal talk about the studio the night before and how they had to return the next night. The conversation then moved to cars. Paul talked about his car, an Aston Martin DB6, parked not far away. They said it was good that Neil hadn't driven them that night; I didn't understand the implications of that comment. Paul wanted to show the New Animal a recording device in the car, and Mal brought it to the front stairs of the club. Dutifully, I followed the group outside to check out the car. It looked dark green with a darkish interior, but there wasn't great light. After a few minutes of admiring this absolute beauty of a car, everyone went back inside, and Mal followed shortly thereafter.

Not wanting to overstay my welcome, not that anyone cared, I edged slowly to the door. Fortunately, the music was blasting, so I didn't have to make any excuses, just gestured that I was leaving. My new friends asked for my phone number should they ever come to New York. Mal nodded goodbye, and Paul let out a "See ya," accompanied with a half salute/ wave. I don't want to be overly sensitive, but everyone seemed OK to see this American teen with the new haircut leave the premises.

About two weeks later, Paul McCartney was at the Bag O' Nails after finishing recording the title song for the *Magical Mystery Tour* album. An American was visiting the club at the invitation of Peter Brown, a personal assistant to Brian Epstein and later author of a definitive early book on the Beatles. She was a New York–based photographer visiting London on assignment to shoot photos of pop musicians. Her name? Linda Eastman.

I returned to the hotel from the Bag O' Nails with a massive headache. I tried to record details about the night in my trip diary, but my head was killing me. My mom suggested that she walk over to the all-night Boots Chemists in Piccadilly Circus to get something to help me out. Not wanting her to go alone at 2 a.m., I got myself together and we headed over, a fast five-minute walk.

Boots was busy. About ten people were sitting in chairs lined up against the wall toward the back. I thought that was very accommodating of the pharmacy to provide seats to customers. There was one empty seat, and because I wasn't feeling well, I asked the people on either side if I could sit down while my mom shopped the aisles. They looked up with no reaction. I noticed they were looking a bit used up, but it was late, and I thought they had been to a club, too!

One by one each person, clutching a small slip of paper, was called up to the counter. Then it was my turn. "

"Your prescription for today," the man behind the counter asked.

I replied, "I don't have a prescription."

"Well, if you need one, we can contact a doctor to help you out tonight."

"Really?" I replied. "That would be great since my head is pounding!"

My mom raced over to the counter as I waited for the man to return with paperwork to be filled out.

"What are you doing?" she demanded as she tugged at my jacket, pulling me away from the counter.

"I'm waiting for a prescription from a doctor to help my headache," I shouted back at her.

She pulled me to the front door and said to look at the people waiting there.

"Yes, I see them."

"They are being dispensed heroin," she said.

"What?" I screamed again.

"Don't you realize you were getting a prescription for heroin?"

At that moment I understood that my mother was pretty savvy. How she knew that Boots gave out government-approved heroin to addicts to prevent them from going the criminal route beats me. Mom paid for the aspirin, and we walked back to the hotel.

We both woke up the next morning to the phone ringing. I hoped it was my dad so I could tell him all about the evening, but no, it was a pen pal I had met through the Beatles Fan Club, John Muszynski from Sherwood Rise, Nottingham. John and I had exchanged letters every month for two years, and we were looking forward to finally meeting. The plan was for John to come down to London, but with the fierce pounding in my head, all I heard is that he couldn't make it. The way I felt, that was fine. Anyway, I wanted to get to the fan club offices before going to Liverpool. I fell back asleep, waking up after lunch.

With my head still throbbing, I needed to get to 13 Monmouth Street. I phoned ahead to let them know I was coming. The same fellow who had answered the phone when I had telephoned previously now told me that the club had closed.

"Closed? How can that be? And where is Anne Collingham then?" I needed to know.

"Didn't they tell you in New York?" he questioned me. I already knew that Anne Collingham, the national fan club secretary, did not exist, but I was surprised that they had moved out of Monmouth Street.

It was Tony Barrow, the Beatles' press officer, who decided during the earliest days that the Beatles Fan Club should have an office based in London at the NEMS office on Monmouth Street. Freda Kelly ran the club in Liverpool out of the NEMS office there, and a young woman, Bettina Rose, ran the southern satellite office of the club from her home in Richmond, Surrey. Again, it was Tony who had created a fictitious name for the national secretary. To arrive at a plausible name, Tony pieced together a street name associated with his secretary and his wife's middle name to create "Anne Collingham." With mail pouring in, the demand for a central figure to answer letters, write articles, and meet and greet fans stopping by the club was essential.

The British club grew so quickly that they took up an extra floor and hired at least six more helpers to sort mail and sign autographs. Yes, sign autographs, the same as in New York. That's why so many counterfeit autographs are floating around. The club was so busy that Bettina Rose left her Surrey office and went to work at Monmouth Street full-time with "Anne Collingham." Fans who stopped by always seemed to find Bettina there; Anne was busy responding to Beatles requests and unable to greet whoever stopped by.

Now, after coming all this way, I felt like the same charade was being played out for me. But . . . I was welcome to come by the office on Argyll Street. "Argyll Street," I repeated excitedly. This is where I wrote Wendy Hanson all the time, and I was so happy to go there to see the offices.

Even though it sounded like a plan, I asked if I could visit the following week. "I'm headed to Liverpool tomorrow," I explained, and I wasn't feeling that well.

"That's fine," he said.

I didn't want to brag. I wanted to go buy Mrs. Harrison a gift.

BACK TO WHERE IT ALL BEGAN

When I figured out that I would be going to England in April 1967, I wrote to many of the people with whom I had been corresponding for three years. Top of my list was Mrs. Harrison, George's mom. Mrs. Harrison was a wonderful person who went out of her way to be part of the Beatles experience and embrace George's fame. I don't remember how I got the Harrison home address, but I started corresponding with Mrs. Harrison in late 1964. We wrote to each other every few months. She let me know what was going on with George, his activities, and marriage to Pattie Boyd, their travels, and visits home to Liverpool. Later, Mr. Harrison wrote about a car crash George and Pattie were in, to let me know that they were fine.

I remember when Mr. and Mrs. Harrison moved to a new home in Warrington, outside of Liverpool. In a letter, Mrs. Harrison called it a "bungalow," but I didn't know what that meant in British terms. I thought that having such a well-off son, a bungalow seemed meager.

Mrs. Harrison would randomly send me pieces of George's old clothes as mementos. I still have a piece of his black sock that Mrs. Harrison affixed to a card, and a plaid shirtsleeve. When I had the exact dates of my trip, I wrote Mrs. Harrison. She replied promptly: I should visit Liverpool, especially because the *clothes were much cheaper up north than in London.* Mrs. Harrison opened her home to me, and with my mother's permission I accepted her kind offer. The plan was that I would take a train from London's Euston Station to Warrington, where she and Mr. Harrison would pick me up for a two-night stay.

I don't think I realized how extraordinary this invitation was, and when I arrived, I received a warm Liverpool welcome. What first struck me about them was how tiny they were—we were about the same height. Mr. Harrison, a city bus driver, had retired. Mrs. Harrison had been a dance instructor at some point in her life but now was a bit chunky, like she enjoyed afternoon cream tea. The home was lovely, white in color outside and very homey inside, with a very English feel. It was spacious,

Dear Debbie,

Thank you for your letter. I would love to meet you both

If you write nearer the time to remind me, (I get such a lot of letters). It's OK to come. You would have to take a train to Warrington from Euston. London 2 hours 20 mins.

George & Pattie are here, they are fine & fit, from the trip to India. Love Louise Harrison

After several letters between Louise Harrison and me, it was decided that I would spend two nights at her home when I visited Liverpool.

AUTHOR'S COLLECTION

not like a bungalow in American terms, with an upstairs room and attic with many windows that looked out on a vast garden and big expanse of land. I remember country music albums in the house, a fireplace, and bookshelves in the living room. How strange I thought—the Harrisons enjoyed American country music when I only wanted to listen to the Beatles and British bands. I have read that George wrote "While My Guitar Gently Weeps" in 1968 in his parents' home. Mrs. Harrison also told me that she loved to sing; when George was young, she would sing and play music for hours.

The Harrisons had recently returned from Florida, and Mrs. Harrison was so enamored of key lime pie that I promised to send her recipes when I returned home. She seemed amazed that I didn't know how to bake a pie, thinking it an American rite of passage that all girls learned how to make pies. Their kitchen was another story; it had the craziest printed wallpaper that made me dizzy.

Besides Mrs. Harrison, I also wrote a letter to Angela McCartney, the woman Mike and Paul's dad, Jim, married. I received a reply asking me to let her know when I arrived in England and my dates in Liverpool: she would try to arrange a time for me to visit. When I arrived at the Harrison home, I showed Mrs. Harrison that letter.

"Well," she said, "tomorrow, we'll ring her up!"

Before I knew it, I was sitting in the Harrisons' car heading to meet Angela and Jim McCartney. The trip from Warrington to the McCartney home on the Wirral Peninsula took about forty minutes. I stared out the car window trying to take in every bit of land. Sheep were grazing along the highway. We passed signs pointing to Liverpool, but we continued straight, leaving the main road and passing well-kept clusters of stone houses and wide-open green fields. It was beautiful despite raindrops falling on the car's windshield. We approached a roundabout, and a minute later we arrived.

As we turned right into the driveway, I remembered having seen a photograph of the house in the teen magazine *Datebook*. The article I read showed Paul and Jane Asher visiting the family. Briefly, when Paul earned enough money, he bought this home for his dad and brother, Michael. They packed up their belongings at midnight in Forthlin Road and headed to the posh side of the River Mersey.

As the car came to a halt, out came Angela and Jim to greet us. This was beyond belief. Two sets of Beatles parents, and here I stood in amazement. My hands were shaking as I reached out to greet the McCartneys and thank them for this lovely invitation. My immediate impression was that the house looked very English, with lots of windows. There were houses in Ridgewood, New Jersey, in a similar Tudor style. While we were still outside, Mike McCartney came running out of the house, late for an appointment in Liverpool. Mike didn't stop but said a brief hello without knowing that I was a visitor from the States.

We entered through the front door. I didn't *dare* take out my camera: this was too personal a visit. Jim was curious where in America I lived as he moved a pile of newspapers from the floor close to the chair where he was sitting. I spoke about my parents in detail; my mom from Winnipeg, Canada, and dad born in New York City's Lower East Side and, of course, my dog, Lollipop. I shared a picture of my dog that I carried in my wallet.

When some shilling notes and pence fell out of the zippered compartment, Jim McCartney quizzed me on giving change. He must have known that British currency was difficult for foreign visitors to comprehend. Everyone laughed because I couldn't get it at all. The Harrisons and McCartneys chatted about various topics, including something about India, and I sat and listened, all the while trying to remember every detail. I was so focused on making memories that I missed out on what was happening.

Shortly thereafter, we left. I still have the ten-shilling note that Jim McCartney used to have fun with me that afternoon. We rode back through Liverpool with Mr. and Mrs. Harrison giving me a tour of the city: the original Cavern Club on Mathew Street, which was still standing; the Catholic church where Mrs. Harrison worshipped as a child; the school George attended. Then we headed back to Warrington. We also passed a sign for a tea shop, Kardomah, and I pointed it out to Mrs. Harrison, telling her that my mom and I had enjoyed tea at a Kardomah the day we arrived in London. It made me feel *one of them* when she said it was a fine Liverpool-based company.

George's older brother, Harold, was supposed to come by, but I think his young son, Paul, who was around seven years old if I remember correctly, wasn't feeling well, so he didn't make it over to visit. That evening I spent time with Mrs. Harrison reading through fan mail and helping her organize the letters that seemed to have been sent primarily from American fans. We talked about all the fans she exchanged letters with and how expensive the postage had become. I also remember telling her how much I treasured the pieces of George's clothing, especially the sock she had sent me a few years earlier. She asked if I wanted more of his clothing. I politely declined, although in my heart I wanted it all.

The next day I was on the first train back to London. We said our goodbyes, promising to write. With abundant "thank-yous," I boarded the train, leaving Warrington in an absolute daze. I finally had the time to enter some thoughts into my trip diary and barely looked out the window at the lovely countryside whizzing by. My mother met me at Euston train

Mr. & Mrs. H. H. Harrison
"Sevenoaks"
Pewterspear Lane, Appleton.
Cheshire. ENGLAND.

12/1/70.

Dear Debbie.

Just a short note in answer to your letter
of 12/8/70. I am sorry for the delay, but mrs
Harrison passed away on the 7th July 1970, and as
I also had had a period in hospital also, (I had
two thirds of my stomach removed) everything just
got on top of me. No doubt the news of mrs
Harrison, will give you a shock, as it did me,
she was very ill for the past twelve months, and
although we tried every way possible to get her
well it all proved useless. I am really sorry
to write you this news, but thought you should
know. I hope you had a nice xmas, and I
wish you every happiness in 1971.

            Sincerley.

            Harold Harrison

Tragically, George's mother, Louise, succumbed to cancer. Mr. Harrison wrote me this devastating letter with the news of her passing.
AUTHOR'S COLLECTION

station, curious to see the clothes bargains I found up north. We had been so busy, there wasn't time for shopping. I'd have to pay London prices if I wanted anything.

I corresponded with Mrs. Harrison for a few more years, and then suddenly there were no answers to my letters. I had had hints that she was not well, sharing that she couldn't put on a Christmas dinner or that she had difficulty in getting to a shop. A letter finally arrived from Mr. Harrison telling me of Mrs. Harrison's sickness, how they had tried everything to save her, but she didn't make it. The news was devastating on so many levels.

Mr. Harrison and I continued exchanging letters, though I was already in college. He gave me strength through my dad's short illness and death and instructed me how it was my turn to care for my mom, never forgetting to send special well wishes to her in each letter. Mr. Harrison passed away eight years after Mrs. Harrison, in May 1978. The Harrisons were the most caring, compassionate couple, and I think of their kindness often, hoping that Dhani Harrison appreciates how *extraordinary* were his grandparents.

MIND THE GAP

Back from Liverpool, I still had much to do before going home two days later. Topping the list was visiting the fan club office. In between all the appointments and Beatles-related activities, we managed to enjoy some of London's finest sites. We took a boat up the Thames to Windsor Castle, explored the Victoria & Albert Museum, Tate, and British Museum, and browsed Foyle's Bookshop, sat with the pigeons in Trafalgar Square, and toured Westminster Abbey and the Tower of London. I also went to the home of my pen pal, Vivien Carter, in Wormley, Hertfordshire, where she drove me to Woburn Abbey. With my mom we all toured Charles Dickens's home and St. Paul's Cathedral on the same day I visited *Fabulous 208*.

I called the fan club office to confirm a time and was told it was fine to come over. Sutherland House at 5/6 Argyll Street was the home of Brian Epstein's company in London, NEMS and an address I knew well as the office of Wendy Hanson. When I arrived, I didn't know for whom to ask except for Bettina Rose. I hoped she was real. I would not want to seem so naive as to ask for "Anne Collingham." That would surely give me away as an outsider.

I was pointed to the fifth floor, where everyone had just relocated. I always knew the fan club to be on the first floor. Stacks of mail were piled high everywhere. Boxes of fan club materials filled every corner. Phones were ringing. People were rushing back and forth. A young woman just about my age approached me and introduced herself as Jo; she may have been the assistant to Tony Barrow, the Beatles' press contact. What about Mary Cockram . . . is she around I asked? Mary aka Anne Collingham. Mary, who modeled Beatles sweaters using the name Anne Collingham. It came together in an instant. Mary, better known as "Cockers," had left the club several months before (1966), but, yes, she was Anne Collingham.

I asked Jo, "Is that your name, or do you go by something else?"

"No, my name is Jo Coburg," she added.

"And what about Bettina Rose? Was she a real person?" I asked. And not missing a beat, "And what about Val Sumpter and Maureen

Donaldson? Or Michael (one of the few guys there) or Monica Stringer or Yvonne?"

Jo seemed to be surprised that I knew these names. Bernice Young had partially clued me in, but I don't think even she knew the full story or cared.

Bettina Rose wasn't around; I think she had a child who wasn't feeling well. I wasn't even sure I should believe that. I was so suspicious that I didn't trust my own judgment. One thing I saw, though, is that it looked like the club was preparing to move again. I asked Jo. She explained that Freda Kelly had taken over completely again, and fan club operations were consolidating and moving back to Liverpool. All that was left in London was a post office box and a phone number. I still own the card she handed me with the contact info for the club: P.O. BOX No1AP, London, W.1. Telephone REGent 0246.

People up north seemed real; here, everything and everyone was unreal. A kind woman from the floor below who was helping move two boxes offered to assist me, but I had no need. I sensed that I was a bother and said that I was going back to the hotel to pack.

I left the fan club disappointed with the entire operation. I had spent so much time dreaming about this visit, with such high expectations. Disillusioned, I left the building. Things would have been so different if Wendy Hanson still worked for Brian Epstein. As the door closed behind me, I noticed a sign next door . . . the London Palladium. Going to a show there was on my list. My favorite poster in my bedroom showed the Beatles posing at the stage door of the Palladium. The Australian group The Seekers was playing there for four weeks, and I purchased two tickets for that evening. A variety show much like *The Ed Sullivan Show* with multiple acts would brighten my spirit. As I walked quickly back to the Piccadilly Hotel, I thought about how I would share this experience with Pam, Sue, and Bernice back in New York. Maybe they would find it disappointing, too, and word would get back to Freda Kelly or Bettina Rose—or better yet, Tony Barrow, who originally conceived the idea to use fake names.

I was ready to go home. I was looking forward to what was ahead— seeing friends, returning to class, and beginning to prep for college.

Looking back from where I sit today, the trip was an experience of a lifetime. It afforded me insight into people and helped set a lifetime goal. I got to meet the Beatles' families and see Brian Epstein just months before his death; hang in a club with the famous, and have a rare opportunity to briefly see half of the Beatles with George Martin at EMI/Abbey Road. It was an amazing adventure with lessons learned that have guided me forever.

Saying goodbye to London wasn't difficult. I knew I would return. I could make that happen.

THE EARTH SHOOK UNDER MY FEET

The harsh realities of the SATs welcomed me home from London, and amazingly, I was ready to take them on. Just ahead was the summer in Peru visiting family followed by college applications. Quickly approaching was the final year of high school and the last fun days of Beatles Fan Club #28 before we all scattered in different directions. I had always wanted to spend time with my mom's extended family in Peru, and so it was decided to send me to Lima for the summer. Except for missing the Beatles, it was a perfect way to spend the 1967 summer of love taking in the exotic culture of the Incas.

Upon arrival I quickly learned that the richness of Peru did not extend to their pop music. The top-selling album was by a band called Los Doltons, five super clean-cut guys known to be part of the '60s South American music scene called "Nueva Ola." "Nueva Ola" was a fusion of American rock and European pop, but it was purely boring retro music that would have appealed to my parents' generation. Strange thing is that I brought the Los Doltons album home from Peru and still have it among my vinyl collection. "Enamorado con una Amiga Mio" was my favorite cut with a salsa beat.

The evening before I was returning home, I received what I thought was a routine phone call from New Jersey. The first words my dad spoke were that Brian Epstein had been found dead in his London home. "What?" I screamed. This was unimaginable. How could this be? My parents must have gotten it all wrong.

My Spanish was OK, and I put on the television. Nothing was on the news. I felt so cut off from the world. What were people saying? This couldn't be real. I had received letters saying that Brian's father had passed away about one month before, and I immediately worried about the shock of this on Brian's mom, Queenie. Was this an accident? It had to be. Morning couldn't come soon enough so I could hear that this was a terrible error.

I had just fallen asleep when I felt a sharp jolt, and the windows rattled in their steel frames. Screams filled the house—shouts to run to the street. As instructed, I ran outside and saw the house shaking on its foundation from an earthquake. Was this an omen of things to come? I still remember looking up at the house thinking, *I don't want to die in Lima*. Nothing was stable: Brian, the ground, the house. It took no genius to comprehend that the Beatles would never be the same without Brian.

A WORLD WITHOUT BEATLES

Inevitably, the Beatles faced significant challenges after Brian's death. So much has been written on this topic that I do not need to reiterate all the sordid details. Already known was the band's inability to continue touring due to the complexity of their music and sheer lack of inertia after the 1966 tour. This, coupled with John's new allegiance to Yoko and Paul's with Linda and her high-powered family, resulted in everyone going their separate creative ways. George was the first member of the group to release a solo album after years of frustration with Paul and John having consistently rejected his musical contributions. Ringo just plain up and walked out. The animosity among the Beatles grew even more apparent to outsiders as they struggled to establish and maintain Apple Corps under Neil Aspinall to oversee their business interests and expand the Beatles empire even with the rancor between the musicians.

But when Lee and John Eastman, Linda's father and brother, respectively (representing Paul's interests), and Allen Klein (having been retained by the other three Beatles, although somewhat reluctantly by Ringo and George) came face-to-face over pending legal and financial decisions, there could be no consensus. Recording the *Let It Be* album and *Abbey Road* was done sporadically while individually each Beatle tended to his own pursuits.

My Beatles Fan Club chapter officially closed in late summer 1968 when I left for college. It was bittersweet to say goodbye to the Beatles friends I had made over the years within the club and among other chapter presidents. I had envisioned a well-defined path after my return from England, and I took that seriously as a student majoring in broadcasting/ film at Boston University.

A curious coincidence happened as I moved into the freshman dorm at West Campus on Commonwealth Avenue. In an adjacent room was another entering freshman—Susie Schaeffer. I was startled because I recognized the name. Susie lived on Long Island. Although we never met, I knew her well via letters. She had been a member of Beatles Fan

Club Chapter #28 for four years. She joined after seeing me promote the national club on the *Clay Cole Show*. Maybe my work would never be fully done, and for freshman year we were there for each other whenever we needed a touch of home or to exchange a knowing glance about the Beatles.

In April 1970, Paul officially announced that the Beatles band was done, and on New Year's Eve 1970, he filed a lawsuit against the other Beatles to terminate their partnership. Since I was thirteen, the group had been the center of my universe. Now I was twenty. It seemed impossible to comprehend a world without Beatles.

HE'S NOT DEAD, SAYS ROSE

The Paul Is Dead hoax and debate wasn't easy to avoid. I won't discuss the clues, except to say that this entire farce began in 1969. The story goes that Paul McCartney stormed out of a *Sgt. Pepper's Lonely Hearts Club Band* session, got into his car, crashed, and died. Yes, there was a crash in January 1967, when Paul let an assistant of Robert Fraser, the art gallery owner, drive his car to a party at Mick Jagger's house in Hertfordshire. Along the M1 highway, the assistant lost control of the car. It was totaled, and the driver sustained major injuries. Also, back on November 9, 1966, Paul had been on a motor scooter and took a fall, resulting in a chipped front tooth that can be seen on some early videos. This is where it all started.

The Beatles supposedly covered up his death for fear of losing popularity even though they also allegedly planted "clues" on the albums, in their music and artwork. Later I heard that the Beatles found the entire episode amusing.

As the story gained momentum, I was already in my second year of college in Boston. My dorm room phone did not stop ringing. Members from the defunct Fan Club #28 called, as did other random people who knew my connection. A newspaper reporter even found me sitting in class one afternoon.

This had to stop. The only way I knew how to resolve the debate was write to Paul at his home on Cavendish Avenue, London. My letter said that if he was still alive, he should sign and return the enclosed "return receipt" to my attention at the dorm, filling out his address and mine. I sent the letter and return card in early October 1969, and by Halloween I had received the "return receipt" dated October 20, 1969, filled in with Paul's house number, but signed by none other than Rose Martin—Paul's loyal housekeeper who worked for him for years. I remember hearing along the way that Rose lived in Queensbridge Road, Shoreditch, London, very close to my friend from *Fabulous 208* magazine. She would share brief updates from Rose's perspective, although nothing was ever relayed about her job. But now, in this dreadful case, there was no need for debate. Rose, via the post office, had put the issue to rest.

I never met Rose but have heard from fans who would wait for Paul in front of his Cavendish home. She was devoted to the McCartney family. Upon Rose's death at age ninety-two in September 2013, Paul took to his website to pay tribute: "Rose was my housekeeper since the early '60s and for many years looked after us and our children. She was a very classy lady with a mischievous sense of *humour*. She was fiercely loyal, and our family and many friends will miss her dearly."

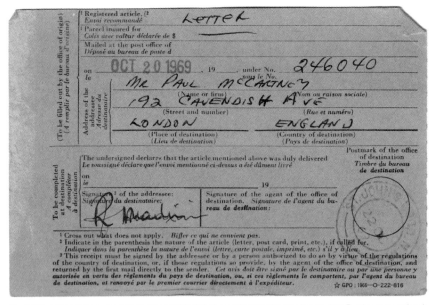

By signing this return receipt, Paul and Linda's housekeeper let me know that Paul was not dead.
AUTHOR'S COLLECTION

YOU CAN'T GET BACK

LONDON 1971

Summer of 1971 was my rite-of-passage student backpacking summer in Europe. As a rising college senior, my primary interest had become making films—films that mattered.

When still in high school during the Beatles craze, I began making short films to illustrate music that I loved. One of my first films was to The Doors' "The End." Karen Wikum, one of my classmates and a fan club member, was the star portraying a disenfranchised young woman contemplating life as she walked along the railroad tracks, dropping roses along the path. My favorite project was a film I shot at the duck pond in Ridgewood, New Jersey, featuring my grandmother sitting solo on a bench while Simon and Garfunkel's "Old Friends" played, her turquoise-colored eyes reflecting in the pond a long life well lived. My English teacher in twelfth grade, John Ianacone, an avid still photographer, was very supportive of my early film endeavors, even driving me to different locales with my camera to shoot scenes for a short, based on the poem "The Love Song of J. Alfred Prufrock." Fairly recently my dear high school friends Beverly and Linda commented that I was among the first to make what became known as music videos. That was 1968.

After three years of producing films in college, I was fortunate to receive a stipend from a university film festival I entered where Terry Melcher, Doris Day's son, and a few other Hollywood types established a film fund for aspiring student filmmakers. The stipend was enough to support my summer plan to produce a documentary in Italy. Together with my artistic co-conspirator, Gary Jaekel, also a film major at Boston University, we went to Italy to shoot a movie we had written based on D. H. Lawrence's most heartfelt 1927 travelogue, *Etruscan Places*, about the Italian Etruscan civilization. The twenty-two-minute film documented Lawrence's path exploring the erotically painted tombs of the Etruscans, whose civilization had been destroyed by the Romans. Exploring the town of Tarquinia, the Etruscan center of activity, was the starting point for the film. Understanding its history as discussed in the movie supported Lawrence's concept that the world was a sex-centric self-indulgent orgy—a premise that he so wonderfully portrayed in novels and by others in films such as *Women in Love*.

Terry Melcher, who I give thanks for making my European summer and film possible, was a versatile talent who played a significant role in tragic contemporary history. As mentioned, he was the only child of film star Doris Day and her notoriously abusive first husband. Terry was eventually adopted by Ms. Day's third husband, Martin Melcher (another sad story—upon his death, it was discovered that he had embezzled many millions of dollars that Ms. Day had earned). Terry, who lived the enviable life of growing up in Hollywood, in the early '60s joined a vocal group called the Rip Chords; by 1964, they had a big hit with the song "Hey, Little Cobra." (The Beatles knocked the song off the charts.) Leaving the performance world, Terry landed at Columbia Records, where he worked with bands such as the Byrds (producing their top hit, "Mr. Tambourine Man") and other notable talents such as Glen Campbell, Pat Boone, and Paul Revere and the Raiders.

Melcher's interest in film and supporting young filmmakers began when he wanted to produce a film about the Manson Family and their hippy compound and lifestyle. Terry met Charles Manson in 1968 through Dennis Wilson of the Beach Boys. Terry had known the Beach Boys for several years, having even sung background vocals on their iconic album *Pet Sounds*. Terry Melcher met Charles Manson at a house Melcher and his then girlfriend, Candice Bergen, rented with Mark Lindsay of Paul Revere and the Raiders fame in Beverly Hills at 10050 Cielo Drive.

Melcher at first promised Manson to support his musical career. But Melcher quickly grew disenchanted with Manson after witnessing the random brutal treatment of people at his infamous Spahn Ranch during talks about the documentary and his music career. Shortly thereafter, Melcher terminated his connection to Manson and moved to Malibu. The owner of the Cielo Drive residence rented his home to new tenants—Sharon Tate and Roman Polanski. Lore says that Manson first visited the Tate/Polanski residence looking for Terry Melcher, but it has been reported that Manson knew that Melcher had already left Beverly Hills for Malibu.

After the brutal Tate murder, Melcher went into seclusion. I read a newspaper report that Manson family member Susan Atkins stated that even though Manson knew that Terry was no longer living on Cielo Drive, he selected the home to instill fear in Melcher that if he did not live up to his promises, anything was possible. Needing something solid to work on after at least one year of seclusion, Terry was looking to support others in the creative arts.

In 1994, the Cielo Drive house was torn down, and a Mediterranean mansion named Villa Bella was erected. Pieces of Sheetrock from the original house were sold at $2 each to benefit an AIDS charity, and the address was changed to 10066 Cielo Drive.

I learned about the young filmmakers' stipend that Terry Melcher was sponsoring through a posting in the Boston University Communications School lobby soliciting applications from film students. My friend Gary encouraged me to apply, believing that I had written and directed a short film the year before for a class on film propaganda that fit the stated criteria. The film was titled *Government for the People*. Shot at the new Government Center building in Boston, it demonstrated how government was not for the people but existed to support the military-industrial complex. Even though the country was submerged in the raging and divisive Vietnam War, with students worried about the draft, the film ended with a positive message celebrating the nation's first Earth Day in Boston Common. Terry Melcher, presenting the award later in the year, told me he supported the underlying message of the film and believed I would produce a companion work of substance. I received two thousand dollars, a good amount of money in 1971, when people were going to Europe on $5 per day!

When we finished the film, Gary and I had enough money left to rent a car and travel from Italy through Switzerland, Austria, Germany to Denmark, and then to our final destination in Sweden for a wedding where a friend of Gary's was getting married. In Denmark we stayed with a friend of Gary's, Søren Groftved, and his family. Charlotte, Søren's younger sister by just a few years, was a worldly sort; while I stayed with her family, she asked to travel to New York City to visit my family.

In 1962, a popular television show that aired on CBS was *Fair Exchange*. Its premise was that two World War II friends had their daughters switch families for one year, one going to London and the other to New York. I loved the series, which starred Judy Carne and Lynn Loring, and with Charlotte going to New York for her adventure, I was living a teenage fantasy of life in Copenhagen.

Finally, we arrived in Sweden for the wedding, which was lovely. After one week in the town of Kiruna, Sweden, above the Arctic Circle where the sun never stopped shining, I found myself thinking about London. It had been four years since my 1967 visit, and I had a strong desire to return. Gary and I were flying home out of London, so I left him with his friends in Uppsala and bought a ticket on SAS Airlines from Arlanda airport in Stockholm to Gatwick for the equivalent of eleven dollars. An International Student Identity Card enabled college students to travel at deep discounts.

Arriving in London late at night, the only place I could find to sleep was a bleak hotel in Earl's Court. When morning came, I did enjoy a traditional English breakfast but then set about to find a happier place to stay. I landed at a charming English residential hotel just north of Oxford Street. The first morning when I entered the breakfast room, two elderly ladies who were enjoying their tea and eggs invited me to join them. They introduced themselves as Candie Mendes of Copacabana Beach, Rio de Janeiro, and Marjorie Moore of Hamilton, Bermuda. By week's end they were Auntie Candie and Auntie Marjorie, and they remained aunties until their deaths. Auntie Candie, who never married, visited London for two months every summer to be close to her nephew, the Brazilian ambassador to the Court of St. James. Auntie Marjorie liked to take in London's plays and cultural scene. The two had enjoyed this summer ritual for twelve years. The friends never ventured far from the hotel, and each evening upon my late return from a day of exploring would serve me the dinner they kept warm with the kitchen staff's help.

For the first three of the six days I was in London, I went to a different train station, Victoria, Charing Cross, or Waterloo to see where inexpensive day excursions were offered. I would select one and take off, never knowing what adventure awaited. The first day I visited the Isle of Wight; I brought the aunties samples of the island's colored sands. That was followed by a visit to Stratford-upon-Avon, returning with pamphlets from a Shakespeare matinee.

The third day I ventured to Stonehenge where the ruins still stood regally without the current signs and barricades advising tourists to keep a distance. Visitors then could go right up to the monuments and touch them unceremoniously, sensing their power and significance for an ancient people. The highlight of the day, though, was to walk Salisbury Plain. This was not merely a random visit—it was a pilgrimage because Salisbury Plain was where the Beatles filmed my favorite part of the movie *Help!* George Harrison's lip-synched song never sounded better than when artfully played on the open space of Salisbury Plain. That day the aunties each received a small rock from Salisbury Plain. It didn't hold much allure for them, but for me it fulfilled a promise.

By the fourth day it was time to revisit the old Beatles haunts that I really had come to see. First stop was EMI, recently renamed Abbey Road Studios. A new sign had been posted over the entrance door. I stood at the now famous album cover crosswalk. It being summer, the street was full of gawkers and fans, many of whom wrote messages on the wall fronting the studio building, declaring their love to the Beatles. It was simply a blank concrete wall when I last visited, the street quiet except for the passing red double-decker bus. I found my way to Panzer's Deli to take

Aunties Candie and Marjorie their daily surprise—this day a box of cookies that could have come from a neighborhood bakery in New York.

The offices on Monmouth Street stood empty; the Bag O' Nails club, deserted. The heroin addicts seemed to have moved on from Boots in Piccadilly Circus; the shops such as Lord John and Lady Jane on Carnaby Street now were either shuttered or cheap tourist traps surviving on their past glory. Perhaps the saddest moments were when I stood outside of 24 Chapel Street, Belgravia—Brian Epstein's regal home. A car was parked in front, with trash cans to the side. The home looked lived in but well kept; Brian would have been pleased. I remembered four years earlier when I had walked down the front steps from the house to the street, so full of excitement at the prospect of seeing George Martin, never imagining that two Beatles would stop by. The day before Gary and I were to meet to return to New York, I went for a walk in Hyde Park. It was a beautiful day. I'd had great weather nearly the entire week. The vibrant red buses. Children playing along the Serpentine with Kensington Gardens in the distance. Pensioners relaxed on the scattered slung-back canvas chairs, rejoicing in the final days of summer warmth. I had made it back to London in four years. What a feeling of accomplishment as I took in the floral-infused air of the park. I felt confident and prepared for whatever adventures were ahead.

It doesn't always work out: the biggest bombshell of my life to date was only weeks away. My dad wasn't feeling well; he went to the doctor, and in two months he was dead. My best pal, who put work on hold to take me to meet Brian Epstein, who fed my Beatles appetite every night for years with magazines, books, and trinkets, who patiently waited hours outside of concert venues, braved the ridicule of his friends, and staunchly defended my taste in music, was gone. He had prepared me, though, for handling life's ups and downs, and I found peace in his manner and solace in his memory. The first night after the funeral, when everyone had left, I sat on my bed in the room where I had felt such joy as a teen and did what a Beatles person would do—I wrote a letter to George's dad, Mr. Harrison. He would understand.

SIBLINGS

MCCARTNEY, BAIRD, AND HARRISON

There wouldn't be a second half to this story without talking about the Beatles' families I've met along the way. Mike McCartney is mentioned throughout this book, so I want to share general background highlights.

To recap, I first met Mike briefly when Mr. and Mrs. Harrison drove me to meet Jim and Angela McCartney at their home outside of Liverpool in 1967. The hello Mike and I exchanged took less than fifteen seconds because he was racing to an appointment in Liverpool. I am confident that he doesn't even recall the meeting.

My second meeting with Mike was two years later in 1969, in Manhattan. I was attending college in Boston and heading home early for the Thanksgiving holiday when I read in the *Village Voice* that he and his very successful satirical comedy/musical group Scaffold were appearing at the Bitter End on Bleeker Street in Greenwich Village. Under no circumstances would I miss seeing them perform. I had not seen Mike live onstage, although I was a fan of his music and Scaffold. I owned a few of his records including "Thank U Very Much," which was a humongous hit in Europe and Britain. The show turned out to be smart and funny, performed in an intimate and memorable venue. After the show I waited to talk to Mike. I remember him saying they were heading by train to Philadelphia to be guests on *The Mike Douglas Show*. Crazy coincidence, because the executive producer of *The Mike Douglas Show* in the '60s is the same EP I worked for on ABC and Hallmark Channel. The evening at the Bitter End showed audiences that Mike is a creative talent in his own right.

At the beginning of the Beatles' rise to fame, Mike joined with two other Liverpudlian artists, John Gorman and Roger McGough, to form a poetry-music-comedy group called the Scaffold. They had several hit singles in the United Kingdom, including "Thank U Very Much," and "Lily the Pink." Curiously, Mike also changed his surname to McGear. Although everyone knew he was Paul's brother, it gave Mike the independent respect he deserved.

Scaffold's appearance on *The Mike Douglas Show* provided viewers with an interesting insight into Mike. Douglas Fairbanks Jr. was Mike Douglas's cohost for a British week. When Mike arrived at the studio in Philadelphia, he wasn't led to the stage to join the show's host but placed in a reserved seat in the audience. The interview started out innocently enough until the next guest was introduced as the DJ whose singular accomplishment was to have started the "Paul Is Dead" rumor. Mike Douglas and the guest reviewed the clues, arriving at the conclusion that Paul was dead.

Then it was Mike's turn for rebuttal, and he blasted the DJ on live television. Being the stalwart Liverpudlian he is, and Jim McCartney's son, he spoke the truth about this whole "con" being rubbish, "based on groundless innuendo and lies." The DJ looked horrified.

For a short time, Mike was involved in another improvisational group called GRIMMS with his two Scaffold partners joining a few other performers, but he left after a short while. Mike then signed with Warner Brothers Records and with Paul released an album called *McGear* that was moderately successful and rereleased to great accolades in 2019.

As the times changed, so did Mike, and he eventually reverted to using his proper name, Mike McCartney. Since he was a young man, Mike would always follow his older brother and his mates around, snapping photos whenever possible. These images tell the early history of the group from the Cavern Club to New Brighton Tower & Ballroom to stills of George standing by his new car or Paul wishing for a pair of shoes on display in a store window. Mike's first book, *McCartney's Family Album*, followed by *Mike Mac's Whites and Blacks and One Color* and *Mike McCartney's Merseyside* and his latest definitive book in 2022 for Genesis Publications, tell a rich story of the McCartney family and Liverpool. Mike's photographic career has evolved, and his work has been displayed and curated around the world. Scaffold reunited for a very special performance at Liverpool's Everyman Theatre in October 2022. It had been decades since I had an opportunity to see Scaffold perform. Knowing that life is all too short, we packed our bags and found ourselves in Liverpool to catch up with our pals. We spent two and a half unforgettable days.

I met Julia Baird, John Lennon's half-sister, just three blocks from my home in Los Angeles at the Wallis Annenberg Center for Performing Arts. It was a lovely April evening in 2019, where both Beatles people and Annenberg subscribers joined together to hear wonderfully insightful stories. Julia and her younger sister, Jackie, had a difficult life, in my opinion, despite having shared their mother with John Lennon. The girls were raised by Julia's youngest sister and her husband, Harriet and Norman Birch, who were given full guardianship of the two sisters. The girls' father, John Dykins, never married Julia Lennon, and upon Julia's tragic death the courts found their aunt to be the best mom. Julia Baird, a mom of three herself, has led a very productive life as a teacher of special needs children and an author. Today she runs Cavern City Tours in Liverpool.

I only saw Louise Harrison Caldwell once. She was signing autographs for profit at a fan gathering. I didn't approach her because I already had her autograph from 1964, on a postcard she was sending to fans in hopes that they would start a Louise Harrison Fan Club. As a young woman, she left Liverpool for Benton, Illinois, where her husband found work at a coal company. In 1963, George Harrison traveled to Benton to visit his sister, and together they tried every means to get airplay for the Beatles to no avail. Louise worked tirelessly to boost the Beatles and George (and herself) throughout her life. Gossip alerted fans that George was not pleased with Louise "putting herself out there," and upon his passing she was excluded from the small monthly allowance he had provided. She passed away at a retirement home in Florida at the age of ninety-one in early 2023.

AMAZED HOW MUCH THEY DON'T KNOW ABOUT YOU

People are always curious about Linda McCartney. Is it because she was from New York, which made her seem more like one of us, or because she and Paul had such a long-lasting, highly visible marriage? And with Linda supposedly being from the Eastman Kodak family, what did that mean to them as a couple?

Whatever the reason, substantial curiosity still surrounds Linda, even years after her sad passing. Yes, we knew each other. I didn't know her well. We weren't friends. Linda always greeted me skeptically. She thought she knew what was in my head. She thought she knew my intentions. I produced segments with her for television twice and had conversations on topics from child rearing to growing up in New York and the Fillmore East. I fought Susan Futterman, ABC TV standards and practices, to allow Linda to describe meat as "dead flesh," and she always gave me credit for winning that fight. And when we were together, we got on well like kindred spirits.

Linda was born in Scarsdale, New York, on September 24, 1941. That made her slightly older than Paul. Her paternal grandparents, Louis and Stella Epstein, fled Russia and established a furniture store in New York City. Their son Leopold (Lee) Epstein, born in 1910, was smart and garnered a scholarship to Harvard; he eventually graduated law school there in 1933. Lee was Linda's father.

In 1937, Lee married Louise Sara Lindner, the only child of Max and Stella Lindner, born in 1911 in Cleveland. The Lindners were a wealthy family of German Jewish descent that owned women's clothing stores. Louise was Linda's mother.

In 1939, Linda's older brother, John, was born, and shortly thereafter attorney Lee Epstein decided to Anglicize the family last name to Eastman, giving birth to the urban legend that Linda was part of the Eastman Kodak family. Asked frequently about the "Eastman" connection, Linda would sidestep the answer. Two years later John was joined by sisters Linda, then Laura and Louise. Lee's law practice grew in prominence,

165

representing painters such as Willem de Kooning. Dinners at the Eastman family home welcomed the biggest names in the entertainment industry. It was Lee and John's legal wisdom, advice, and expertise that strategically contributed to making Paul not only the extremely wealthy entertainer but music publishing/copyright holder he is today.

On March 1, 1962, tragedy struck the Eastman Family. Louise was flying from New York's Idlewild International Airport (renamed JFK in December 1963) to Los Angeles for a short vacation in Palm Springs. From what I have read, Lee always had them travel separately, and for good reason. Moments after takeoff, American Airlines Flight 1 crashed directly into Jamaica Bay. All eighty-seven passengers and eight crew members were killed upon impact. The investigation determined that there was a short circuit defect in the automatic pilot system. Louise Eastman was just fifty years old. It was a devastating loss.

In season 2, episode 2 of AMC's popular fictional series *Mad Men*, that crash is central to the plot because adman Pete Campbell learns his father is among those on board.

Linda had studied art at the University of Arizona. While there she met geologist John Melvin See, and they married in 1962. They had one daughter, Heather, who Paul later legally adopted. Linda first studied photography while in Arizona and in 1965, Linda, now divorcing John See, returned to New York with Heather and took an apartment at 140 East Eighty-Third Street in Manhattan. She worked at *Town & Country* magazine as a receptionist, snitching the invites to gala openings where she had easy access to celebs to supplement her photographic portfolio. After a short time, Linda left to work as a professional photographer. She gained unique access to concerts and photographed all the big names of the '60s, including Jimi Hendrix, Bob Dylan, The Doors, and Neil Young.

Linda was on assignment in London to photograph rock stars when Peter Brown, Brian Epstein's assistant, invited her to go to the Bag O' Nails club. There she met Paul McCartney, just days after I had been there in May 1967. Their second meeting took place at Brian Epstein's home on Chapel Street at a party for the launch of the *Sgt. Pepper's Lonely Hearts Club Band* album a day later. I've read many accounts of this second meeting, but I don't know if Linda manipulated her invitation, as many say. It's not important. One year later they met again while Paul and John were in New York to announce the formation of their new company, Apple Corps Ltd. Not long after they were married, in March 1969.

I bring nothing new to this discussion on how they traveled together always and raised their family of four out of the limelight in humble English countryside surroundings. Linda's vegetarianism, fight for animal rights, and her inclusion in all of Paul's musical endeavors is legendary.

Linda's passing was a profound loss for those who knew her and for everyone who knew of her.

KISS IT ALL AWAY

After college I returned to New York City and started my television career at CBS. I was so proud to be part of the CBS family, where I had spent time as a teen at *The Ed Sullivan Show*. My job initially was at entry level in the Walter Cronkite newsroom, but soon I moved to the entertainment division. I worked at CBS for fourteen years—six in New York, and after a transfer in 1978 to Television City in Los Angeles, eight more.

When I arrived in New York, the vibe was very different from the one I had come to know as a teenager patrolling the streets, from fan club headquarters to radio stations to concert venues. It was the era of disco and Studio 54. Washington Square, close to my apartment on lower Fifth Avenue, still had its share of lingering '60s hippies and '50s beatniks, but my world at CBS rocked to a different rhythm.

Moving back to the New York area also provided me the opportunity to reconnect with family and friends, including my babysitter, Frances, now called Fran. The daughter of my mom's best friend, Fran had gotten married and had two children, a daughter and son. Sadly, the marriage fell apart just as Fran began working as the office manager for a band just starting, KISS. Fran moved into the city with her two children and on her $150 weekly salary could afford only a small one-bedroom apartment, where the children shared the bedroom and Fran slept on the pullout sofa.

Fran was efficient and thorough and ran the office with the utmost professionalism. To the unknowing, her desk appeared to be a mess, but she knew where everything was and could locate any document in mere seconds. Fran's boss, Bill Aucoin, was credited with discovering KISS and managed the group for ten years into superstardom. When I stopped by the office to visit one night after work, it was a drug zone. Everyone there was doing something except for Fran. She was a mom who took her responsibility for two children seriously. Fran partied, but she stayed away from the drugs. The others in the office kidded Fran about it, but everyone respected her antidrug stance. During one after-hours office visit, I shared with Fran my experiences with Beatles fan club that closely approximated some of her work for KISS. Strange that maybe watching *American Bandstand* all those years before did have some lasting influence on us both.

Because we all knew Fran didn't do drugs, we were shocked by a phone call that Fran's father, received early one morning from a NYC police detective. He was calling from Fran's apartment—Fran was dead, sprawled face down on her sofa, and had been discovered by her children. The detective said it was a suspected drug overdose. Her dad phoned my mom that he was taking Fran's mom to the doctor's office, where they would break the news to her. He believed she would need immediate medical care.

I was angry. Angry at the drugs and angry at the music industry that glorified and enabled this monster that devoured good people. There was no autopsy because Fran was Jewish, and the next day at Fran's funeral service I sat in a pew next to Gene Simmons; Paul Stanley; Bill Aucoin, Fran's immediate boss; and Sean Delaney, who worked with KISS and was the self-described creator of the band and Fran's confidant. My heart hurt for Fran, a life cut too short, her children, and Fran's two siblings, who felt like my sisters. The cause of Fran's death never seemed right or logical. When drugs were in play, there always was some clue. I only recall Fran talking about financial hardships in connection with Casablanca Records. Fran innocently may have learned too much along the way.

I was done with music, bands, concerts, fans, and even the Beatles, who had suffered through the ugliest of breakups. Even when I was offered VIP tickets to see Paul McCartney's new band Wings at Madison Square Garden, I passed on the invitation. Only once did I see the McCartneys with their manager at the Lee Witkin photography gallery on East Fifty-Seventh Street. For the few years until I was transferred to Los Angeles, I thought little about the Beatles and never spoke of them or other bands. Professionally, any mention of my Beatles past was looked at as frivolous and immediately tagged me as a groupie. I pretended the Beatles had never happened.

Outside of work I volunteered for a nonprofit called Friends of Cast Iron Architecture. Under the direction of preservationist Margo Gayle, we saved historic buildings and street artifacts in New York's Soho district from destruction. I welcomed the new members and occasionally led Saturday walking tours of the endangered buildings. I also volunteered at the Lower East Side's Henry Street Settlement instructing teens in the art of Super 8mm filmmaking. Henry Street held special significance because my dad as a child went there nearly every day after school. It was time to give back.

After Fran's passing my mom's best friend picked herself up and carried on, heartbroken. After all, there were Fran's two young children to care for, though they went to live with their dad on Long Island. Years passed, but my closeness to the family remained. After my mom's passing, her friend came to Los Angeles to await the birth of my daughter and be there to help as any mom would do. We talked about the Beatles album she had brought, how it affected my entire teenage years, the fan club dance, and from time to time we would talk about Frances. It was a sensitive topic for us both. We especially loved talking about the day when Fran was exploring the attic and fell through the ceiling below, only to land directly in the middle of her bed, unhurt. Those were the good times.

PURE CLASS

WALTER SHENSON

In late January 1978 I received a phone call from my supervisor at CBS, Steve Sohmer, who was in Los Angeles attending meetings. Steve was a big, hulking guy who intimidated and bullied me by closing his office door and puffing his cigar smoke directly in my face. With at least two failed marriages that I knew of under his belt, he married soap opera diva Deidre Hall, from whom he is now also divorced. He is best recognized as a Shakespearean scholar, not a television guy. When I picked up the phone, Steve asked what the weather was like in New York City. I looked out the floor-to-ceiling window of my office on the twenty-seventh floor and replied, "It's gray and dark with snow falling."

"Well," Steve said, matter-of-factly, "it's seventy-three degrees out here, and you're gonna love it! See me on Monday when I get back." He hung up before I could ask questions.

By Wednesday morning, the Seven Santini Brothers Moving Company was at my apartment, estimating how many boxes were needed to pack for my move to California. My gym membership was bought out, as was the lease on my most wonderful apartment at 25 Fifth Avenue in Greenwich Village. I said sad goodbyes to my mom, who rationalized the move as a two-year experiment; my former roommate, Vivian; and my boyfriend, who was left trying to figure out what he might do for work in California. In less than three weeks, I was living and working in Los Angeles.

I was nervous about the move as I had no friends or family in Los Angeles, had only visited three times, all work related, and was terrified of earthquakes, remembering the temblor in Lima. However, there were a few people living in Los Angeles who figured prominently in my past with whom I was anxious to connect.

It was May, and I had been living in Los Angeles for about three months. I enjoyed attending CBS affiliates meetings, cocktail parties at the beach, and private film screenings, but nothing came close to the excitement of driving from CBS Television City along Beverly Boulevard to see

Walter Shenson at his office in Beverly Hills. Walter was the producer of the two feature films with the Beatles, *A Hard Day's Night* and *Help!* Walter and his family had returned a few years earlier to Los Angeles from London, settling on Bel Air's toniest street, St. Cloud.

When I parked in front of the office, I was surprised to see that it was an understated two-story building. The second-floor office had a large window overlooking El Camino, the street below and the courtyard driveway leading into the Beverly Wilshire Hotel. The Wilshire hadn't yet achieved international fame as the primary location for the film *Pretty Woman*, which thrust Julia Roberts into superstardom.

I entered the doors to the building and walked up the flight of stairs. At the desk was Ellen Brodax, Walter's assistant, who welcomed me. Coincidentally or not, Ellen was the daughter-in-law of Al Brodax, producer of the Beatles' animated TV series that aired on ABC and the film *Yellow Submarine*. Ellen was always kind, helpful, and efficient, and I enjoyed our conversations when I visited the office. I studied the room carefully, expecting to see posters of *A Hard Day's Night*, *Help!*, or even lobby cards highlighting Walter's film legacy such as *The Mouse that Roared*, starring Peter Sellers and the controversial Jean Seberg, which he had produced. I had imagined the place overrun with Beatles film memorabilia and testaments to his long-standing relationship with the film's director, Richard Lester, and other Hollywood icons. The surroundings seemed humble for such a respected producer.

I snapped to attention when I heard him ask me to come in. There, standing behind the desk, was Walter Shenson.

We looked at each other—had we met in 1964, when I was overseeing the fans camping out at night around the Astor Theatre? I don't specifically remember meeting him then, and he didn't quite remember me, but who cared? This meeting was special and the beginning of a unique relationship between a legendary movie producer whose stellar reputation preceded him always and me—Beatles fan and CBS transplant working in the feature film department (where I purchased theatrical movies for the network's *Saturday Night at the Movies*, or Thursday, or Sunday).

Walter was among my most favorite people, and it was an honor to consider him a friend and colleague. As we got to know each other, we shared wonderful lunches at Don Hernando's in the Beverly Wilshire. If you sat next to us, the conversation would be about what film did you just buy and how much did you pay ($6.8 million, with a built-in escalation clause); why Neil Aspinall was not returning Walter's phone call (he was upset with the film residuals); to the immense pride he had when his son, Douglas, was accepted to medical school at Tulane. Walter would talk glowingly about his talented photographer wife, Geraldine, and how together they helped Paul McCartney buy an elegant velvet couch for his home on Cavendish Avenue. Walter was always ready to share the details: Paul and Jane Asher had been dinner guests at the Shensons' London home and loved their velvet sofa. They wanted one. The following day Geraldine took them shopping for the identical couch.

One morning Walter called and asked if I could meet him for lunch at Don Hernando's. I never said no to his invitation. Over a tostada, Walter shared that the complete rights to the Beatles film *A Hard Day's Night* had reverted to him. The United Artists deal, made back in 1963, was that after fifteen years in release, the film would become Walter's sole property. More about this in a later chapter.

Right around this time I got the idea to teach a class on the Beatles, their influences and music, for UCLA Extension. The first person I turned to for advice was Walter. He offered to let me show either *A Hard Day's Night* or *Help!* to the class. All he asked in return was to attend the class and share his experiences with the students. This was Walter: always generous.

I advised Walter on a few of his projects from my CBS feature film perspective. *Reuben, Reuben* starring Tom Conti was one script I read easily five or six times for him, along with his other movie, *Echo Park*, which starred *The Partridge Family*'s Susan Dey. I visited Walter on the set a few times while this was being filmed on the streets of Los Angeles. The final project Walter discussed with me was the film *Ruby Jean and Joe* that he worked on for several years. We spent a lot of time on the title of the film—I still have a copy of *Ruby Jean and Me*, the original name. It starred Tom Selleck. Walter was always on top of his game unless it came to dealing with one individual—Neil Aspinall.

Aspinall, the Beatles roadie who was now CEO of Apple Corps, was the subject of many of our conversations. The two men had a very contentious business relationship. As head of Apple, Neil needed to enforce the Beatles image around the world, including Walter's ownership of the movies. Personally, though, it was a very different story.

One of Walter's friends while he was living in England was Bud Orenstein, who headed the United Artists office in London and was the executive overseeing both Beatles movies. Bud's daughter Suzy was a perfect match for Neil, and Walter introduced the young Suzy to Neil. They eventually married. It always seemed strange that with such a strong personal connection, Neil consistently presented obstacles to Walter. We had long talks about Neil's motivations, never reaching a definitive conclusion. Suzy and Neil had a long marriage, with four children. When he was young, Neil had fathered a child, Vincent Roag Best, with Mona Best, ex-Beatle drummer Pete Best's mother. Roag is the ultimate Beatles supporter in Liverpool and recently has refurbished the iconic Casbah Club into a Beatles-inspired place to stay with suites named after each Beatle.

Among most cherished memories of Walter was when my daughter was born. Walter was the first person to have a huge bouquet of flowers delivered to my room at Cedars-Sinai Medical Center; and when I got home, he was an early visitor. I was that frazzled first-time mom when Walter stopped by the house one morning. The first thing he commented on wasn't the baby: it was my framed poster of *A Hard Day's Night* that hung on the dining room wall.

He said, "Because I own all the rights to the film, that poster is my property!"

I responded, "You see that two-tone blue Rolls-Royce parked out front? That's really mine based on all the times I saw the movies!"

We always enjoyed each other.

That same morning, I also learned that Walter didn't own *A Hard Day's Night* movie poster. After he left, I contacted a Beatles memorabilia collector and had a one sheet delivered to the office on El Camino. A few weeks later my husband and I passed a frame shop on Little Santa Monica Boulevard, where *A Hard Day's Night* poster caught my eye. We stepped inside the shop and took a quick peek: Walter's name was on the receipt. The next time I visited his office, the poster was displayed prominently on the wall.

Now this is the way I imagined Walter's office should be decorated.

THEY'RE FROM MAPLEWOOD, I'M FROM OAKLAND

I had just returned to my office from my usual lunch at the Farmer's Market at Third and Fairfax when I got a phone call from Vic Petrotta, a prop master at Universal Studios. He had heard that I owned Beatles memorabilia he needed for a movie shoot. I asked Vic what the movie was about, and he said some kids from Maplewood, New Jersey, trying to get to see the Beatles on *The Ed Sullivan Show*. It sounded like my life, only I was from Oakland. With all four Beatles still alive, I asked if they were going to be in the movie. Maybe.

What was the film called? *Beatles-4-Ever*. Who was involved with the film? A young guy, Robert Zemeckis, was the director; two women whose names he couldn't remember, and another guy . . . Steven Spielberg, "Ya know," he said, "from *Jaws* and *Close Encounters of the Third Kind*."

"What pieces of memorabilia do you need, and would they be safe, because my collection is precious," I added.

Vic assured me everything would be treated with special care. "In movies," Vic added, "this is done all the time."

What things was he looking for? First was a ticket to the Sullivan show. I explained that to my knowledge no tickets still exist; we had handed them in to a ticket taker. I did ask to keep mine but was told that every ticket had to be accounted for. I did know what they looked like and could remember the design. I frequented the Sullivan show, so I had many tickets over a three-year period. He wasn't interested and said he'd have to get creative. The producers requested such interesting relics as Beatles talcum powder, the two pristine Beatles bubble baths, badges, magazines, a three-ring notebook, a Beatles shoe (boot)—I only owned one, which they used; my "Flip Your Wig" game, a Beatles pennant, and newspapers that I might have quick access to. He already had a few Beatles wigs, albums, and sweatshirts. In return I'd receive a stipend and a screen credit of thanks.

"OK," I said innocently. "I'll loan you what you need."

"How about dropping everything off tomorrow," Vic asked. That seemed workable. "I'll leave you a drive-on at Universal Gate 3 right off of Lankershim, and the guard will show you to the bungalow," he added. Vic wasn't sure if he'd be around when I got there. The whole thing sounded cagey, but to have my memorabilia featured in a Beatles movie was exciting.

The next day I loaded the memorabilia into two boxes—one flat for the papers and magazines and notebook, another for the talcum powder, bubble bath plastic containers, badges, the game, canvas boot, and a few other things I thought might add an extra touch. When I got to the office no Vic, but there were two people who were expecting the drop-off. They thought I was from a rental prop house because I asked for a receipt for the items. I was worried about leaving my memorabilia and thought I shouldn't have gone along with this request, but it was too late.

The industry trades were always around our offices at CBS, and one morning I was browsing through the *Hollywood Reporter* and right there in the production notices was that *Beatles-4-Ever* has a new title, *I Wanna Hold Your Hand*. Wondering what was up, I found the phone number on the receipt, phoned, and was told Vic would get back in touch, which he did the next day. They were done with the props, and the items would be delivered by an assistant to my apartment in Studio City.

I used that time to find out about the people who were involved with the film. I wanted details. It was cowritten by Bob Gale and Robert Zemeckis. I had not heard of either. How did they come up with the idea of kids from New Jersey trying to get into the Sullivan show? And Steven Spielberg? It was his first time as an executive producer. Because Zemeckis was a first-time director, Spielberg promised the execs at Universal that if Zemeckis wasn't working out, Spielberg would direct the movie.

Both boxes came back plus a third. The assistant knew nothing about the Beatles appearing in the film, the creative team, release date, my stipend, or end credit. I didn't bother to inspect the two boxes with the memorabilia because I was so curious about the third box. The assistant said inside the mystery box were some of the props they created for the film that Vic thought I would like for the collection. Inside were the prop tickets to the show, two copies of the front page of the fictitious *New York Daily Herald* with the headline "They're Here" and a 16 x 20 color photograph of Ringo that was shown hanging inside a closet in the Beatles Plaza Hotel suite that Nancy Allen (Pam in the film) spotted and jumped back from in fright.

After the assistant left, I opened the other two boxes. I picked up the Beatles talc tin, and it was practically empty. I had never used it; it was full when I delivered it to Vic; the bubble bath containers had been emptied of the liquid soap, too; the badges were OK, but the real New York *Daily News* announcing the Beatles' arrival was ripped and improperly folded.

My heart sank; I knew in my gut that I should not have loaned the items. My precious possessions were ruined. I called Robert Zemeckis's office, but no one answered. To this day, no one has acknowledged the damage to my memorabilia. When I worked on the Universal lot for six years, I sometimes walked over to Robert Zemeckis's bungalow and left notes. I wasn't invited to an early screening or the premiere of the movie in Westwood, but via CBS connections I managed to get on the invite list anyway. The scene with Eddie Deezen jumping on the bed with my original Beatles talcum powder spewing from the tin still makes me cringe. My other artifacts, in perfect view, gave authenticity to the film. I spotted the two empty plastic bubble bath containers in two scenes, the Flip Your Wig game on the floor, pennant on the wall, and scrapbook on the bed.

Last year I was perusing an auction house catalog that had many original Beatles items up for bid. I loved seeing the Beatles dress from Holland, 1964 Christmas flexies, and a Shea Stadium concert poster ready to be auctioned. What shocked me was a ticket to the February 9 Ed Sullivan show—not the real ticket, of course, but the fabricated prop. I called the auction house to let them know it wasn't real, only a prop from a movie. When I checked after the auction, the description still called it an original from *The Ed Sullivan Show*. It sold for more than $5,000. Even reputable auction houses can be duped.

Although the film did poorly in its initial 1978 release, it has become a cult classic. In 2019 I was contacted by the Criterion Collection to help with their rerelease of the movie. Knowing that I was affiliated with *The Ed Sullivan Show*, they asked for assistance in licensing the entire Beatles performance on February 9 for inclusion as bonus material on the DVD. Unfortunately, the deal did not happen.

P.S. I never received the stipend, nor was my name listed on the credits.

P.P.S. Eddie Dezen via a DM recently let me know that the talc scene was his favorite in the film!

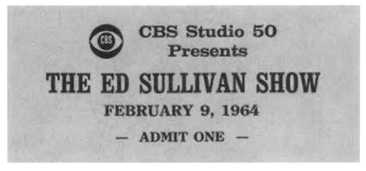

This is a prop used in the movie *I Wanna Hold Your Hand*. Many think it's real, but this is not how tickets to *The Ed Sullivan Show* ever looked.
AUTHOR'S COLLECTION

I styled this photograph to display some of my memorabilia for an article on the passing of John Lennon that never made it into print. You can sense the overall sadness.
AUTHOR'S COLLECTION

In 1982, a BBC crew came to Los Angeles to interview Beatles fans for a documentary they were producing for television titled *Beatlemania!*
AUTHOR'S COLLECTION

"Beatlemania" 1982 : Liverpool / L.A fans reminisce ...
YouTube · Steven Rutter · Jun 20, 2016

UK TV presenter Noel Edmonds featured me on his show *Noel's Addicts*. I didn't appreciate being referred to as a Beatles addict. This photo shows us prepping for the interview.
PHOTO BY JILL JARRETT

In the spring of 1983, when I was seven months pregnant, I taught a second series of classes on the Beatles at UCLA. Each week, students were treated to insightful guest speakers. In this photograph addressing the classroom are Walter Shenson, producer of both Beatles movies; and Marc Behm, the screenwriter of *Help!* Marc also wrote the story for the movie *Charade* starring Audrey Hepburn and Cary Grant. PHOTO BY JILL JARRETT

This snapshot was taken at the Bonaventure Hotel during Beatlefest '83 just before joining three other Beatles fans for a *Life* magazine story on the Beatles' twentieth anniversary.
AUTHOR'S COLLECTION

Mike's shirt needed
a touchup before his
appearance on KPIX
San Francisco.
PHOTO BY JILL JARRETT

With Linda at Beverly Hills Hotel before
she headed to Burbank for Paul's guest
spot on the *Tonight Show*.
PHOTO BY KEVIN WINTER

Paul leaving the Beverly Hills
Hotel and heading to the *Tonight
Show* with Johnny Carson.
AUTHOR'S COLLECTION

This picture was taken at the Jill Youngblood Gallery in October 1985. Elliot Mintz joins Mike McCartney for Mike's photography exhibit.
PHOTO BY JILL JARRETT

During "A Day with the Artist" at the Youngblood Gallery, Mike had a chance to meet fans.
PHOTO BY JILL JARRETT

Auntie Gin was the matriarch of the McCartney family. Mike McCartney graciously drove us to tea at her home. Gin was welcoming, and made a great cuppa. Here she is at her front door as we said good-bye.
AUTHOR'S COLLECTION

I booked Mike McCartney on a TV show in San Francisco. The show flew us up, and Mike was anxious to explore the city, but it was pouring rain. After getting soaked, we spent the evening enjoying Irish coffees at the Buena Vista. Here we are heading back to the hotel. AUTHOR'S COLLECTION

Here I am with Cynthia Lennon at the Hard Rock Café in LA celebrating the premiere of the feature *Imagine*, directed, written, and produced by none other than Andrew Solt.
AUTHOR'S COLLECTION

In 1991, I was working on a morning TV show. With the opportunity to join my husband on a trip to London, I contacted Jane Asher, who owned a cake shop there. Here is a photo of Jane with my daughter taken in her shop.
AUTHOR'S COLLECTION

I generally knew better than to bring my camera. It sounds strange but I learned early on—and Linda McCartney confirmed my suspicions—that even though she was a photographer, cameras were *not* welcome by everyone. This time, at the Fahey Klein gallery on La Brea in LA, Linda was the center of attention with her exhibit "Sixties: Portrait of an Era." I took this opportunity for a quick shot of Paul—he seemed surprised!
AUTHOR'S COLLECTION

Walter Shenson, producer of *A Hard Day's Night*, decided to rerelease the film in the mid-90s. Here I am at the premiere near UCLA being interviewed by Bob Heath of *Entertainment Tonight*.
PHOTO BY JILL JARRETT

It was an honor to find my name on the front page of the *New York Times* for a story on the fiftieth anniversary of the Beatles on *The Ed Sullivan Show*. This photograph appeared on page A3 to accompany the article.
PHOTO BY J. EMILIO FLORES

A Grammy Museum panel on the traveling Beatles exhibit. Pictured are (left to right) Bob Santelli, Grammy Executive Director Russ Lease, me, Chuck Gunderson, Bob Eubanks, and Bruce Spizer, all talking Beatles. PHOTO BY JILL JARRETT

The Beatles: Eight Days a Week - The Touring Years (2016)

Directed by: **Ron Howard**

Stars: **Paul McCartney, Ringo Starr, John Lennon, George Harrison, Larry Kane, Whoopi Goldberg, Elvis Costello, Eddie Izzard, Sigourney Weaver, Richard Lester, Kitty Oliver, Howard Goodall, Jon Savage, Debbie Gendler, Richard Curtis, Malcolm Gladwell, George Martin, Neil Aspinall**

see less

Category: **Film**

Genre: **Documentary**

Language: **English**

Streaming Date: **Unknown**

After two years of scheduling mishaps, I was finally interviewed for Ron Howard's film *The Beatles: Eight Days a Week—The Touring Years*, ending up on the accompanying DVD "3 Fans." Here I am listed in the credits.
AUTHOR'S COLLECTION

Gary Smith, pictured here, was producer of NBC's *Hulabaloo*, where I sat in the audience frequently. Brian Epstein had a weekly spot taped in London and rolled into the show. I met Gary at the memorial service for my cousin David Winter, who was the choreographer on *Hulabaloo*. Here's an unused ticket. I must have had a cold that day.
AUTHOR'S COLLECTION

My local paper had an announcement that John Lennon's half sister, Julia Baird, would be talking just blocks from my house. After her presentation, I introduced myself, and we shared a few stories about Aunt Mimi.
AUTHOR'S COLLECTION

Every year Ringo celebrates his birthday at Beverly Garden Park in Beverly Hills, where his "Peace & Love" statue is located. I live three blocks away and on July 7th, 2021, I walked over at noon and snapped this photo. I think he looks better now than in the '60s.
AUTHOR'S COLLECTION

Tidying up after tea at the McCartney childhood home on Forthlin Road, October 2022.
AUTHOR'S COLLECTION

Studying the famous Forthlin Road drainpipe that afforded the McCartney boys easy exit from the house.
AUTHOR'S COLLECTION

AFTERMATH

12.8.1980

I was just leaving a work-related Monday-night film screening at Grauman's Chinese Theatre on Hollywood Boulevard when I heard the news that John Lennon had been shot. Horror, outrage, disbelief. Racing home through the streets of Hollywood, I charged into the house to join my mom and husband, who were already glued to the TV.

Overnight reports were that a fan had shot him. A fan? How could that possibly be? As a generation, we all had experienced too much gun violence. Violence against public figures seemed pervasive throughout our society: JFK, Martin Luther King Jr., Malcolm X, Robert Kennedy, Harvey Milk, and now John Lennon. It seemed unconceivable.

I went to work the following day in a complete daze. Nothing seemed right in the world. That afternoon I received a phone call from a reporter at the now-defunct Los Angeles *Herald Examiner*, Suzan Nightingale. The paper started by William Randolph Hearst in the early 1900s was the alternative to the *Los Angeles Times*. Suzan contacted me because she had heard that I had met John Lennon. Suzan was exactly my age and a Beatles fan. When she arrived at my house to conduct the interview, Suzan thought the story was much bigger than she had anticipated. After about two hours of talking and going through some of my letters and memorabilia, Suzan called for a photographer to take photos. The story would appear the following day with other tributes to John Lennon in the *Herald Examiner*, possibly syndicated across the country.

The next morning my husband raced to the newsstand to pick up a copy of the paper. I was just out of the shower when he came in to tell me that the article wasn't there. He had gone through the paper a few times but concluded that the article hadn't made the editor's cut. It was a time to mourn John and not look for publicity. My husband was finishing his cereal when I walked into the kitchen where the crumpled paper sat on the butcher-block countertop. There I was, pictured on the front page. My husband had not looked there!

The article and photo led to a few other interviews, including a story on KABC Channel 7 6 p.m. news. I thought that the article was good; however, it gave way too many details of where I lived and worked, and details about the Beatles memorabilia that at the time filled my house. A few nights later when I arrived home from work, a suspicious-looking person was sitting in a parked car across the street. When my husband arrived thirty minutes later, the car and driver were still there and as we left for dinner, nothing had changed.

As we drove away an uneasy feeling befell both of us, so we made a U-turn and headed back. The car was now directly in front of our house. The driver quickly stepped on the gas, racing to the alley. We chased the car at high speeds through the streets for about ten minutes, trying to get his license plate number. All I had was California plate "NRAY . . ." before the driver got away. We never saw the car or driver again.

One month after John Lennon's passing, I received a phone call from a man named Jack Crane. He said he had read the article in the newspaper, he was a big fan of John Lennon's, and wanted to meet me to discuss John. That seemed plausible, and I was always encouraging fans. I invited him to my house late on a Friday afternoon. Looking back, I would not do this today, but my mom would be present.

Jack arrived at the set time. No car was parked out there. Dressed in business attire, he stood at the front door, tightly clenching a briefcase. He sported a military-style haircut and chewed gum nonstop. After Jack politely introduced himself, he sat down confidently on the sofa and fired off rehearsed questions for which he demanded immediate responses. It was more like an interrogation than a fan wanting to talk about John Lennon and his legacy: When did I first meet John Lennon? What was he like in person? Do I remember what we discussed?

Jack kept drilling me about John. Then he asked to use the bathroom. Strangely, he picked up the briefcase and took it with him to the bathroom. Briefcase to the bathroom? He returned to the exact same spot on the sofa and nervously kept asking questions for another half hour. Abruptly he stood up, said it was time to go, and left, walking rapidly up the street. I went into the bathroom after he had gone; nothing had been touched. Had he changed a tape in the bathroom and was recording me? It was very odd.

A week passed, and I received another call from Jack Crane. He needed to return to ask me a few more questions. I asked for his phone number, and he gave it to me. But Jack called the next day before I had the chance to call him to set a date for the meeting. This time I made it for Saturday at 4, to make sure my husband was home. Jack returned, briefcase still in hand, and he placed it strategically in front of my chair. After a few short questions about the Dakota apartment building and other random thoughts on John Lennon, Jack said he had all he *needed*. *Needed* for what?

Very curious, my husband asked where he was going. Because he had no car, we offered to give him a ride. Jack seemed flustered, but then agreed. We got into the car, with Jack in the backseat, and he told us he was headed to the San Fernando Valley. He directed us to Lankershim Boulevard in North Hollywood. At a light Jack asked us to drop him there, in front of a vacant storefront. Barely saying goodbye, he quickly got out of the car and was gone. Later that evening I tried the phone number he had given me. It was disconnected, with no forwarding number. I never heard from Jack Crane again.

During the interview, *Herald Examiner* reporter Suzan Nightingale had asked my first impression of John Lennon when I saw him in person. The answer had to be at *The Ed Sullivan Show* while the Beatles were performing "All My Loving." Although a Paul song, the image still fresh in my mind is of John dutifully playing his Rickenbacker guitar, looking up and smiling at us screaming girls in the audience. A seemingly innocent smile that I will remember forever.

I have read in several reports that Stephan Lynn, head of emergency medicine at Roosevelt Hospital, now Mount Sinai West, and Dr. David Halleran who attended John Lennon on this horrific night, commented "that, at the moment Lennon was pronounced dead, a Beatles song, 'All My Loving,' came over the hospital's sound system."

There wasn't much to smile about anymore.

A GOOD TIME GUARANTEED FOR ALL AT ONLY $15.95

As a new arrival in LA, weekdays were fine and busy at CBS. I had a lot to do—find an apartment, buy a car, and explore a new city. The weekends were rough and lonely. With my mom in New Jersey and my boyfriend in Brooklyn, I spent more time on the phone than anything else. Coming with me to Los Angeles, though, was my assistant, Paul Dobbs. Personnel at CBS had asked if I wanted him along. Paul was married, and the move for him would be more complicated. But after a day or two of consultation with family and friends, Paul and his then wife, Linda, made the move west.

One lunchtime about four months after our arrival at CBS Television City, Paul and I walked up to Melrose Avenue. Across from Fairfax High School was a venerable record store, Aaron's Records. Besides having the best collection of used, vintage, and imported albums and singles, Aaron's had a bulletin board where people who bought and sold and traded records and memorabilia posted their contact information. One of the business cards tacked to the bulletin board was "Felice Lipsky, Dealer in Buying, Selling and Trading Beatles Memorabilia." Knowing my Beatles history, Paul decided that "Felice Lipsky" should become my friend. He removed her card from the bulletin board and pocketed it while I was sorting through the records.

The next Friday Paul asked what I was doing that weekend and I just shrugged, implying nothing. He pulled Felice's business card out of his desk drawer and said, "Call her." At first, I dismissed the idea as being weird, but by Sunday evening, bored beyond belief, I thought, *why not.* The Beatles were a good enough reason to meet. When I phoned Felice, her husband answered and told me that Felice's mother had just passed away and she was back home in Detroit. We talked for an hour about Felice's Beatles memorabilia business and how she made a great living selling Beatles items. Selling Beatles memorabilia was a new concept, which piqued my curiosity. She returned a week later and phoned. We agreed to meet at a diner on Laurel Canyon Boulevard, in North Hollywood.

I was amazed at the scope of the business she ran out of her North Hollywood living room: mail order; the monthly Capitol Records Swap Meet; and Beatlefest, which I had not heard of before. Three times a year Felice would pack her records and memorabilia and head to Beatlefest—New York City in February, Chicago in August, and Los Angeles over Thanksgiving weekend—to sell Beatles memorabilia and records.

When I met Felice, Beatlefest had already been going on for four years. Starting as an idea of Beatles fan Mark Lapidos in 1974, he looked for a way to honor the Beatles, their tenth anniversary coming to America, and to profit along the way. After obtaining John Lennon's blessing, Mark held the first Beatlefest in New York City in September 1974. It was a time for Beatles fans to celebrate the group in a meaningful way.

Beatlefest weekends were a resounding success with thousands of fans in attendance. By 1976, Beatlefest had moved to other cities. Now called The Fest for Beatles Fans due to legal issues, I assume, with Apple Corps, the Fest has been operating for fifty years. I will always call it "Beatlefest."

Mark and Carol have had the pleasure of welcoming thousands and thousands of Beatles fans and now second- and third-generation fans to Beatlefest. And they have had nearly everyone from the Beatles world speak—from Harry Nilsson to Wings' Laurence Juber, Peter Asher, George's sister Louise, Cynthia Lennon, Pattie Boyd, Pete Best, Clive Epstein (Brian's brother), actors from the Beatles movies, film producer Walter Shenson, and Mickey Dolenz, just to name a few.

I attended Beatlefest for a few years, helping Felice behind her table selling her memorabilia and authenticating items. Assisting Felice gave me something to do, although I always felt somewhat awkward not sharing details of my backstory, but in time bits leaked out. The record and memorabilia dealers, and I include Felice, were a brutal group. The competition was fierce between them, and the can-you-top-this stories were laughable and unbelievable. They would try to outsmart and outbid each other with jealous rage.

Over a Beatlefest weekend in Los Angeles, Felice would easily gross $15,000. I was never paid, but I enjoyed being with the fans, selling Felice's memorabilia, and sharing insights. And I made forever friends. I met burgeoning photographer, now noted rock photo guru Jill Jarrett, at a record swap meet, but our friendship continued over many Beatlefests and far beyond.

As the old memorabilia and records sold out, Felice and her colleagues fell into selling Beatles bootlegs and manufacturing Beatles pins and badges and other types of merchandise. This proved a big problem for me. I had just gotten married, to someone I had met after moving to Los Angeles. He was a lawyer, and his specific expertise was copyright and trademark law. How ironic that my friend with whom I had spent so much time was working with people who manufactured Beatles bootlegs. It was a definite issue, and my husband asked me to end the friendship.

As Beatlefest grew, Mark and Carol cornered the market in Beatles goods, not just charging admittance of what I remember was approximately $15.95 per day back in 1979, but to limit dealers from selling items they manufactured. Felice and her colleagues kept the manufacturing going, creating a demand for more and more.

Simultaneously, once a month a record swap meet was held in Hollywood at the parking lot adjacent to the Capitol Records building on Vine Street. The Capitol Records Swap Meet was held on the first Saturday/Sunday of the month. It started at 11 p.m. Saturday night after the parking lot officially closed and went until 11 a.m. the next day. Cars, trucks, and vans would pull in and put out their records, memorabilia, and other rock-related items such as posters, pictures, and pins and sell through the night. Many of the same local Beatles dealers who sold at Beatlefest would bring their items to the Hollywood meet. Bootleg records were rampant as were used records, imports, cassettes, and tapes for sale. I had a blast every month no matter what the season.

Our ritual was that at about 8:30 p.m., we would meet for dinner at the old Tick Tock Restaurant on Cahuenga just north of Hollywood Boulevard for a nourishing warm meal. Then we would head over to wait for the lot to shut down to claim our parking space. By 2 a.m., when the clubs closed, the parking lot was packed with hundreds of people browsing by flashlight through boxes of merchandise and records. In winter months at 3 a.m., as the winds picked up, I huddled under blankets in Felice's car trying to stay warm. At 4 a.m., you could see drummer Bruce Gary from the Knack or David Lee Roth walking the crowded parking lot.

We got to know Bruce Gary well. He showed up nearly every month and consistently left with several bootlegs not just of the Beatles, but other artists including Cheap Trick, Joe Jackson, or the Cars (Ric Ocasek even browsed the parking lot once). During these early-morning conversations, Bruce, a studio drummer for Bob Dylan, Bette Midler, and George Harrison, shared stories.

Eventually Capitol Records found out that bootlegs were being sold and shut down the parking lot. The Capitol Records Swap meet moved from location to location after that, never finding a permanent home. One Saturday night at the Hollywood Roosevelt hotel all the dealers had just put out their items. Buyers were lined up in the hall to enter the smaller ballroom, poised for another night of selling and trading. Instead, the Hollywood police marched in and confiscated several hundred boxes of bootlegs and arrested many sellers—including Felice. Even though she had her resale number prominently displayed, it had no impact on the arresting officer. Always feisty, Felice argued with the police officer as he led her off in handcuffs.

I phoned my husband to meet me at the Hollywood Police Department. Felice and others needed legal advice ASAP. As I sat on the hard wooden bench at the entrance to the police station waiting for my husband to arrive, I sensed movement inside my abdomen. I was five months pregnant, and a police station was no place to be at midnight. My husband was right—it was time for it to be over.

CELEBRATING THE MACS

I read the ads announcing Michael McCartney's appearance in Los Angeles. I had met Mike twice, first briefly outside his home in Liverpool and again a few years later when he was in New York City performing at the Bitter End in Greenwich Village with his comedic improvisational group the Scaffold. In the intervening years Mike had become a dad to three daughters, divorced, and was raising the girls on his own. The notice said Mike was coming to Los Angeles to promote a book he had written called *The Macs: Mike McCartney's Family Album.*

I wanted to do something extraordinary for Mike and the book's release. I appreciated Mike's talent; and his dad, Jim McCartney, had been welcoming and gracious when I visited Liverpool. I hoped to reciprocate.

I spoke with my husband and mom about hosting a book signing party for Mike at our house. We all decided it would be great fun, especially because my mom was undergoing chemotherapy treatments, and this might take our minds off the inescapable ending. The following day I tracked down the book publisher, Delilah Publications, based in New York City. Delilah's co-owners, Stephanie Bennett and Jeannie Sakol, were immediately receptive to the idea if it didn't cost them any money. I agreed to foot the entire event, except Delilah Publications would absorb the cost for the design and printing of the invitation. The Delilah girls were pleased to have a home in Beverly Hills where they could invite key industry professionals to meet Mike and further their company's objective to publish other rock 'n' roll titles.

Jeannie Sakol had written romance novels, and we got along just fine. Stephanie Bennett was primarily business-oriented, direct and determined. I preferred to deal with Jeannie in setting all the details. Delilah did a great job on the postcards, and together we sent out about 150 invitations. We selected Tuesday evening, December 1, for the party.

What I didn't know when organizing the event was that on Sunday Mike's three daughters were coming to stay for a few days' vacation and would be here for the book signing party. Their presence would make it even better.

Replies came pouring in, and I had to plan the menu for the evening. I decided to put on a great spread and made everything, cooking and baking right through Thanksgiving Day without even a thought of turkey. We had more than one hundred RSVPs. My house would be jammed. Jeannie and Stephanie arrived from New York City and were very pleased to see Mike's book selling so well wherever it was displayed. On that Sunday I decided we needed a new dining room chandelier and bought one without hesitation. Then we needed additional comfortable chairs for the living room and impulsively bought two new plush chairs. The house had to be perfect.

Mike's daughters arrived from Liverpool a few days later, accompanied by Rowena Horne. Mike lighted up when he welcomed Rowena into the living room. It was wonderful to see the girls with their loving dad. Rowena, Benna, Theran, and Abbi had plans to go to Disneyland, see the sights, and have a fun family vacation while dad worked. Also planned was a visit to the set of a television show.

Rowena was wearing the most magnificent beehive-collared beige coat—even today the image lingers. She was stylish and beautiful with a sparkling innocence. She was shy and reserved. Rowena was taking it all in silently. Whenever possible, I bombarded her with questions, especially about the coat she designed; and after learning she was from Liverpool, questions nonstop. During my 1967 trip to Liverpool, I didn't see many of the important sites. I probably was too brash and invasive for Rowena, who seemed very private and guarded, but that is a trait that burdens many who hail from New Jersey.

It was nearly 6:30 p.m., and people started to arrive. The new chandelier was sparkling over the table filled with goodies to be devoured. Wine and beer were self-serve. The living room was packed to capacity, and the overflow crowd kept expanding to the dining room, to the kitchen, and beyond to the back deck. Scattered about were British and Scouse accents. Rowena, Benna, Theran, and Abbi found a comfortable place on the living room sofa.

I looked around in complete amazement. Graham Nash was standing next to my piano. Leaning against the dining room wall was Badfinger's Joey Molland being admonished by my mom for flicking his cigarette ashes onto the dining room's hardwood floors. Moments later, I caught him bending down to clean up his mess. I turn my head only to see Spencer Davis of the Spencer Davis Group standing next to the bookcase. It became impossible to move through the house. Capitol Records executives showed up, as did reps from Warner Brothers Records, Mike's label.

Even a former nightclub owner and his son from Liverpool then living in California stopped by. I spent a good deal of time talking to the dad, Jim Ireland. Mike was happy to see him. Jim had owned a jazz club in Liverpool in the late '50s and '60s called the Mardi Gras. It was a sister club to the Cavern, where bands and jazz musicians would play and hang out. The Beatles, Gerry and the Pacemakers, Cilla Black all played "The Mardi." The club could hold around seven hundred people and had a dance floor for three hundred. I knew Jim was an important part of the Mersey music scene when he told me he also managed bands along with Brian Epstein. Jim's most famous group was the Merseyside band the Swinging Bluejeans of "Hippy Hippy Shake" fame. I was so impressed. Not long after our meeting. Jim fell ill and left California for Liverpool. Before the move Jim contacted me with his address, kindly offering his hospitality and encouraging me to visit him at 56–60 Seel Street. I remember Mike calling to let me know that Jim had passed away not long after his return home.

We may have received one hundred RSVPs, but by estimates we had 250 people in attendance. As the host, I tried to welcome everyone to the house and be sensitive to all the guests' needs, but that proved impossible. I noticed that Mike's jet-lagged girls were beginning to fall asleep on the couch and tried my best to forge through the crowd to see if I could encourage them to the bedroom where they might be more comfortable. Abbi liked the idea, and as I led her toward the bedroom, over my shoulder I saw the star of the hottest show on television, *Dynasty*'s Joan Collins and her daughter, Katy, sitting in the new chairs. Joan's husband, Ron Kass, was standing alongside in front of the fireplace. How happy was I that we had bought those chairs. Kass was the American head of Apple from 1968 to 1969 until Allen Klein forced him out, claiming financial impropriety. Two years after Mike's party, Joan Collins and Ron Kass divorced, although they remained on good terms until his untimely death at age fifty-one in 1986.

In addition to her husband, Joan Collins had another significant connection. Her father, Joe Collins, was a well-respected London theatrical agent. In 1963, Brian Epstein had approached him for advice concerning booking the Beatles into a specific London venue. Joe Collins in the early days was very helpful to the novice Beatles manager. It was appropriate that Ron and Joan came by to welcome Mike. I was excited for Mike that they showed such interest in his career.

By now the signing was winding down, and Mike had no more books on hand to autograph. The Delilah gals left the party, calling it a resounding Hollywood success, and from their perspective, it undoubtedly was. A year later Delilah Publications came out with *The Compleat Beatles*, a best-selling compilation of Beatles sheet music with commentary. Later

Jeannie and Stephanie published books on girl groups, Bruce Springsteen, Kenny Rogers, and Blondie. Jeannie eventually returned to writing romance novels, and Stephanie continues today producing documentaries that included the classic Everly Brothers 1983 Reunion at Royal Albert Hall, London.

I packed up my homemade lemon bars and pumpkin bread for departing guests to enjoy with their morning tea. As the McCartney entourage packed into the car to return to their hotel, a white stretch limousine pulling up in front of the house caught our attention. The car came to a stop, the back window opened, and out came an arm holding, of all things, a Bible. Mike walked over to the car and bent down to see inside—it was Little Richard. He was an inspiration to all the aspiring musicians in Liverpool, and it was an honor for him to stop by to congratulate Mike on the book.

After the Little Richard frenzy subsided, the gang returned to their car. Exhausted, we all said our goodbyes until the morning. As the McCartney car pulled away from the curb, with Mike and Rowena in front and the girls in the back, I sensed that a new chapter was about to be added to *Mike McCartney's Family Album.*

SECOND TIME AROUND

In early 1982, I was having lunch with Walter Shenson at the Beverly Wilshire when he mentioned that Universal wanted to do a rerelease of *A Hard Day's Night*. It had been several years since I had seen the film, and I was excited to learn that the movie would be out again. The deal Walter had made with the Beatles, Brian Epstein, and United Artists in 1963 was this: fifteen years after the theatrical release of the movie, all rights would revert to Walter. I remember Walter saying shortly after I reconnected with him in 1978 that the film's rights were his and thinking how amazing it was that I knew the person who owned *A Hard Day's Night*. Although Walter's sons Douglas and Richard sold the two masterpieces to the Karsh family, my connection to the films' ownership lives on, being an acquaintance of Martha Karsh. Martha, also a fan, published the book *The Beatles A Hard Day's Night: A Private Archive*, written by Mark Lewisohn, in 2016.

Jim Katz, who worked in publicity on the original release from United Artists in 1964, would be involved in the rerelease as well. The Beatles, Walter added, were behind the project, as was Neil Aspinall, who ran Apple. No new scenes would be added because outtakes from the movie had been destroyed shortly after production was completed. By 1982, it was common knowledge that the film was made so that United Artists could own a Beatles album, and there was always a slight suspicion that their popularity would fade.

There would be one new music addition. The song "I'll Cry Instead," cut from the original film (but not the soundtrack), would be added over a montage of still photos from the movie to form a new prologue. A big movie premiere would mark the occasion. I quickly added that I would be happy to *help in any way*. I remember Walter laughing at that comment. Always very attuned to language usage Walter said, *Help!* Would be the next film released.

I did help Walter in many ways—supplying him with copies of the original oversized tickets that I had saved from the movie's early press

screenings in 1964 and assorted other memorabilia that they could repli-
cate for the film's reissue. Walter had T-shirts and caps made to promote
the film and worked with Universal publicity to bring the top entertainment show on TV in 1982—*Entertainment Tonight*—to the movie's premiere in Westwood, California.

As I had done in 1964, I organized fans to be outside the movie theater.
It was a great evening filled with fun and excitement. The film was better
than ever, and people congregated at the theater for the premiere even
asked for my autograph.

TEACHING AND TESTIFYING

Beginning in or around 1981, a group of Los Angeles—area Beatles fans would gather frequently at my house to talk about the group. We would meet between Beatlefest conventions. Based on these get-togethers, I thought that a serious, in-depth class on the Beatles would interest those who were curious about the band and wanted to examine the craze many still called Beatlemania.

Who would want to sponsor a class on the subject? There were no degrees on the Beatles yet or even respected classes on the band as a legitimate subject. The year before, I had taken a class at UCLA Extension on motion picture finance and thought that was a place to start. After making a few calls to UCLA, I reached two women who seemed intrigued—Ronnie Rubin and Sharon Wilkinson House. Wasting no time, I put together a syllabus that would span eight weeks, breaking it down into topics ranging from the Beatles' beginnings to the impact of their music and films on culture, fashion, politics, and society. It would be both enlightening and entertaining because I included guest speakers for each session. Beatles film producer Walter Shenson would speak in addition to former Wings guitarist Laurence Juber and the film editor on John and Yoko's art movies, Doug Ibolt.

When Ronnie and Sharon saw the class outline, they immediately agreed. Sharon came to my house for a meeting. As we talked about the class, Sharon suggested that we should do it first as a weekend seminar. Sharon's thought that we would meet Saturday from 9 to 5:30 at a classroom on the UCLA campus. On Sunday, the school could rent the ABC Shubert Theater in Century City for an exclusive screening of the movie *Help!*, which had recently been remastered and was about to be rereleased. We would also play clips from *A Hard Day's Night*, *The Beatles in Tokyo*, *Let It Be*, and *The Beatles at Shea Stadium*.

Joining us to introduce the film and then do a Q&A after the showing would be the film's producer, Walter Shenson; and Jim Katz, the film's original publicist now at Universal. Richard DiLello, former staffer at

Apple Records; and James Bacon, the entertainment columnist at the Los Angeles *Herald Examiner*, hopefully would complete the panel. Cost of the weekend was $55, which included all classroom materials.

UCLA had a sizable turnout, about eighty-five people. In the winter of 1983, we did it again, but this time as a six-week structured class with all the guests I had originally proposed and others—Beatles historian John Stark; and the screenwriter for *Help!*, Marc Behm, who happened to be visiting Walter Shenson. Other guests included Philip Norman, author of *Shout!*, a history of the Beatles; and Rip Rense, pop music critic/reporter also for the Los Angeles *Herald Examiner*.

An amusing incident includes Rip Rense, stepson of the iconic editor of *Architectural Digest* Paige Rense, although he refused to admit it.

As a thank-you for Rip's participation as a speaker, I invited him to join my husband and me for dinner at an Indian restaurant on La Cienega Boulevard. When we drove up to the restaurant, the place looked like it had seen better days. Rip and my husband were both giving me a hard time for even suggesting such an uninviting place. Once inside, we could select any table: we were the only people there. Just as I was saying yet again how sorry I was, a limousine pulled up, and we could see four people coming into the restaurant. How relieved I was. As the foursome entered, we looked up to see Mick Jagger, Jerry Hall, Shelley Duvall, and Kim Cranston (son of US senator Alan Cranston) sit down right behind us. Stunned, we finished our dinner in total silence. I had no need to apologize again.

Three years later I was leaving home when a well-dressed man got out of his car, approaching me carefully.

"Debbie Gendler?" he asked, with a slight doubt in his voice.

"Yes," I replied, concerned for my child inside the house with her sitter.

"Please sign for this."

It was an official envelope with the return address California Superior Court, Los Angeles County. Before I could comment, the man drove off. I opened the envelope: I had been subpoenaed to testify in the *Apple Corps Limited v. Beatlemania* trial. I ran back into the house and immediately phoned my lawyer husband. He thought this was the greatest thing; I was upset. My husband explained that it seemed like I was being called as a witness for the defendants against Apple Corps.

The trial was followed closely by all tribute bands and others centered on issues of the right of publicity of the Beatles name, image, and likeness, and their misappropriation in the Broadway stage production, touring productions, and feature film of *Beatlemania*—not the real thing but an incredible simulation. The musical on Broadway, featuring twenty-nine Beatles songs performed by a look-alike tribute band, was a huge success and ran for two years. After Broadway, there were traveling tours of the show, and in 1980 a film version of *Beatlemania* was produced. The stage play could somehow get away with it, although the production seemed sloppy—the images projected on the back screen didn't match the songs, and the four "Beatles" seemed like cheap replicas. When the feature film was released to a wide audience in August 1981, after John Lennon's death, it didn't hold up creatively. Critics were horrified, with one influential reviewer, Jonathan Rosenbaum of the *Chicago Reader*, saying "his idea of hell is being forced at gunpoint to resee this 1981 atrocity."

The Beatles themselves and their legal team decided enough was enough and took producers Steven Leber, David Krebs, Beatlemania Ltd., Ely Landau, Ely Landau, Inc., and The This Is The Week That Beatlemania Was Company, Inc., to court.

I didn't understand why I was called to testify but soon learned that the defendants were using the classes I taught at UCLA as an example of other entities that exploited the Beatles name and image to make money without paying Apple a license fee. The classes were not intended to exploit the Beatles, and UCLA didn't make a significant profit. I was only paid $375 total for the six-week class and even less for the earlier weekend double session.

The attorneys for *Beatlemania* invoked many maneuvers—First Amendment claims and fair use rights. I was deeply offended by having to give testimony that might harm Apple's case. I did what any loyal fan would do, and I called Apple's attorney in Los Angeles. The firm arranged for their legal counsel, Robert Marshall, to come to my house to ready me for trial as a hostile witness. I spent an entire afternoon with Mr. Marshall preparing for my day on the stand.

When called to the witness stand, I answered all the defendant's lawyer's questions truthfully and to the best of my knowledge, but still the *Beatlemania* attorney, Joel Smith, grew rather upset with my testimony. It slowly backfired on his case. He then verbally attacked me on the stand, just like Perry Mason, by insinuating that I was a hack who had no Beatles knowledge. I was deeply offended.

As a last attempt to discredit me in front of the judge, the lawyer reached for the only question he could instantly come up with that he believed would show I was *not* an expert: "Who wrote the song 'Taxman?'" he asked smugly, thinking he got me.

With complete confidence I fired back at him without hesitation . . . "George Harrison!"

Joel Smith looked stunned, defeated. He turned his back to me, dropped his hands at his side, and I was dismissed.

I didn't win the case for Apple, the evidence did, but I felt good about my court appearance. When Judge Paul Breckenridge on June 3, 1986, ordered the producers of the *Beatlemania* stage show and film to pay Apple Corps Ltd., $10 million, I celebrated my own personal victory.

Apple Corps Limited v. Leber, et al., 229 U.S.P.Q. 1015, California Superior Court Los Angeles County, No. C 299149, Decided June 3, 1986,

    Action by Apple Corps Limited, against Steven Leber, David Krebs, Beatlemania Ltd., Ely Landau, Ely Landau, Inc., and The This Is The Week That Beatlemania Was Company, Inc., for misappropriation of right of publicity. Judgment for plaintiff. Bertram Fields, Robert F. Marshall, and Greenberg, Glusker, Fields, Claman & Machtinger, all of Los Angeles, for plaintiff. Joel M. Smith, Gary L. Swingle, and Leopold, Petrich & Smith, all of Los Angeles, Calif., for defendants. Breckenridge, Jr., Judge.

GIVE MY REGARDS TO BEVERLY HILLS

Paul McCartney's much anticipated feature film, *Give My Regards to Broad Street*, was finally set to premiere in Los Angeles in October 1984. Not dissimilar to *A Hard Day's Night*, the film centers on a day in the life of Paul McCartney when the master recording tapes of his upcoming album were believed stolen by an employee who had a questionable past. The plot had real-life implications because Paul's trash from his home in London had been regularly sifted through for years and sold for big money to collectors. And like *A Hard Day's Night*, the film was primarily a soundtrack in search of a script.

Since making two films and a television movie, *Magical Mystery Tour*, for the Beatles, Paul wanted to get back into the feature world. Although *Give My Regards to Broad Street* was touted as being his first foray into the theatrical world in many years, Paul had produced his own rock concert films. With the three other Beatles having gone into the feature world, I believe that Paul wanted in, too.

John and Yoko had produced films such as *Two Virgins* and *Rape* going back to 1968 and 1969, respectively, and then *Fly* in 1970, just to name a few productions. John also was the actor in Richard Lester's *How I Won the War*. George Harrison partnered with Denis O'Brien in 1978, to establish HandMade Films to finance the film Monty Python's *Life of Brian*. That venture eventually evolved into HandMade Films producing their own successful feature in 1981, *Time Bandits*. Other films followed throughout the 1980s until George and Denis O'Brien had a falling-out due to financial tensions. Ringo, who was the Beatle most interested in acting, it seemed, appeared in films and television as diverse as *Caveman* in 1983, and much later as the narrator in the popular children's television show *Thomas the Tank Engine & Friends*.

When I heard that Paul and Linda were coming to Los Angeles for the film's premiere in Westwood adjacent to the UCLA campus, I thought it a great opportunity to see them.

Through a paparazzi friend I knew, they were ensconced in their favorite bungalow at the Beverly Hills Hotel, a tradition since the earliest days of their getting together in 1968. I wrote a letter letting them know I would like to say "hello" and dropped it off at the front desk. When I returned to my car, parked on Crescent Drive, I was assured that Paul and Linda were guests because I recognized the security staff close to their bungalow. Two days went by, and I received no response. I also knew that on the afternoon of October 23, Paul was booked as the lead guest on *The Tonight Show* with Johnny Carson.

Not wanting to lose any more time, I left work early and drove to the Beverly Hills Hotel, parked again on Crescent Drive, and followed the side pathway to their bungalow. Linda was closing the door, heading to the main hotel. She didn't seem surprised to see me. Timing couldn't have been better. She was going down to the sundry shop to pick up a throat lozenge, and I walked along. We talked primarily about my old Nikon camera that dangled around my neck. I knew it was best not to bring a camera, but I couldn't resist the temptation. After all, this town was home, and I didn't think that taking a few photos would intrude. It seemed to have gone down well with Linda; she took the camera from my neck and looked through the lens.

Returning to the bungalow, we walked up the green-carpeted stairs and out the double doors to the right of the entrance to the world-famous Polo Lounge. Walking along the path with the bungalow in sight, Linda dashed back in, saying they would leave for the studio in five minutes, and I should wait to say hello to Paul. Sounded super to me.

But in a flash, just as Linda shut the door, fifteen pushy photographers appeared with a few fans on Crescent Drive. Simultaneously, a black Corvette pulled up with John Hammel, Paul's go-to guy, behind the wheel. John had worked for Paul since 1975, joining the Wings crew, and was an invaluable asset to Paul for years. (He's now remarried and in Utah after living in Belize.) As the car pulled up, Linda motioned for me to come back just as Paul stepped out of the bungalow. Paul and I chatted a few moments primarily about the Broad Street movie and his hope that it would be well received. Meanwhile, the photographers pushed each other to get a better angle of Paul, who was wearing a great-looking blue sports jacket.

Paul was in full PR mode, happy to sign autographs and pose for photographs. Linda was carrying copies of *Club Sandwich*, trying to get attention for the glossy newsletter. *Club Sandwich* was the official publication of the Paul McCartney Fun (Fan) Club and full of great information on McCartney tours, music, and their pro-animal vegetarian activities. Started in the 1970s, *Club Sandwich* stopped publication shortly after Linda's very sad passing in 1998.

As the paparazzi rushed Paul and company, darting past the crowd was John Hammel with a pink bakery box in hand. I overheard him telling a few photographers that Paul was taking the box to the Carson show. Inside was a cake for Johnny Carson, whose birthday it was, October 23rd. Paul would surprise him with the cake on the show. As cameras flashed, Paul made it to the driver's side of the Corvette. John Hammel placed the cake in the car's trunk and hopped into the passenger seat beside Paul. Linda got into another car following behind. They were off to Burbank, and I stood on the sidewalk waving goodbye with the gathered group.

Paul did a fine job promoting the film on the show and blew out the candle on Johnny Carson's cake. *Give My Regards to Broad Street* premiered in Westwood that evening and drew a large enthusiastic crowd outside of the theater, with Paul and Linda arriving regally. Unfortunately, the film was a box-office disaster. The soundtrack did well, though, and had a breakout hit, "No More Lonely Nights," that reached #1 in the British charts and peaked at #21 in the States.

When I arrived home that afternoon from the Beverly Hills Hotel, a letter was waiting from Shelagh Jones, assistant to Paul and Linda, responding to my letter. Shelagh had written,

> Paul and Linda have asked me to reply to your letter of yesterday's date . . . unfortunately, on the trip they have been too busy for anything but press and TV interviews. However, they thank you for your letter, and wish the warmest regards to you, Paul and the baby, and as they themselves said— "hopefully next time . . ."

Yes, definitely, next time.

BEANS ON TOAST

Shortly after the big Delilah book party at my house in 1981 for Michael McCartney's book launch, Mike and Rowena married; then their first son was born. Through it all, our friendship grew, and I truly came to appreciate them, not because of their connections but as the wonderful, good-hearted, down-to-earth people they are. Mike also trusted my advice on projects he had in development and started to depend upon my husband for his knowledge of copyright law.

Liverpool, my personal "mecca," played a big part in our growing friendship. I always felt a connection there, and over the years I became a devoted Anglophile. *Seventeen* magazine once noted in a column, "How far will they (fans) go? Beatlemanics in Oakland, New Jersey, have even set their clocks ahead five hours—they're on London time!" That was me. I kept a small Union Jack windup alarm clock at my bedside always on London time.

While I was advising Mike on an upcoming project, we all agreed that it might be a good idea my husband, Paul, two-year old daughter, and me to travel to Liverpool. First, timing was perfect: my husband had a legal conference in Augsburg, Germany, in June. Second, wanting a newer, safer car, we had purchased a BMW locally, to be picked up at the factory in Munich. We could easily shorten the time on the continent to go to Liverpool. After the conference we drove through Germany to Belgium to visit friends, leaving the car in Antwerp for shipment back home. We then took the hovercraft from Ostend to Dover and train to London, on to Liverpool. The first night when we arrived, we went directly to a hotel in the city center, near the partially constructed Albert Docks. Mike thought it would be good for us to experience Liverpool first, then stay at his house for a few days. We took in some of the sights including a "Ferry Across the Mersey," after which my husband immediately went to Marks & Spencer's to buy a warm jacket. He hadn't anticipated how cold Liverpool could be in June.

On day two, our bags packed, Mike picked us up, bound for the posh part of Merseyside. It had been eighteen years since I had visited Liverpool and been welcomed into a McCartney home. This time it was Mike's home, not Jim's. Sitting in Mike's backseat I could feel the excitement all over again. A lot had happened since I had traveled these same roads with Mr. and Mrs. Harrison in 1967: marriages, deaths, births, moves, and then out the window I saw the roundabout . . . the same left turn . . . passing Jim McCartney's home.

"Is that Rembrandt?"

Mike seemed surprised that I could pick it out so quickly from all the others on the road.

"Had I been here before?" he asked.

"Yes, in 1967 with Mr. and Mrs. Harrison, and briefly met you when I visited your dad and Angela."

"Amazing," Mike replied as he quickly rounded the bend in the road. He didn't remember our first meeting.

Mike's family was there to greet us with their young son, just months older than our daughter. It was near teatime for the children, and beans on toast was served. My daughter didn't appreciate this new exotic dish. We left Mike's children at the table enjoying their tea and our daughter with tears in her eyes, just staring at the plate of beans as we moved on to plan the next day.

The following morning Mike loaded us into his car, and we were off to meet the immortalized and much written about Auntie Gin. It was Auntie Gin who was there to help her brother Jim raise the young Mike and Paul after their mother's devastating passing. As we stepped out of the car, a smiling Auntie Gin in a floral housedress was standing in her doorway.

Joining Auntie Gin at home was Cousin Mike Robbins, who had stopped by. As most Liverpudlians do, first thing we were offered a cup of tea, which we accepted appreciatively. I wish I could remember more of our conversation, but I was in awe just to be sitting there in Auntie Gin's living room. Because Auntie Gin was the family matriarch, her home was where many McCartney family celebrations were held. Auntie Gin was the mom of cousin Ian Harris, so important in the family's life.

At one point Mike's son and our daughter, both two years old, began to chase each other back and forth between the multicolored plastic streamers that framed the front doorway. Auntie Gin seemed none too pleased, and Mike sternly told them to settle down. It was so cute to see the two children step back and sit down together, wearing impish grins but trying their best to behave.

We said our thanks, hugged, and waved goodbye from Mike's car. Just before leaving, Mike Robbins suggested that we adjourn to his house. I was still reeling from this meeting. It felt like Mike had brought us to meet the family matriarch to gain her approval, and I hoped we had passed the test.

On to the home of cousins Mike and Bette Robbins, where we found Auntie Millie shelling prawns in the kitchen. Millie and Gin were sisters, and it was Millie who also helped raise her brother Jim's two young sons. We were welcomed warmly and accepted as if we had been part of the family for years. I read years ago that Beatrice Millie, Paul's daughter with Heather Mills, was named after Auntie Millie. Aunt Millie was married to "Uncle Albert," immortalized in the McCartney song "Uncle Albert/Admiral Halsey" from the *Ram* album.

We stayed two more days with Mike and family. We met Rowena's talented artist mom, Audrey, and her charming husband, Ron Robinson. Audrey remains among my most favorite people without reservation. She had the most exquisite taste and appreciated the things I also love— English pottery, afternoon tea, and British mysteries. Audrey painted magnificent watercolors inspired by her travels around the world and her Liverpool backyard. Her passing was sorrowful, and when I visited Liverpool in October 2022, I especially felt her absence.

Mike and I, along with my husband, Paul, had time to talk in depth about future projects. Mike shared iconic photographs he had taken as a very young man with a camera I think called a Rollei Magic.

The photographs were masterpieces that captured moments before anyone envisioned their future historical significance. I told Mike he had to do something with these iconic photographs. Remembering Linda McCartney's excellent exhibit at the Molly Barnes Gallery back home, I suggested a gallery show of his photography in Los Angeles.

"If you find a place to do it, I'll come to Los Angeles," Mike said.

With an inspiring visit at a close, I was returning to Los Angeles with a mission—to find a reputable gallery where we could launch Mike's first Stateside photographic exhibit. It felt exhilarating, like my former teenage self!

As we left Mike's home, heading down the long path from their door to our car rental, the Wings song "Let 'Em In" played loudly in my head— Auntie Gin, Brother Michael, Cousin Ian—thank you for letting us in.

MIKE MAC ON DISPLAY

Back in Los Angeles after my first visit to Mike McCartney's home in Liverpool, I wanted to make good on my promise to find a reputable gallery to launch an exhibit of his photography. Lining La Cienega Boulevard were several galleries, and during my lunch break I would scour West Hollywood for an appropriate space. A few years before there was a gallery on La Cienega called the Molly Barnes Gallery, where Linda McCartney had had a photograph exhibit. I wanted Mike to have his own identity as a photographer, so I didn't consider that gallery. But one afternoon I decided to look at the Molly Barnes space, only to discover that it had closed. Across the courtyard, however, I saw the Jill Youngblood Gallery with photographs on display. From the look alone, this space seemed to be a real contender.

I remember telling my former assistant at CBS, Paul Dobbs, about the space. My recollection is somewhat unclear on a few details. Paul came with me to check out the Jill Youngblood Gallery the next day. I'm not sure if this is when Paul met Jill for the first time, or he already coincidentally knew Jill. It wouldn't be important except for the fact that one year later they got married. Jill came from an influential and prosperous family in La Jolla that developed mini malls throughout Southern California, and she had attended the swanky Bishop School in La Jolla. Paul came from the Bronx and later Orange County, New York. The opposites thing must have worked out, because I think they are still together.

After phoning Mike about the gallery prospects, he seemed really jazzed that this was becoming a reality. I sent him photos of the space, and he and Jill eventually spoke. They decided fall 1985, probably October, would be a good time for the exhibition. Thursday, October 24, would be a big evening opening; then, on Saturday, October 26—a Day with the Artist—Mike would be present to meet fans, sign photographs, and talk briefly. Mike and Jill also thought that because his photographs would be somewhat pricey, they would create a poster for the exhibit that Jill would sell and have Mike autograph each copy of it individually. As for the logistics, Mike would stay at my house for three weeks as he had other projects in development and wanted to set meetings while he was in town.

Mike had been a photographer going back to the early '60s before most people had ever heard of the Beatles. He nearly became the band's drummer, if not for a broken arm. We have Paul to thank for helping Mike on his photographic journey. Paul brought back from Hamburg a camera for Mike that he always referred to as his Rollei Magic. With it, Mike snapped the iconic early photographs we marvel at today for their historical insight. Mike has published several photographic books displaying revealing images he has shot all over the world. Even while traveling as part of his successful group, the Scaffold, Mike's camera was always at his side.

Mike arrived on Tuesday, October 22. My husband Paul and I picked him up at LAX in our new car. Mike had heard all about the car because we visited him in Liverpool right after sending the car to the States. He couldn't believe how well the car did during the nearly three-month trip from Antwerp, where its journey to Los Angeles began. We loaded the trunk and drove directly to Jill Youngblood's house to hand over three additional photographs for framing for the exhibit. The opening was just two days away.

We were there less than twenty minutes. When we returned to the car, we saw broken glass all over the street. The driver's window had been smashed, the radio was missing, and Mike's carry-on was gone from the backseat. Fortunately, his suitcase and stage clothing were safe in the trunk. Everything was replaceable, except for the sentimental value. Mike, welcome to Los Angeles!

Instead of spending a leisurely morning the following day, we were all over town replacing the stolen items. The car had made a perfect ocean crossing from Antwerp just a few months earlier, only to get beat up on the streets in daylight. To celebrate Mike's arrival, that evening we went to the original Spago still on the Sunset Strip to catch some Hollywood action. Actress Lisa Hartman (before Clint Black) who at the time was starring in the CBS show *Knots Landing* was there; Rick Springfield seated at another table. We all enjoyed a great Wolfgang Puck dinner.

The opening went spectacularly well. Jill had spared no expense; she even hired a limo to drive us to the gallery. Attendees at the opening included Elliot Mintz, Yoko Ono's PR representative; Jackie Lomax; Spencer Davis; Peter Altshuler, Murray the K's son; Wings' guitarist Lawrence Juber; Gordon Waller of Peter & Gordon fame; and Graham Nash, who at the time was heavily into collecting photographs. People bought photographs, mingled, and enjoyed the fine wines and hors d'oeuvres served.

We all had a great evening, and Mike wished that his family could have been there sharing in the fun. Local news outlets and *Entertainment Tonight* were outside reporting on the opening, and when the limo pulled up at the end of the evening, we jumped in. The TV monitor was playing a video of none other than Maharishi Mahesh Yogi lecturing to disciples. We laughed at his ridiculousness and high-pitched voice. Mike's only comment was, "What a night!" The limo took off.

Saturday at the gallery was a lot of fun. Many people showed up for a Day with the Artist, primarily due to the extensive media attention the opening had received. Selling posters was a great idea because people were pleased to be able to afford a piece of Mike's work that he would inscribe. Mike took time talking with each person in attendance. They had stories to share about photography or travel to the United Kingdom. He patiently posed for pictures, gave lengthy explanations of the circumstances surrounding each photograph, and stayed well beyond the gallery's usual closing time. The British community in Los Angeles also supported the event, showing up in strong numbers along with fine art collectors.

In 1992, I was told that QVC would dedicate one hour to selling Beatles memorabilia. Two hundred posters remaining from the exhibit were crated and shipped to the QVC representative at a company called Catch a Rising Star Collectibles in Cherry Hill, New Jersey. When the posters were put up for sale the night of October 9, 1992, in four minutes they sold out. I must confess that I have about ten posters carefully tucked away.

BE SURE TO WEAR FLOWERS IN YOUR HAIR

After the successful gallery launch of Mike's photographs in Los Angeles, we were headed to San Francisco. I had arranged for Mike to be a guest on KPIX's Channel 5 popular morning show. George Dobbins was Mike's producer, who arranged to fly both of us up to San Francisco the day before the interview and put us up at the ritzy Clift Hotel. Being the final days of October, the weather in San Francisco was rainy. But the rain didn't stop Mike from wanting to see the sights, so we dropped our luggage at the hotel and took off to see the city.

Any time of year San Francisco is the most beautiful city, but that day with all the rain, clouds, and fog it seemed barely visible. We trudged through Union Square to the Marina district to Ghirardelli Square. For dinner we found a neighborhood Italian restaurant in North Beach that had scrumptious bruschetta, mozzarella marinara, and spaghetti Bolognese, a McCartney home specialty. We drank lots of red wine and headed back toward the hotel, but it was still early.

With rain coming down in sheets and only knowing the tourist sites in the city, I suggested we revisit Mike's Irish roots and go directly to the Buena Vista Café at Fisherman's Wharf to enjoy a perfect Irish coffee. The Buena Vista is a San Francisco landmark known around the globe for authentic Irish coffee with the perfect collar of lightly whipped cream. We had a good laugh while downing several traditional coffees. I barely slept courtesy of the caffeine.

The show went well, and the next day we went back to Los Angeles for a slew of meetings I had set in connection with Mike's projects.

RELATIVELY SPEAKING

SFO Airport was experiencing rain delays when Mike McCartney and I arrived for our flight back to Los Angeles. The producers left word as we checked out of the hotel that they were very pleased with Mike's segment. Even after the director called it a wrap, the staff and crew continued posing questions to Mike about his famous brother. After an additional hour delay, it was time to board. We took our seats, and as we buckled up, someone dressed as Marilyn Monroe walked down the aisle. We looked at each other and realized it was Halloween. Mike leaned toward me to say it was not just Halloween. I knew what day it was: the anniversary of his mother's passing. As the plane took off through very choppy air, Mike talked about Mary and the dinners she had fixed for the family. We talked about jam butties (jam sandwiches) and her recipe for scouse—a family favorite.

Scouse is a Liverpool tradition, and everyone prepares it differently, but basically it is a lamb or beef stew that uses all the week's leftover veggies and potatoes. Cooked and stirred for hours, it is sumptuous and served with cabbage, pickled beets, and dense bread.

When the plane hit very choppy air, we calmed our nerves by thinking that a cookbook of traditional McCartney family recipes would be an interesting project. We could quickly put together a one-sheet proposal to pitch a cookbook where appropriate. During the next eight days we had scheduled meetings with various Hollywood producers and agents, and they might find this concept interesting, especially if Mike's brother decided to stop in for some good McCartney home cooking—veggie, of course.

The first meeting was with Joy Tashjian at DIC in Burbank. Joy was VP of merchandising for the company that specialized in animation, and we decided DIC was a perfect place to begin pitching. Mike had created a wonderful animated children's project with significant adult appeal called *Rainbow Rabbit*, and Joy was excited about the possibilities the concept presented.

We had several other meetings over the days but none as important as the upcoming pitch at Paramount syndication. Mike had an idea for a television series called *Relatively Speaking* that he would host. As the sibling of a superstar for most of his life, Mike knew the challenges and advantages this relationship presented to others like him. This syndicated talk show would explore these issues. We would get to meet people who sometimes live in the shadow of others and how they have forged their own identities. In 1985, when we worked on this project, it was breakthrough television. The only other entertainment series on the air was *Entertainment Tonight*. This show would be a new spin on insightful information about the day's hottest talent without the need to get them to the studio.

Before Mike's planned trip for the photography exhibit at Jill Young-blood Gallery, I called the biggest TV syndicators. Since I was still working at CBS on a police-action drama series called *T. J. Hooker* (starring William Shatner and a then-unknown Heather Locklear), I spoke with the show's executive producers and other executives at the network to get an idea with whom we should meet in Los Angeles. As anticipated, the McCartney name was magic, and no one turned down a meeting. This affirmed the premise of the show—that viewers would find the topic interesting.

Mike put together lists of interview possibilities that I included in a formal show proposal. Missing was a female cohost. Mike and I discussed this in depth until he suggested Rona Newton-John, Olivia Newton-John's older sister. Brilliant! Mike may have met Rona in London at some point, but I needed to arrange a meeting while he was in Los Angeles.

My contacts at *T. J. Hooker* proved invaluable: someone at William Shatner's office knew Rona. Mike also reached out, and together we were able to schedule a meeting. While Mike was visiting, I brought work home most nights because I still had job responsibilities even though he was in town. One of the important duties of my job on *T. J. Hooker* was to screen each episode. At night I would pop a cassette into our tape player and Mike, my husband, Paul, and two-and-a-half-year-old daughter, Kate, would critique the show. I made notes on dialogue, their leather wardrobe, plot, edits, and so forth. Kate would listen intently and enjoy watching all the sirens and police action on the TV screen.

Rona and Mike decided that dinner would be a good idea for their first official meeting. The plan was for Rona to drive to our house, pick up Mike, and take off for dinner. We were watching clips of that day's *T. J. Hooker* episode where Heather Locklear knocks on someone's door to conduct a search. I had just made a comment about the scene. Right at that moment, we heard a knock at our front door. My daughter ran to the door, opened it, and there was Rona Newton-John.

Mike, who had gone to the guesthouse to get a jacket, asked, "Who is it?"

Kate shouted in his direction, "Hooker!"

"What?" shouted Mike, like he didn't hear it the first time.

"Hooker," Kate said.

We rushed to the door. Rona stood there in complete shock. Dressed in black leather with blonde hair, she looked just like Heather Locklear right out of an episode of *T. J. Hooker*! Amazing what can come out of a two-year-old's mouth. It was a quite an introduction. and Rona was the ultimate sport.

Sadly, Rona passed away far too soon in 2013. Years later, I booked Olivia Newton-John to appear on the Hallmark TV show where I headed the talent department. I mentioned the incident to her manager, Michael Caprio. He didn't want to cut me off but said he had heard it many times before. It was one of Rona's favorite stories to tell.

IMAGINE . . .

CYNTHIA AND YOKO TOGETHER

In October 1988 the much-anticipated premiere of the feature documentary *Imagine: John Lennon* finally was coming to theaters. With Yoko Ono's full cooperation, the film would document John's life from the early days in Liverpool through the Beatles era and solo years up to December 8, 1980.

Several months prior to the premiere, Julian Ludwig from Andrew Solt's office called, asking for help with the project Andrew and David Wolper were working on about John Lennon. Andrew had questions about the Beatles along with inquiring about licensing a few of Mike McCartney's early photographs of the band and John.

After work I stopped by the office, bringing a copy of Mike's latest book of photographs to see what images Andrew would like to incorporate into the documentary. From the book Andrew selected about eight photographs that would help tell the story of John's life in Liverpool as a teen. I went back to Mike with the request, and after a few days of going back and forth, Andrew and Mike agreed upon a license fee for use of three or four images. I was happy to do both a favor.

Premiere of the film took place in Westwood at the National Theater, and I remember seeing Olympians Greg Louganis and Janet Evans standing in the crowd. Warner Brothers, which distributed the documentary, gave a premiere party at the Hard Rock Café, to which I was invited. When I arrived, it was only half full of guests. Yoko Ono with Elliot Mintz was standing in one corner, Timothy Leary in another, and sitting alone at a back table was Cynthia Lennon. I first approached Elliot and Yoko. It hadn't been that long since I had last seen Elliot, so it was easy to start a conversation with him and Yoko. It had been eight years since John's passing, and this was the first time I had seen Yoko since the unimaginable. We spoke briefly about the film and my contribution to the project. Yoko seemed pleased to know I had helped obtain the early photographs of John, commenting that they were beautiful. I told her I would let Mike McCartney know she appreciated his early work.

Then there was Timothy Leary. How could I resist talking with Timothy Leary? Tune In, Turn On, and Drop Out? Richard Nixon had called him "the most dangerous man in America." Working in the entertainment industry I had met many celebrities, but meeting and talking with Timothy Leary was beyond special. He wasn't featured in the film, so I was curious why he was present—except for the fact he was Timothy Leary. I didn't have to ask the question because he let me know immediately that his son worked there as a waiter. The child of Timothy Leary a server at the Hard Rock Café in the Beverly Center? Timothy added that he lived close by in Laurel Canyon and that he came to the Hard Rock nearly every day. Elliot saw us talking and came over. I learned from the conversation that Timothy Leary was at the recording of John and Yoko's "Give Peace a Chance." It was now making sense.

Across the room, Cynthia Lennon was seated alone, observing from a distance yet keeping an eye on Yoko. During the height of Beatlemania, I didn't meet Cynthia. Brian Epstein always kept Cynthia apart from John when in the public eye and by 1966–1967, she was sadly relegated to a minor role in the Beatles saga. I introduced myself, and we chatted a moment. She was soft-spoken and chose her words skillfully. We spoke briefly. We had enough time to take a picture together, and she happily obliged. The situation wasn't right to mention my correspondence with Aunt Mimi that took place during the time Cynthia was married to John. I sensed that Cynthia was being cautious as Yoko seemed to be the evening's focus for attention. Cynthia had been there and done that; sometimes there isn't much to say.

A week later my cousin Sue, her then husband, Bob, and family visited us in Los Angeles. It had been several years seen I had seen Sue, and when it came time to grab a bite, Bob suggested the Hard Rock Café. It was the newest place in town and close by. We all agreed it would be fun.

As we were waiting for our order to be brought to our table, I spotted Timothy Leary at an adjacent table. Bob, who taught art at the university level on Long Island, was especially intrigued. "Timothy Leary over there," he said as he gestured in his direction.

"You want to meet him," I asked.

"What?"

"Yes, I know him!" I replied.

Bob looked at me strangely. How could I possibly know Timothy Leary? Among the family I was still that dumpy cousin from New Jersey. We walked over to Timothy's table where he was seated with two young adults who could have been his other two children. Timothy stood up and gave me a hug; he remembered me from the previous week. Bob was blown away meeting the high priest of LSD, saying it was the highlight of his trip to Los Angeles. I never divulged how we knew each other.

THANKSGIVING DAY AT THE FORUM, AND WE'RE A SIDE DISH

It was the first time Paul McCartney had been back on a stage in the States in thirteen years, and the concert kicking off the tour was to be at the Great Western Forum Los Angeles on Thanksgiving Night 1989. Even better, Mike McCartney would be in town hosting a second photography exhibit at the Legends Gallery on San Vicente in Brentwood.

I had a dilemma: I was hesitant about purchasing tickets for the concert because it would seem strange with Mike here to say, "I am headed to see Paul in concert," or even worse, to hand Mike a ticket I had bought, but I would never exclude him as he was staying at our house. And I would never be so desperate as to ask Mike to get us tickets. I resolved to do as I had done in years past: just wait it out.

Besides having been off the US stage for thirteen years, this was a very important tour for Paul. *Give My Regards to Broad Street* was a theatrical flop, with only one song from the soundtrack making an impact. Critics thought this might be his final tour, but many of us who followed Paul closely knew otherwise. After John's death, many articles had been written about John being the single creative force behind the Beatles. In time, Paul felt the need to change that perception. He had his work cut out for him because it was challenging to confront the Lennon legacy. He started in the most obvious way, embracing his Beatles past by including fifteen Beatles songs of the twenty-nine played at each concert venue. Paul also gave long interviews where he answered reporters' questions with thought, meaning, and conviction. I was frazzled over how to get to the show. Here I am with Michael McCartney, Paul is playing in town, and I can't get there?

Just two days before Thanksgiving Mike and I were driving along Wilshire Boulevard to Legends Gallery, where his photos were being installed.

"Let's go to the concert," he said.

"Really?" I replied casually, trying to mask my excitement. "It would be great to go."

Mike was invited to join us in celebrating his first Thanksgiving at my friend Ronnie Weinstock's house. Ronnie is a terrific host and was very happy to include Mike in the festivities. We had a great dinner, enjoying all the traditional fixings. After the spectacular meal—including four desserts—Mike said he now understood why the early settlers left England for America. It was 5:30 p.m.; we had to leave for the concert. Mike and I got in my trusty Toyota Camry station wagon and headed to the Forum, near LAX airport. Parking was already a nightmare, but we managed to find a spot far off in the lot.

We walked toward the entrance, where we were stopped by ticket takers. Mike told them why we were there without tickets. I guessed that in the United Kingdom, if Mike attends a Paul concert, it is under very different circumstances. Not until one of Paul's people, PR guy Joe Dera, spotted Mike at the door did security allow us to enter the building. We quickly were taken past backstage crowds, down gray hallways. A door opened, and there stood Paul with Linda, Stella, and James. Something was going on with Paul prepping his calluses?

Two couches were in an "L" shape, a large TV screen to the left. We were welcomed as part of the group. Paul and Mike shared a brotherly hug, and I took a seat on the couch, trying to keep my composure. Stella was seated to my right, and Mike sat down to my left. Paul ended up sliding in between Stella and me, and he was obviously happy to have Mike there.

At the next moment Paul then stood up and I noticed his shoelaces were untied.

I said, "Your shoes are untied."

Paul turned and snapped, "I like them that way!"

OK, I thought to myself, *best to remain quiet*.

At that same moment there was a knock at the door, and Michael Douglas came in to see Paul and Linda with his then wife, Diandra, and son Cameron. Cameron sat down next to James, who at age twelve was enraptured playing Nintendo on the big TV screen. Standing up to shake their hands, I was excited to meet Michael Douglas.

Paul and Michael Douglas talked with our Michael joining in the conversation. I tried to talk to Stella about school, as we were seated alongside of each other, and that went OK. She was dressed casually and stylishly, but there was no evidence of the award-winning couture designer she has become. Bill Bernstein, the MPL official photographer, was taking photographs. Paul could sense that I was excited to be in a picture with Michael Douglas.

So, there I was posing backstage standing between Paul, Mike, and Michael Douglas. I've never been given a copy, and I know somewhere in the 1989 tour archives are the originals. I would love to see them. In

November 2019, I contacted Bill in New York City about the photographs. He clearly remembered taking them and shared his general procedure: after each roll was shot, Linda would take them away for safekeeping. My chances of ever getting a copy were "probably never."

The Douglases left, saying they would see Paul and Linda at the after party.

"Enjoy the show," Paul replied. He was standing in the middle of the room, Mike next to him, when I injected an innocent comment in the conversation.

I don't remember the subject or what I added, but Paul again looked at me and said, "Isn't that lyrics to one of my songs?"

I couldn't win. I walked away not knowing what I had said or what lyrics I had repeated.

Linda gestured to join her; she was getting clothing together. Linda quietly commented on how I got to be backstage and gave me this groupie insider-like smile, seemingly knowing what I was trying to accomplish. This entire backstage thing was strange.

When Paul said he had to finish getting ready, I was relieved to get out of there and head for our seats. The Forum was packed. As we took our places, Mike acknowledged someone sitting right behind us: Geoff Emerick. He politely introduced me. The situation wasn't conducive to mention that we had already met at EMI/Abbey Road Studios back in April 1967. Anyway, that was a lifetime ago. Others from Paul's staff all acknowledged Mike.

The feeling in the arena was electric. The audience was full of anticipation for the show about to start. The lights dimmed, and up came Richard Lester's eleven-minute film projected on a huge screen, with images of fans screaming at Shea Stadium and other clips of Paul and the Beatles from their most notable and iconic moments. The film unquestionably cemented Paul's Beatles' contribution that many of the John fans were beginning to downplay. The audience went wild.

Then out came Paul and the band as he hit the first notes for "Figure of Eight" from his latest album, *Flowers in the Dirt*. My daughter and I really love that album; we call it our traveling music. Shortly after the album came out, we spent one week at a picturesque English cottage in Kent. While touring the sights we played the cassette in the car as we drove to writer Vita Sackville West's home, Sissinghurst, and to the Bloomsbury Group's Charleston Farmhouse. The music even accompanied us to Burwash, the home of Rudyard Kipling, quite a contrast to *Jungle Book*.

Midway through the show, Paul launched into "Things We Said Today," and I leaned toward Mike to say it was one of my favorites. "He's playing it for you," Mike said jokingly. For a mere second my correspondence with George Martin about that song flashed in my head. How far I had come to be here on this amazing night.

As we approached the end of the show, Paul introduced the next song as a dedication to some people who were present . . . James, Stella, Mike, and Fleetwood Mac. The song was "Live and Let Die." It was awesome sharing the concert with Mike. Back in 1964, at the Sullivan show, I would never have imagined this.

Emotions were running high as everyone streamed out of the arena after an amazing show. Mike spotted someone he knew from Paul's entourage, and he decided we should follow him. That got us to a door with the sign VIP Forum Club. Fortunately, Mike is tall, and I think it was Paul's manager Richard Ogden who identified Mike among the masses. Taking us each by the hand, he pulled us in the door one at a time.

The room was crowded with people lined up around the bar. Mike and I stood to one side. Paul and Linda with Stella and James came in right after the band members—Hamish Stuart with his very identifiable look from Average White Band; Paul "Wix" Wickens; Robbie McIntosh, whom everyone seemed to know from the Pretenders; roadies; and the undeniable LA women who looked like they crawled out of a rock 'n' roll time capsule to see Paul. For this I don't blame Linda for keeping such a close eye: they were all over him. So many people crowded Paul that he and Linda escaped for a while to a secluded room.

For a short time, there was talk of us heading back to the hotel with Paul and Linda in their limousine. Mike asked if it would be OK to leave my car in the parking lot overnight. It was fine with me. We stood on the sidelines just taking in the scene. All the maneuverings to get Paul's attention were laughable; the fast-talk jargon about deals he should fund didn't end. It was late, and we were all tired. It was already past 1 a.m., and Paul, Linda, and kids called it a night. Mike and I did, too. We all said our goodnights and saw them off in their limo. Paul had another show the next night, and Mike had his art opening.

Slowly walking back to the car, we agreed it had been quite a night. Far off was the Toyota wagon in the middle of a now-deserted parking lot, a single security light shining down from above.

A SONG HEARD ROUND THE WORLD

YOKO ONO

Ideas were being discussed for John Lennon's fiftieth birthday celebration on October 9, 1990. Jeff Pollack, an international radio consultant, met with Yoko Ono in New York about how to appropriately pay tribute to John on his birthday. Riding in a cab after the meeting, Jeff heard the song "Imagine" on the radio. At that instant he knew that a worldwide celebration should be planned around that the song.

Jeff went back to Yoko, and together they came up with the plan. To honor John, they would arrange a simultaneous worldwide broadcast of "Imagine" on more than one thousand radio stations—rock, news, talk, and classical formats; and MTV, spanning more than fifty countries. On October 9, 1990, at exactly 10 a.m. Eastern Time, "Imagine" would be heard on every continent by millions of people.

Kicking off the day, Yoko would give a short address at the United Nations immediately before 10 a.m. Introducing Yoko would be none other than DJ Scott Muni, who had hosted my Beatles Fan Club dance *twenty-six years* before! By this time Scott had left WABeatleC (WABC) and now was at WNEW-FM, never far from his Beatles roots.

On the daily television series where I worked, part of my responsibilities included looking for contemporary topics for segments. I thought interviewing Yoko about the upcoming birthday celebration would be meaningful. I pitched the idea to the producers, who agreed. ABC Network executives suggested that I contact Yoko directly.

The following day I called Yoko at her apartment in the Dakota. I was surprised to hear a man's voice on the other end of the phone: Sam Havadtoy. Sam became associated with John and Yoko in the late '70s when he was working at an interior design shop in New York City where they purchased a set of Italian Egyptian revival chairs. Sam, who was born in London but raised in Hungary, was just twenty-four years old when he met John and Yoko. He went on to design their apartment in the Dakota, along with a country home they had purchased in Upstate New York where I understand Yoko is currently living. After John's passing, Sam grew close to Yoko, eventually moving in with her and Sean. Through Yoko's celebrity status, Sam was spotted with people ranging from Andy Warhol to Keith Haring, for whom he also designed homes.

I read that Andy Warhol in his diary in 1984 wrote, "I can't figure out if it's her boyfriend or what" of Yoko and Sam. Whatever it was, they were together for twenty years, longer than she was married to John. They separated in late 2000, and the last I heard, Sam lives in Italy and Budapest running his own art studio, Gallery 56, the name Yoko gave the business, representing artists and his personal works.

When Sam answered the phone, he sounded like he was acting in an official capacity. He listened to my pitch and patiently explained that traveling to Los Angeles to be on the show would be impossible due to Yoko's schedule in New York City; however, she might do a satellite interview. Sam suggested that I contact Elliot Mintz in Los Angeles to work out the details.

Mintz is a publicist, media consultant extraordinaire, and radio personality based in Los Angeles who hosted programs on KPFK, KLOS, KLAC early in his career, moving on to television as the Entertainment Reporter on KABC. In 1971, he met John and Yoko and became a close confidant of theirs in addition to acting as their official press liaison. Elliot and I knew each other. Elliot had attended Michael McCartney's two Los Angeles photo exhibits. Our paths also crossed again at a few other Lennon-related art events and at the Andrew Solt/David Wolper *Imagine* film premiere.

Elliot was totally on board with the interview via satellite, so it looked like it would happen. We would do it the day before the official John Lennon broadcast, so viewers could join in with the millions around the globe to listen to "Imagine" on John's birthday the following day.

As I boarded the Friday-night red-eye to New York City for the Yoko interview, I was especially happy to know that Elliot would be present. Ever since my first meeting with John in 1965, I was cautious with anything John connected. At age fifteen John had mimicked and ridiculed me for being a Beatles fan, and it left a forever sting.

To ease my pain and embarrassment at that young age, I took a note from my letter exchange with George's mother, Louise Harrison, and kicked off a correspondence with John's Aunt Mimi. Although portrayed as strict, Aunt Mimi Smith was a lovely lady who would respond promptly. We wrote for several years, although as she grew older living in Dorset after a move from Liverpool, our letter exchange slowed. After I returned home, I wrote Mimi about my experience producing this segment, but I didn't receive a response. She passed away the following year.

John's Aunt Mimi Smith and I exchanged postcards for a few years. Although reports always said she was strict, I found her warm and sincere in all her correspondence. Here is our very first exchange.
AUTHOR'S COLLECTION

October 8 was Columbus Day, a holiday celebrated every year in New York with a big parade on Fifth Avenue. Many of the side streets were blocked off, so I needed to leave the hotel extra early. Yoko's was the first segment up, and because we went live at 11 a.m., Eastern time, there was no room for mistakes. The producer in the LA studio told everyone to be there by 10:30 a.m. to test the satellite connection. The address I had been given was Com-Tech, 77 Lexington Avenue. Knowing New York, I thought that was a strange address, but that was on my call sheet and written down by our tech people at our studio. Yoko had done other interviews from the Com-Tech studio, so she was familiar with the building, as were Elliot and Jeff. Yoko would arrive in her own car because she had other interviews scheduled in various locations throughout the city.

I stayed at the Mayflower Hotel right on Central Park West and left at about 9:20 a.m. Traffic was slow, and when the taxi pulled up to 77 Lexington Avenue there wasn't even a front door to the building. Everything was boarded up. I looked at the address, which was on the call sheet, so I paid the fare and left the taxi. Looking around, I realized this had to be the wrong place. I went through all the paperwork from my correspondence with Elliot and saw the real problem. The correct address was 770, not

To Debbie,

Another year over

And a new one just begun

Have a good one!

Joy,

John & Yoko Xmas '92

Yoko and I exchanged season's greetings for several years after I worked with her producing a TV segment. This is one from the early '90s.

AUTHOR'S COLLECTION

77 Lexington. The segment producer and studio technicians had made a mistake.

It was already 10:05 a.m., and I frantically waved for a cab to stop. One finally pulled over, and I told the driver to please hurry, I had to get to the studio at 770 Lexington fast. It didn't seem out of the ordinary for him to drive like a madman.

When I arrived at Com-Tech, Yoko, Elliot, Jeff, and Sam were all there, along with a room full of video technicians. With less than thirty minutes to air, I had missed the entire satellite run-through. Fortunately, having been at that studio before, Yoko, Elliot, and Jeff hadn't needed to check the address. Elliot was curious why I was late, but I hadn't time to explain.

Although I had had brief sightings of Yoko in the early 1970s when she and John were making movies downtown where I lived, it was my first opportunity to work with her on a project. We became acquainted, exchanging seasonal holiday cards for several years thereafter. Yoko was exacting and demanding as I had been warned, but her collaboration made the segment better. It is said that more than one billion people listened simultaneously to "Imagine" that day. By bringing Yoko's message to our television audience, I was still helping spread the word.

TRY A LITTLE TENDERNESS

LINDA MCCARTNEY

After fourteen years at CBS, the time finally came to say goodbye. The department I was working in was being downsized due to a financial hit on the network when Ted Turner tried to purchase its stock. The senior VP said that because I was married, it was decided I was the one to leave the department; my coworker, a single man, would remain. In 1986, laws hadn't been enacted yet to protect women from workplace discrimination. I considered the people I worked with family; I had given up my life in New York to move to the West Coast at their request. Many were guests at my wedding. In my book, being asked to leave was a betrayal.

Because I had a young child at home, I was encouraged to become executive director at Women in Film Los Angeles. Having been a member of the organization since I was transferred to LA in 1978, I believed that the group functioned as a resource where women in the entertainment industry could come for career mentoring and celebrate the successes of female achievement in film and television, both in front of and behind the camera. What I found was nothing of the kind. Many of the women who made up Women in Film at that time were, from my perspective, perhaps the most backstabbing, brutal individuals I have ever known in the industry. Meetings were contentious and lengthy, most lasting past midnight.

I tried to bring civility and meaning back to the organization, but it proved impossible. After the monthly board meeting, I would go home and cry. When offered a position to work on a new syndicated television series (by one of the understanding Women in Film Board members), *On Trial*, produced by Woody Fraser, I jumped at the opportunity. Woody, who I'm told is now retired to Ojai, lives on the fence between sheer genius and television's never-ending demands. He has taught thousands of television wannabes the ropes, his way. I knew of Woody Fraser because of his association with *The Mike Douglas Show*. Mike McCartney had been set up as a guest on the show and was used to reinforce the Paul Is Dead hoax. A very typical Woody stunt. In February 1972, John and

Yoko cohosted the show with Mike Douglas for one week. The week was very insightful, showing Yoko to be direct and discriminating whereas John was gracious and passive. I was surprised to see John this way, so very different from the sarcastic, stinging person I had encountered a few years earlier.

I thought I'd give the job a go. The prospect of working for Woody was intriguing. *On Trial* was way ahead of its time as the first program to bring cameras into the courtroom; Court TV, created by Steve Brill, took its inspiration from the series. Here's the premise: we would go into a courtroom where permitted by state law and tape the trial proceedings as it unfolded. I learned a lesson early on when one of my trials in Rhode Island ended in a short jail sentence for spousal abuse. A few months later the accused was set free and phoned to tell me he was en route from Cranston to meet with me in Los Angeles. Next, he called to tell me he had arrived in Las Vegas, but fortunately I never heard from him again. After one season, when the show wasn't renewed, I was the first person to raise a hand to leave.

My last day was on a Thursday in late 1988. On Friday morning I received a call from Woody Fraser. He asked where I was.

"At home."

He replied, "Time to get back to work."

What work? Woody told me to get over to the studio at Sunset Gower, where his new show, *Home*, was taping. The series was for ABC, and shortly after I joined the staff, we moved to the ABC lot at Prospect in Hollywood. I was well suited to the show's demographic: women with children, concern about family and household topics ranging from finance to fashion.

By Monday morning I was working full-time at the *Home* show. Eventually my relationship and experiences with the Beatles would be discovered. I was there for just over one year when I celebrated my fortieth birthday. That day at the studio I received a most magnificent bouquet of flowers in a hand-painted Italian earthenware receptacle. The card was signed "With love from the Mike McCartneys." My secret was out.

From that day forward, every two weeks I was asked about when Paul and Linda were going to be booked on the *Home* show. A few months later I learned that Linda's cookbook, *Linda McCartney's Home Cooking*, was being published. I called London and talked with the publicity people at Bloomsbury Press, who were releasing the book in Britain. I knew this would make a wonderful segment for *Home,* and I offered it to our senior producer, Marty Tenney, who said, "Let's book it."

Reaching out to the US publisher, Arcade, I was told the book would be released in this country in October 1990 and that Linda would be doing a media tour. I called Paul McCartney's publicity person in New York, Joe

Dera, and was told the book tour was being handled by Planned Television Arts (PTA). Fortunately, I had worked with them previously and had no trouble arranging the interview and cooking demo to take place in New York City via satellite. The date was set for Friday, October 19.

I was put in contact with the PTA publicist to work out what Linda would be cooking. That is when the problems began. Linda wanted to prepare two dishes and discuss turning "veggie." We didn't have enough time in a single six-minute segment to do it all. After going back and forth, we finally decided upon Chili-non-Carne and Sloppy Joes. The Sloppy Joes would already be prepared, and Linda would talk about it while she prepared the Chili-non-Carne on camera, adding "go veggie" comments throughout.

Everything was moving forward until Linda phoned me early one morning at home to say she wouldn't do the segment unless she could refer to meat as "dead flesh." I went to Marty Tenney, who told me to call Susan Fetterman at ABC's standards and practices. Dead anything was disturbing language for this cozy morning show.

After checking with network executives and a tense phone call with Susan, standards and practices approved Linda's saying "dead flesh." When I phoned Linda at her farm in the English countryside, she was quite pleased, calling it our victory. During the same phone call, she told me other ingredients she would need on set, including TVP. Later I learned that the letters stood for textured vegetable protein. Linda used TVP in many of her dishes in the cookbook. What she didn't tell me was that TVP was also the primary ingredient in Hamburger Helper.

The senior producers decided that I should fly to New York to be in studio with Linda. I needed to be there at least two days early because I also had to find someone to prep the food and the final food beauty shots. With a friend's help I contacted Vera Kaltinick. Vera was a home chef who cooked only vegetarian dishes; Linda had made it very clear that she would not tolerate food coming from a nonvegetarian kitchen.

When word got out that Linda would be on the *Home* show, I received a phone call from Archer Daniels Midland, the manufacturers of TVP. They wanted me to take a gift to Linda—twenty-five pounds of TVP. No way could I take twenty-five pounds of anything on the plane. But I agreed that if they sent me a smaller package, I would deliver it to Linda. It all worked out; they shipped it directly to my hotel in New York City.

I was staying again at the Mayflower Hotel on Central Park West and Sixty-First Street. Paula McClure, a semi-regular on the show, had been assigned as our on-camera correspondent who would ask Linda the questions during the segment. My first night in New York I made a shopping list for Vera and called her to go over everything. I also made time to meet my best friend from Oakland, Beverly Don, who lived in New York City.

Being with Beverly the evening before producing the segment with Linda was meaningful and the culmination of much of my professional work. Bev had shared so many Beatles experiences with me back when the Beatles Fan Club was active. She had tried to manage the crowds at the Beatles fundraising dance in Oakland, had stood with me trying to catapult the band US into superstardom. Now, I was here to work with Linda McCartney. And when Michael McCartney and family came to Los Angeles to attend my daughter's wedding in 2014, I was so excited to seat Bev, who flew in from New York, in what I regarded as the best seat in the house right next to Mike.

It was an early morning call on Friday, the 19th. Realizing that having Linda on the show was a great booking, the producers scheduled two segments for a total of twelve minutes beginning at 10:58 a.m. I packed all my things and headed to HBO Studios at 120A East Twenty-Third Street between Park and Lexington. This time I made sure the address was correct, remembering the Yoko screwup. When I arrived there, I went right to the Green Room to make sure that all was good with Paula. She hadn't arrived yet, which made me nervous. I checked the satellite link, and all was fine.

Back in Los Angeles at ABC Prospect, where we produced the show every morning, cohosts Gary Collins and Dana Fleming were getting ready. I spoke by phone to Marty Tenney. letting him know all was OK except that Paula hadn't arrived at the studio. We didn't have cell phones yet, so I just had to be patient. Vera had delivered the food, prepared exactly to Linda's specifications, to the studio at 9:30 a.m.

Just on the other side of the wall, I could hear Linda's voice. I didn't want to intrude as she was getting ready, but I slowly rounded the corner, and she caught me with TVP in hand. Big hug. As I handed over the package of TVP, she seemed curious. First thing she mentioned was "dead flesh" and our victory; Linda was preoccupied with the concept. I was so pleased that I had gone to the trouble to clear this with the network. Sitting close by was Linda's daughter, Mary, and Robert "Robbie" Montgomery. Robbie was Paul's manager at the time, and he spoke about Paul and his upcoming projects. Stella and James were also in New York but at their uncle John Eastman's law office for the morning. They were all going for dinner that evening to Shun Lee Palace Chinese Restaurant on East Fifty-Fifth Street, and would I like to join him? Robbie said it was a favorite.

Robbie was very much the businessman. He presented me with his card listing his address and phone in London and in the countryside close to where Linda and family lived. He talked proudly about the goats he raised there. It was reminiscent of my formal first meeting with Brian Epstein and Walter Hofer.

Helping me was Elaine Angel; I hadn't known her until that morning. Elaine was at the studio to conduct an interview with Linda after my show was over, and we just started talking. Elaine was very supportive in trying to find Paula, who was still missing. Later that day, I went back to her apartment on the fortieth floor of a building on West Fifty-Seventh Street, which had the most amazing view looking northward. Elaine said she was married to the brother of Bob Iger from ABC, but frankly I didn't know if Bob Iger even had a brother. I never knew how Elaine showed up. Was it because our show aired on ABC, and she found out about Linda's interview and waited, hoping that Paul would show up? Not too long afterward, Linda told me that Elaine never did the interview. I tried to contact Elaine but didn't receive a call back.

Linda was getting anxious that Paula wasn't there yet, and she wanted to go over the questions. The previous evening after dinner with Beverly, I had returned to the hotel and written out the cue cards, so I offered to run the cards with Linda. She liked the idea. Mary helped with the cards while I directed Linda. Some of the questions were:

What convinced you to become a vegetarian?

Why a vegetarian cookbook?

Is it hard to keep your family on a vegetarian diet?

Critics say a vegetarian diet isn't healthy for children—your thoughts.

Linda started to talk, and she really got into the subject, explaining how and why she became a vegetarian. Here's the story: She and Paul were eating lamb and spied lambs outside their window. Shortly after that, they were driving behind a truck that had chickens piled into the back, where they could not move. At that point, they stopped eating "dead flesh." Linda must have repeated "dead flesh" at least five times during the rehearsal. After we were finished and Linda was feeling confident in what she would be doing on camera, we just chatted about New York, the show at the LA Forum, Auntie Gin and family dinners at Cousin Ian and Jackie's house, and their beautiful view of the River Mersey. Paula showed up ten minutes before air, saying she had been stuck in traffic. The demo went well: Linda cooked and answered the rehearsed questions while cohosts Dana and Gary simultaneously tasted the Chili non-Carne and Sloppy Joes (made with textured vegetable protein), in Los Angeles, prepared by our studio chef according to Linda's recipe. If you would like to sample Linda's recipe for Chili non-Carne, it's in *Linda McCartney's Home Cooking*. It's delicious even for nonvegetarians.

As the double segment ended, and Linda said her final words, "Go veggie," Gary and Dana began to "throw" to the upcoming segment— Wisconsin's fastest-talking DJ, Joel Whitburn, who was there to discuss his collection of more than 100,000 albums. The throw to the next guest felt inappropriate in front of Linda. It cheapened the entire segment. Were we some rock 'n' roll crazed show? She could sense that I was embarrassed. I wanted this to be perfect to show that I was not just a fan or groupie but a television professional.

Linda was starting to wrap it up and didn't realize we were still live when Gary Collins asked her, "What's your favorite top song between the years 1955 to 1985?" Linda turned to the camera and said without hesitation, Otis Redding's "Try a Little Tenderness." Linda surprised everyone in the studio, especially Gary Collins, who was left speechless. He had thought it would surely be a Beatles song.

INDICATIONS OF THE FUTURE

When Paul McCartney moved into Jane Asher's elegant family home at 57 Wimpole Street in London, he was already famous. Up to that time from what I saw via Mike McCartney's Forthlin Road photographs, original Picassos, Renoirs, and Degas did not fill the McCartney lounge walls nor did guests such as Bertrand Russell and Harold Pinter stop by for tea. When Paul arrived at the Asher home an entirely new world of art, music, literature, and culture opened, and he embraced it fully.

Peter Asher, Jane's brother, was a friend of Barry Miles and John Dunbar (who was at the time married to Marianne Faithfull). In 1965, Barry and John were both in attendance at a poetry reading at Royal Albert Hall of American Beat poets including Allen Ginsberg and Gregory Corso. After the reading, the two were so jazzed that with silent partner Peter Asher they decided to jointly open an art gallery/bookshop—a place that ultimately became a trendy meeting place for Swinging London in the mid-1960s. Peter brought along his houseguest, Paul, to the bookshop/gallery during construction. It has been reported that Paul famously helped with carpentry work, designing the shop's wrapping paper, and was the bookshop's first paying customer. The shop's inventory was kept in the Asher basement, and Paul would go downstairs to browse and select books, leaving payment behind.

The store space become known as the Indica Gallery/Bookshop and found its place in rock history as the location where in 1966 John Lennon met Yoko Ono while he was standing on a ladder looking at writing on the ceiling. This was Yoko's first exhibit in London sponsored by art buyer Robert Fraser. However, Paul McCartney can also lay claim to Indica as his territory. The Indica wasn't a traditional art gallery—it was a place where you could hang out and experience fun parties, all against a backdrop of exhibits and books by nonconformist experimental artists from all over the world. Allen Ginsberg, William Burroughs, Timothy Leary, the Fugs' Ed Sanders, Alan Watts, and Lawrence Ferlinghetti are just a few of the authors the bookshop carried and who visited there when in London.

It is also where Paul got to know Robert Fraser, who advised him on acquiring fine art. Robert brought to Paul's attention the works of Belgian surreal artist René Magritte and invited him to Paris to meet Magritte's representative. While there Paul purchased two of his surreal oil paintings. Magritte passed away only one week before Brian Epstein. Just a short time after Magritte's passing, Robert brought one of Magritte's final works to Paul's home for his consideration. The painting was called *Le Jeu de Mourre*, which translates as *The Guessing Game*. You can do a search to see the painting. If it looks familiar, it is. The artwork served as inspiration for the Apple logo and company name.

Robert Fraser would be famous just for this accomplishment; however, his connection to the rock world didn't end there. Robert was arrested with Mick Jagger and Keith Richards at the infamous 1967 Redland heroin bust. Robert, the former Etonian, pleaded guilty and served prison time, whereas Mick and Keith, also found guilty, managed to serve no time. Robert was plagued by drug addiction for years.

Around the same time, it was Robert Fraser who suggested to the Beatles the artist Peter Blake to create the cover for the Sgt. Pepper album. Sir Peter Blake was an artist whom Fraser also represented at his gallery; he was an intriguing fellow. Robert never fully recovered from his unfortunate addiction and died of AIDS in 1986. He will always be remembered as the person responsible for staging Yoko's art show at the Indica and the person who invited John Lennon to the gallery where he met Yoko.

When I visited England in 1967, I visited the Indica Gallery. Anne Wilson, the editor's assistant at *Fabulous 208* magazine, said I shouldn't miss it. The Indica was close to Hotel Piccadilly, where my mom and I were staying. So, though it was pouring rain, we walked over—a good plan for a bleak afternoon. The exhibit at the time was a set of uniform brown bags with very strange lights in and around the bags casting a shadow over Sanskrit lettering. My mom and I tried our best to make sense of it. The bookshop had moved, which we were disappointed to learn. At the time of our visit, there was much about the location I didn't know—that the Indica was the place where John had met Yoko the previous year, and that Paul had helped in its creation. John was still happily married to Cynthia as far we fans knew.

A 2006 article in London's *The Guardian* newspaper described the gallery: "Indica . . . marked the point where the counterculture met the new pop aristocracy." It was the place to be seen.

No one embodied that description more eloquently than co-owner Barry Miles, who has made sure that the Indica maintains its place in history. When speaking of London in the 1960s, it is impossible to have a conversation without including author and pop culturist Barry Miles's name. I have not met him but hope to one day. Barry oversaw Zapple, a division of Apple that dealt with their spoken-word product. He was at Sgt. Pepper photo shoots, he was the conduit for song lyrics for "Tomorrow Never Knows" (from Timothy Leary), and was a friend of Allen Ginsberg and his contemporaries.

As a journalist, Barry Miles was enamored with New York's *Village Voice* newspaper. The epitome of the counterculture New York scene, the *Village Voice's* motto was "expect the unexpected." As described in its subscription solicitation, every issue of *The Voice* uncovers what's new and controversial. *The Voice* is the weekly newspaper dedicated to free opinion on just about everything.

Barry wanted to start an alternative paper in London like the *Village Voice* to serve as a place of record to announce avant-garde events. To accomplish this Barry Miles, only twenty-four years old, enlisted a few friends, including John "Hoppy" Hopkins and Jim Haynes. Hopkins had graduated from Cambridge and began his career as a nuclear physicist but ended up as a photographer, researcher, and political activist instrumental in launching Pink Floyd. Hoppy is a 1960s icon.

Jim Haynes, an American originally from Louisiana, found himself in Scotland in the mid-1950s and stayed. In 1966, after participating in the founding of the Edinburgh Festival, Jim ended up in London. There he became involved with Barry Miles and Hoppy Hopkins and two others in launching the *International Times*, which became known as *IT* after *The Times* of London threatened lawsuits over the possible confusion of the paper's name. *IT* fulfilled all that Barry Miles hoped it would.

Through Indica and the newspaper, Barry became acquainted with Paul McCartney. In the early days especially, Paul helped *IT*—he funded the paper by designating money for a competition for experimental film scripts. McCartney also struck a professional friendship with Jim Haynes; and as a show of solidarity for the paper's causes, he paid £1,800 for an ad placed in *The Times* on June 26, 1967, to protest drug laws. Michael McCartney's friendship with Jim soon followed. Jim was known to hang out at "Spanish Tony's" drinking bar off Oxford Street with Mick Jagger, Keith Richards, Brian Jones, Paul McCartney, and Robert Fraser, all enjoying punch spiked with LSD. So that's the "Spanish Tony" everyone at Bag O' Nails was talking about!

In 1992, my husband, Paul, was in Madrid attending a legal conference when he heard that Mike McCartney and his daughter were going to Paris for a school assignment at the Rodin Museum. Encouraged by Mike's invitation to join them, my husband booked a room at the same hotel. When Mike said they had dinner plans arranged with Jim Haynes and his friend Kyle at Le Petit Prince, a neighborhood Parisian restaurant, my husband thought, *OK, who's Jim Haynes?* Haynes was an interesting character. Besides being the cofounder of *IT*, he wrote books, taught at the university level, and opened his house every Sunday evening to complete strangers from the 1970s until his death. Well over 145,000 people were at Jim's house over the years. Every Sunday a friend prepared a virtual feast in Jim's kitchen. On a summer night he could accommodate about 120 people; in winter indoors, 60. Everyone contributed twenty Euros for the dinner, and the party began. Jim sat on a stool adjacent to the open kitchen, checking off each guest as he entered. The joy for Jim was introducing people to converse, mingle, and explore each other's minds. When my husband returned from the trip, all he talked about was Jim Haynes and his Sunday supper.

The following year my husband and I were in Paris and made sure that we stayed over a Sunday night just to attend Jim's soiree. As anticipated, we met people from all over—Budapest, Amsterdam, a student from Bologna. The following year Jim visited Los Angeles promoting his book series, *People to People*, where he compiled lists of visitors who attended his Sunday dinners and who would then open their homes to others who might visit their city. I experienced Sunday evenings at Jim's house six times over the years and sent friends visiting Paris there to enjoy their Sunday evening. When asked how I found my way to Jim's, I was cautious about revealing my connection, but Jim, always understated, responded, "She's a friend of the McCartneys." Jim passed away in 2021 leaving a void on Sunday nights in Paris. His legacy was to bring people together, and he lived his mission every week.

THINGS WE DIDN'T SAY

JANE ASHER

As I write this, today is April 5, and that means it is Jane Asher's birthday. Every year on this day I think about Jane, so it is only proper that I write about her and our meeting.

Jane was Paul McCartney's girlfriend at the height of Beatlemania. She was the most envied girl in the world for several years. Paul met Jane in 1963, days after she turned seventeen, when she reviewed a Beatles concert at Royal Albert Hall. Jane was the second of three children born to Dr. Richard Asher, a physician at Central Middlesex Hospital; and his wife, Margaret, who taught oboe at the Guildhall School of Music, where George Martin had studied for three years. When Jane met the Beatles, she was already famous, having begun acting at age five in films and later television. From what I have read, all the Beatles fancied Jane. Each was surprised to see that she had beautiful red hair because all they had ever seen was Jane on a black-and-white television set.

Jane was cultured, educated, and had refined taste, preferring classical music to pop/rock. I also read in Barry Miles's book that Paul, coming from a working-class Liverpool family was intrigued by the Ashers' manners, sophistication, and social status. When it became impossible for Paul to be out freely due to his fame, he moved in with Jane and her family in their stately home on Wimpole Street, London, an address worthy of a doctor's family and a famous Beatle.

In addition, Jane's older brother was Peter, who later was half of the singing duo Peter and Gordon. Peter later became a very successful music producer and manager of talent such as Linda Ronstadt and James Taylor. Jane's younger sister, Clare, today is a radio presenter and was then still at home. Paul lived with the Asher Family for three years and wrote many of the Beatles' most famous songs including "Yesterday" there. By 1965, it was time to leave the Asher residence, and Paul purchased a house at St. Johns Wood close to Abbey Road. The couple moved in together.

Jane was an independent professional who wanted to have her own career and identity. This didn't exactly sit well with traditional Liverpool boys, but Paul seemed to overlook that for the present. As Beatles fans, we had love/hate relationships with the women in the Beatles' lives. We all fantasized that we would be the "one," but realistically, we all accepted certain truths. I liked Jane the best of all the Beatles' girlfriends. I respected her professionalism and dedication to acting despite being Paul's girlfriend. I felt like she got her jobs on her own merit and talent. I always wanted to meet Jane, but her acting didn't take her to New York as far as I knew.

When I went to England in April/May 1967 and saw Paul, he had just returned from visiting Jane in Denver for her twenty-first birthday where she was appearing in a play. When she returned to London after her five-month tour across America, things had changed. Paul had been living the bachelor life, and he had met Linda Eastman and several others. I read that Jane sensed things had shifted, but by Christmas 1967, she and Paul were engaged.

Although Paul was officially off the market, he really didn't live like it. Many women were in and out of his life. In May 1968, Paul and John went to New York to announce the formation of Apple Corps and at a press conference, Linda Eastman appeared, slipping Paul her phone number. Paul phoned Linda as he and John were heading to the airport, and she rode with them. But when Paul arrived home, Linda seemed to be in the past and all seemed cozy with Jane, according to the press.

Now engaged, Jane went back on the road appearing in a play. Meanwhile, Paul picked up with American Francie Schwartz, who had come to London to interest Apple in funding her screenplay. While still seeing Francie and with Jane away, Paul headed to New York and Los Angeles for business. In New York he left a phone message for Linda, telling her he was on his way to the Beverly Hills Hotel in Los Angeles. Before he knew it, Linda was waiting for Paul as he checked into the hotel. Reporters followed them around town, trying to figure out who the mystery woman was.

Returning to London, Paul picked up with Francie; she had been living in his home while Jane was still gone. One morning, there was a knock on the bedroom door. Jane entered, only to find Francie in bed. Jane left, furious. A few hours later Mrs. Asher arrived to collect her things. On July 20, 1968, Jane announced on the BBC TV show *Dee Time* that her engagement with Paul was off, and that is the last time she spoke publicly of the split. Paul and Linda were married eight months later.

From the time of the breakup, I followed Jane's career. She married artist and illustrator Gerald Scarfe, who designed the famous album cover for Pink Floyd's *The Wall*, had children, and continued her acting career. Jane also built a very successful baking business called "Jane Asher's Party Cakes," wrote several books on children's parties, costumes, how to move a home, and cake baking and decorating—a British Martha Stewart.

In 1991, I was working on the *Home* show on ABC, the year before I produced separate segments with Linda McCartney and Yoko Ono for the show. Now, I had the opportunity to join my husband on a business trip to London and thought Jane would be an ideal guest to have on the show to share her expertise on party planning, sewing, along with cake decorating. At the time Jane's brother, Peter, was living in Los Angeles and running a successful personal management company. While planning the trip, I spoke with the executive producer of *Home* show about inviting Jane to be a guest when she next visited Los Angeles. He gave me the go-ahead.

I had not met Jane but thought it was worth a try to meet while in I was London. Enough years had gone by that it didn't feel awkward. I phoned Jane at her shop, Party Cakes. She was open to meeting, and we set a date to talk when I arrived in London; Jane said she would call me at the hotel.

On the day Jane said she would call, my husband and daughter went on a conference-sponsored trip to Cambridge, but I stayed at the hotel to wait. By 3 p.m., and still no call, I was sorry that I hadn't gone to Cambridge with the group. I stepped out and, of course, she phoned. The next morning, we touched base, and Jane suggested we meet at Party Cakes the following day, have lunch, and talk about the show and her possible guesting. I asked if I could bring my daughter, and she thought it was a brilliant idea. When I hung up the phone, I thought how lovely she was.

The following morning my daughter and I hailed a taxi, bound for Jane Asher's Party Cakes at 24 Cale Street, Chelsea. From our hotel near Victoria Station, it was about a twenty-minute ride in the late-morning traffic. For London, it was exceptionally hot. Jane was waiting for us at the bakeshop with a welcoming smile. I introduced my daughter, Katie, only to learn that Jane's daughter was also a Katie. We talked about the show, what Jane could bake and decorate, that we could produce a segment on creative children's birthday parties.

We had such a fun time talking and planning that we nearly forgot to have lunch. Enjoying sandwiches in a small adjacent garden, I began to feel guilty. I was not being totally transparent regarding my motives in wanting to meet this lovely woman and have her as a guest on the show. We talked and talked the entire afternoon, like we had known each other for years, and planned to continue the conversation when I got back to Los Angeles. She loved the idea of a working holiday, where she could also see her brother and his family.

During the conversation, I had mentioned that my husband's birthday was the next day, the day we were flying home. Just as my daughter and I were about to leave, Jane stopped us. She asked us to take a walk and

THE RUBENS
Telephone: 071-834 6600

Message for ___Ms. Supnik___ Room No. 303
Message from ___Jane Asher___

Telephone ☑ Please call back ☑
Called to see you ☐ Will call again ☐
Wants to see you ☐ URGENT ☐

Telephone Number (071)

Message ___Please call Ms. Asher at home this evening or Tomorrow at the shop.___

___Shop number: (071) 584 6177___

Taken by ___G.N.___ Date ___05/09___ Time ___17:17___

Jane Asher kindly left me this message confirming our meeting at her cake shop.
AUTHOR'S COLLECTION

come back in about twenty minutes. We did. Upon returning to Party Cakes, Jane was waiting with a small cake packed for travel. "This is for your husband," she said. "Wish him happy birthday from me."

On the plane we carefully opened the box containing Jane's cake and when we sang "Happy Birthday," I felt bad that I hadn't fully disclosed everything. Jane, though, was adamant about not wanting to discuss her McCartney past. Because of that I respected her wishes. Jane never made it to Los Angeles, and shortly thereafter Peter moved to New York City for a position at Sony Music.

About two years after our meeting in London, I was doing development at Weller/Grossman co-owned by my friends Robb Weller and Gary Grossman. We were creating shows for the launch of HGTV. Still believing in Jane's creativity, I developed a half-hour series featuring Jane and her multiple talents. I called her about the possibility of hosting a thirteen-week series, and she was up for the challenge. But after the development process was completed, HGTV network executives passed on the show concept; they didn't want on-camera talent with an accent. Obviously, that decision was eventually overturned with the advent of new network executives, who brought on a bevy of Brits.

A KRAY Z THOUGHT

When I was fifteen years old, I read a lot about England. I was completely consumed not just with the Beatles and other British groups but also the culture of the country. Shortwave radios were still in use, and for people from afar wanting to listen to BBC News like I did every evening, it was invaluable. International coverage wasn't easily available, and to keep on the cutting edge of British culture, I had to work at it.

Among the most headline-grabbing news stories of the era was coverage of the twin brothers at the helm of London's East End gangster crime syndicate—Reggie and Ronnie Kray. The Kray Brothers brutally terrorized London throughout the '50s and '60s at the same time they supposedly ran a bodyguard service for Hollywood elite visiting London, including visitors such as Frank Sinatra, while dabbling in other so-called businesses.

During those years the Kray Brothers' names popped up in newspapers and on the BBC news frequently, primarily in connection with prestigious individuals. To a kid in New Jersey, far from the Krays' intimidation, the brothers were unimportant, yet during the Swinging '60s they had free rein over London. The Krays were off my radar until 2015, when the film *Legend* was distributed internationally. The film was based on John Pearson's book titled *The Profession of Violence: The Rise and Fall of the Kray Twins*. The film starring Tom Hardy, who played the dual role of the twins, chronicling the brothers' criminal activities and psychopathic behavior ordering vicious assaults and shakedowns throughout London and affirming their supremacy in the gangster underworld.

As an American member of BAFTA (British Academy of Film and Television Arts), I can vote on the United Kingdom Awards and was sent a screener of *Legend* to view for voting on the 2016 Awards. I remembered the Kray name but not much more. As I watched the film, things began to click. References to Swinging London, the dress, hairstyles, dialogue felt strangely familiar. By the film's conclusion, I was visibly upset. My husband looked over at me and didn't understand my reaction. I just blurted out, "The Krays are responsible, if not directly, then indirectly, for Brian Epstein's death."

Speculation about the circumstances surrounding Brian's death was hot news in August 1967. At seventeen having seen Brian in London only four months prior to his death, people thought I had some special insight. I didn't. I heard the theories just like everyone else. Had he feared that the Beatles wouldn't re-sign their managerial contract with him in the fall of 1967? Had the merchandising losses, rumored at $100 million dollars, that his lawyer David Jacobs had negotiated back in 1964 factor in? Had his gambling debts mounted? Was excessive drug use in play or his gay lifestyle? Brian's father had just died the month before Brian, and many believed that he would never intentionally bring additional grief upon his beloved mother, Queenie. It didn't make sense to me, even at age seventeen.

After watching the film, I began an internet search to look for possible connections. One article, written in 2009, was headlined "Crime leaders Kray Twins schemed to take over as the Beatles' managers!" My overactive imagination was moving in the right direction. Others seemed to have reached the same conclusion. The article said, "Ronnie and Reggie had been introduced to Epstein one evening at a gay club in London. . . . It was suspected they [the Krays] had evidence he [Epstein] was having a gay affair with a musician. He [Brian] was keen to keep his sexuality secret. At one point Brian was told that the Krays were taking the Beatles "off him." Using Brian's gay lifestyle as blackmail was not beneath the Krays' seemingly unchecked power.

Additional research shows that the Krays had influence with members of Parliament, where their blackmail tactics were commonly accepted. As the Krays were widely known to supply young boys to the upper crust for sex, this left Brian Epstein vulnerable to their exploitation and desire to control England's most famous export—the Beatles. From 1885 to 1967, homosexuality was illegal in Britain; the maximum sentence for sodomy was life in prison. In 1967 homosexuality was partially decriminalized, but arrests were still commonplace.

With Brian's five-year contact with the Beatles up for review in the fall of 1967, and if the gossip was anywhere near correct, Brian was feeling the pressure. In 1966 when I saw Brian at the hospital in New York, things seemed in disarray; now it made sense why he was nervous and shaky. He scared me. During my brief visit in April 1967, he was clearly unwell. Did the prospect of the Krays' power, the threatened exposure of his hidden lifestyle, and the upcoming Beatles management contract, possibly send Brian into a tailspin that resulted in his overdose?

What also makes sense in this context is the sudden departure of Wendy Hanson from Brian's employ. Wendy and I corresponded regularly about my visit to England scheduled for April 1967. When I received her letter in December 1966 informing me that she was leaving her job without significant notice, it didn't seem right—the suddenness of her departure, saying that that she could no longer protect Brian from himself. Wendy, it is not unreasonable to surmise, could also have been frightened by the Krays, but this is only conjecture on my part.

The final piece of evidence was the horrific and questionable suicide of Brian's lawyer, David Jacobs. Like Brian he was gay, dabbled in recreational drugs, and was well connected. Jacobs was a respected London solicitor, who represented notable and high-profile celebrities. When the Kray Brothers asked Jacobs to represent them in late 1968 on a pending charge of double murder, he declined. Shortly thereafter, in December 1968, Jacobs was discovered hanging from a wood beam in his garage only sixteen months after Brian had died. It was the same home in East Sussex Jacobs had loaned to Ringo and Maureen for their honeymoon. Many observers have found the connection between Brian's death and David's demise suspicious.

It's been so many years I am not sure how important Brian's passing is to the public, but for me it remains disturbing and leaves me wondering.

ADRIAN HENRI

POET, PAINTER, TEACHER, AND SINATRA FAN?

In early 1992, I received a message from Mike McCartney that his friend and Liverpool legend, poet and painter Adrian Henri, was coming to Los Angeles, and he thought it would be good for us to spend time together. My husband and I had met Adrian just briefly one afternoon while visiting Mike in Liverpool about two years earlier. Mike was driving us around to iconic sights when Adrian stepped out of his front door at 21 Mount Street as we were passing by. He was still in a bathrobe and black knitted booties, though it was two in the afternoon. Adrian looked like he had just awakened. Adrian and Mike exchanged a few scouser words that were difficult to understand.

As we drove off, Mike explained that John Lennon lived with Adrian in that house while he was an art student at the Liverpool College of Art. Adrian was influential in helping John develop his artistic gifts and gave him a place to live. Beside John, Adrian was also an artistic influence on Paul McCartney. Liverpool's favorite son writer, Willy Russell, and Allen Ginsberg were Adrian's close colleagues. In the early 1970s, Mike McCartney's group the Scaffold joined with Adrian and Neil Innes, Viv Stanshall, Andy Roberts, and others in an expanded other group called Grimms—a respected and well-known, comedy ensemble.

Adrian was a local icon, a free spirit who stayed in Liverpool instead of moving to London when the opportunity for greater fame and fortune presented itself. Adrian was part teacher, performer, rock 'n' roller, and playwright besides painter and poet. Adrian married once but had no children. He was closely associated with other pop artists of the 1960s and in 1967 formed a poetry band call the Liverpool Scene that didn't meet with much success except in 1969 opening for Led Zeppelin. Adrian, it was said, would get out of control onstage to the point of frightening the audience and other performers.

When Mike let me know that Adrian was coming, the welcome mat was out. I was told Adrian was headed to Los Angeles to see friends who lived in Laurel Canyon. My husband and I spent a lot of time thinking about where to take Adrian for dinner and finally decided on Wolfgang Puck's newest LA restaurant, Eureka. It was a casual restaurant—a fore-runner of gastropubs serving on-site manufactured beers. We thought Adrian would enjoy the atmosphere. It was loud, crowded, and very hip.

Adrian arrived at my house with his student/girlfriend/collabora-tor Catherine Marcangeli, who lived in Paris. Catherine was lovely and treated Adrian with deserved reverence. My friend Shirley Bennett also joined us for the evening. We made small talk about last names, with Adrian repeating my friend's last name "Bennett . . . Bennett . . ." continu-ously. We stood and chatted as Adrian didn't want to sit down. Finally, it was time for the drive to West Los Angeles. We all squeezed into one car and headed down Wilshire Boulevard.

As we drove, we gave Adrian and Catherine a tour. They were very interested in the city and its history. They didn't quite understand how downtown was far from the ocean. We explained that Santa Monica was a magnet for Brits since it seemed like Brighton. Adrian was enraptured with the city's aura and wanted to absorb it all.

During dinner Adrian and Catherine spoke of their work, a joint proj-ect where Catherine was helping Adrian put together another book of his poetic works. Adrian was an engaging teacher, and we listened as he spoke on diverse topics.

After dinner we took the long way back, circling through Hollywood. Adrian took the opportunity in front of Grauman's Chinese Theatre to sink his feet into several celebrities' footsteps. I couldn't help but think this is where I was when his friend John Lennon was shot. Now I was standing at the same spot with his mentor. Adrian took in the neon lights and action of Hollywood Boulevard. He posed for pictures with the street actors dressed as Spiderman and Snow White who lived off tourists' tips. There was something so naive about Adrian, yet wise like an old soul.

When we arrived back at the house, and we were saying our goodbyes, Adrian spotted a jar of pasta sauce on the kitchen counter. Frank Sinatra had come out with a line of signature pasta sauces based on his family recipe, and I was planning to use it the following evening. Adrian looked so longingly at the jar that I asked him if he would like it.

"Yes, I'd like to bring it back to Liverpool."

How strange I thought, but, hey, this was pure Adrian Henri. I wrapped the jar in plastic bubble wrap ready for the suitcase. We said our good-byes, and they were off with Catherine driving back to their host's home in Laurel Canyon. I still am not sure whether the evening had a purpose, but I hope it was to enjoy each other's company.

In preparing this chapter, I emailed my friend Shirley Bennett to go over some of the details of the evening. She wrote back, "If I recall correctly, Adrian sent you a thank-you note for his visit, specifically mentioning your gift of the Sinatra pasta sauce, saying it was displayed on his mantelpiece admired by all." It would take someone unique like Adrian, or Andy Warhol, to display a jar of spaghetti sauce as a work of art.

During one visit to Liverpool, I spent time at the Museum of Liverpool. While walking through it, I came upon a wonderful display of Beatles memorabilia with a tribute to the arts that came out of the city. Featured prominently were works by Adrian Henri; Adrian's name was surpassed only by John Lennon and Paul McCartney as contributors to Liverpool's artistic heritage.

It was apt that the night before Adrian's death in 2000, the city of Liverpool conferred on him the well-deserved Freedom of the City medal. We will never know whether Adrian consumed that jar of pasta sauce or was a just devoted Frank Sinatra fan.

THE SIXTIES AT FAHEY-KLEIN GALLERY

Linda disliked coming to Los Angeles, or so I've been told. I attribute this to all the women who would come of out of the woodwork to throw themselves at Paul. Linda, the forever groupie, didn't appreciate these women. Frankly, neither did I.

It was embarrassing to witness. The example that illustrates this point was the opening night of Linda's photographic exhibit at the Fahey-Klein Gallery on La Brea Avenue in Los Angeles. "The Sixties" was a photographic retrospective of her work. Her portfolio is an extraordinary document of the era; photographs of Mick Jagger, the Grateful Dead, Jimi Hendrix, and naturally, the Beatles, were featured in the exhibit.

The evening of the opening, my daughter was home with a raging fever. A sitter was with her, but I felt guilty. She was old enough to tell me I should go to the opening because these invites rarely happen. We arrived in appropriate style, handing the valet the car keys, and made our way into the gallery among outlandishly dressed women. One can never look too happy to be at an event such as this; a more sour demeanor means you'll be better accepted.

Even though we arrived on time, the place was already packed with Paul's followers, Linda's fans, and tons of security. Linda spotted us across the room but didn't reach us until later in the evening. Paul was surrounded by people standing three deep wanting autographs, photos, you name it. Paul's assistant, John Hammel, was rushing around, desperately trying to enlist security to clear the way so others could gain access to Paul.

With all the crowding, I felt responsible for bringing my husband and wanted him to have a fun evening. It was difficult to move, let alone reach Paul to say hello and congratulate Linda on the exhibit. We just stood in one place and let the action revolve around us. When I turned around at one point, Paul was right next to us. The moment had finally arrived. It was somewhat awkward to even talk with people pushing, but in a very uncharacteristic move I pulled out my camera and flashed it in his face.

I had had many opportunities over the years to take pictures, but I had refrained; I felt like the camera violated the unique position I had been granted, but here I was acting just as poorly as everyone else.

Paul seemed surprised to see me with a camera. I am pleased in retrospect that I was bold enough to get a few photos. Truthfully, if Linda hadn't been pushy enough to take the photos in "The Sixties," none of us would have been there that evening.

UK INTERVIEWS

BEATLEMANIA AND *NOEL'S ADDICTS*

Over the years I had the chance to be interviewed by various media, but I was always very reluctant. I had learned my lesson early when *Seventeen* magazine wanted to do a story on the Beatles and contacted me to be interviewed. *Seventeen* was the leader in trendy fashion and style for teen girls at the time, and it was an honor to be asked. The media in 1966 wasn't anything like today's gossip-hungry reporters, yet I was hesitant because I didn't know what they would ask, and I didn't feel comfortable sharing details.

I passed on the *Seventeen* opportunity. The Beatles organization found out that I declined, and from that time on I was invited back to events. Many years later I found myself in Linda McCartney's company; we talked about interviews, and I shared with her what happened with *Seventeen.* Linda confirmed that it was the smartest thing I ever did.

Another incident was when *Time* magazine was doing a twentieth-anniversary story on the Beatles, and they sent a reporter to interview me at my house. I agreed to the interview and posed for photos. After the reporter and photographer left, it just didn't feel right. I phoned my husband and asked him to rush to the *Time* office located at the corner of Santa Monica Boulevard and Roxbury Drive in Beverly Hills to stop the story. He got there just in time.

However, along the way television opportunities presented themselves in which I did participate—CNN, ABC's *World News Tonight, Entertainment Tonight,* Bill Maher's first late-night show, Grammy Awards/CBS fiftieth anniversary show, *The Night That Changed America,* and Ron Howard's feature documentary on the Beatles, *The Touring Years,* to name a few. Some of these I have briefly mentioned in other chapters, but the details of the following two interviews are fun.

In 1982, I was interviewed for a BBC documentary called what else . . . *Beatlemania!* The BBC sent a crew to the States, and they convened in my living room like a swarm of locusts. I brought in from my storage facility two steamer trunks full of Beatles memorabilia for them to shoot as B-roll.

241

They spent three hours asking me questions about meeting the Beatles. It was simple, straightforward, and I was glad to read that the three Beatles appreciated the show when it was televised in the United Kingdom.

The next interview I did for BBC television was ten years later. Noel Edmonds was coming to America to interview collectors for his popular primetime show *Noel's Addicts*. I really didn't like the name of the show, but Noel was a much-loved television presenter in the United Kingdom, respected like Dick Clark was here. So, I agreed to the interview. Noel did his best to portray me as a crazed collector of Beatles memorabilia who would stop at nothing to add to my collection. John Lennon probably would have agreed. Although I didn't see the show, something very interesting came out of it.

About four months after the program aired, Andrea Miller, the segment producer, forwarded a letter from a viewer who had contacted her via the BBC. The viewer claimed he knew me and wanted my address. Before giving out any information, Andrea wanted to be sure she had my permission. The letter was from Michael Kemble, one of my British Beatles pen pals with whom the English fan club connected me around 1965. We had exchanged letters for about two years and then lost touch. We had not met or talked, but his letter explained that his wife was watching *Noel's Addicts* in another room, and he overheard my voice. He just had a feeling it was me. Sure enough.

I gave the producer the go-ahead to divulge my contact information, and in no time, I heard from Michael. As luck would have it, we had a trip planned to visit Michael McCartney and family in Liverpool and then drive back to London. Instead of going directly, we arranged to stay overnight in the quaint Cotswold town of Chipping Camden, and Mike Kemble drove from his home in the West Midlands to meet us.

Although I was a little reluctant, meeting Mike and his daughter turned out just fine. We talked about our Beatles connection and how they were still the greatest band. Mike grew up Merseyside just outside of Liverpool, so he was present from the beginning. In catching up on our lives, it made me uneasy when Mike told us about serving in the military in Northern Ireland. His politics seemed ultraconservative, which made me personally uncomfortable. As Paul McCartney wrote, wasn't it time to give Ireland back to the Irish? Upon my return home we exchanged a few letters, but what more was there to say?

MOTHER NATURE FOR THE ENVIRONMENT

Celebrating Earth Day has always been a very special day. I was still at Boston University when the first Earth Day was celebrated in April 1970. Twenty million Americans across the country marched to bring attention to potential dangers environmental pollution was causing. We in Boston were no different, and after marching we gathered in Boston Gardens for a peaceful and meaningful afternoon.

I had just left the daily ABC TV *Home* show for the PR firm when I learned that Earth Day Los Angeles would be celebrated on April 16, 1993, with an important star-studded event at the Hollywood Bowl. The promoters called it Concert for the Environment, and the lineup featured k.d. lang, Natalie Merchant, Bruce Cockburn, P.M. Dawn, Don Henley, Kenny Loggins, and taking a break during their New World Tour—Paul and Linda McCartney. I phoned the senior producers on my former show and let them know I could finally deliver not just Linda cooking, but Paul as well. Even though I was gone, I really wasn't.

I had Paul and Linda's country home phone number from having several calls with her during the cookbook segments for the show, so I simply called. If I could get the word out to "go veggie," to put a halt to animal testing, and to protect the environment, they were in. The entire concert would be solar powered, and the concession stands would sell only vegetarian food.

This concert was momentous not only because of the messages being sent to the world, but this marked the first time McCartney was back at the Hollywood Bowl since the Beatles in 1965. The afternoon of the concert I met the show's crew at the Bowl, and they began to set up. I also brought along my camcorder. The performers were doing press in a marquee adjacent to the stage, and Natalie Merchant was responding to questions when Paul (in sunglasses) and Linda entered. I charged over to them; my reward was two hugs and kisses. The show's crew were able to get a brief one-on-one interview with Paul and the promoter before he sat down to share his message. Meanwhile, Linda was already onstage for the soundcheck. During the concert, no video cameras would be allowed because the promoter had hired a crew to capture the entire event.

Paul left the press room to join Linda for the soundcheck, and I left with him. I headed for one of the box seats, camcorder slung over my shoulder. Paul, Linda, and band began to play "Mother Nature's Son." It was sounding really good, and I positioned myself holding the camcorder in a strategic location to get a clear shot. Suddenly, two security guards showed up and wrestled the camcorder out of my hand. A slight scuffle followed, and I guess I was quite loud because soundcheck came to a halt. Paul could see that I was having a rough time and told the guards that I had special credentials to video his set.

At the very end of Paul's final song, "Hey Jude," from the wings out came Ringo to a tremendous roar of the crowd as the entire cast gathered behind them. Simply amazing to witness these two former Beatles embracing on the Hollywood Bowl stage. I recently transferred the videocassette to a digital link to keep it intact. "Mother Nature's Son" never sounded sweeter.

MEETUP AT MIDEM

Without Tony Barrow we would never have had the name "The Fab Four"; as the Beatles' press officer, he came up with the moniker. Widely known as the record reviewer for the local newspaper, the *Liverpool Echo*, still read by every Liverpudlian today, Brian Epstein relied upon Tony's expertise from the outset of the group's rise to fame. Tony came on board early, arranging the band's first London-based auditions at Decca Records, where he worked. Shortly thereafter, he organized the publicity for the Beatles' first UK single release of "Love Me Do." Tony eventually joined Brian Epstein working for his Northeast Music Stores (NEMS) management company doing publicity not just for the Beatles but also Brian's other groups and individuals such as Billy J. Kramer and the Dakotas, Gerry and the Pacemakers, and Cilla Black.

Tony was an innovator, an out-of-the-box thinker. Tony was the creator/originator of all the fan club materials given to members; he transferred the club operations from Liverpool to London and set and oversaw the press conferences for the Beatles around the world. To Tony we owe grateful thanks for coming up with the concept for the Beatles to record Christmas messages sent out to all fan club members (the flexies) and the pictures and one sheets made available through the club. It was also Tony who suggested alternate names for many working within the Beatles empire. Shortly after Brian's death, Tony left to open his own public relations/publicity firm, where he repped top British bands and some American performers when they toured in the United Kingdom and Europe, namely, David Cassidy and the Jackson 5.

It wasn't until the Warwick Hotel press conference in 1965 that I met Tony Barrow. Seeing Tony enter the Warwick Room, where the press conference was being held, I knew the Beatles' entrance was near. Tony first walked to the dais, testing the microphones with utmost precision, wanting everything to be perfect. Tony methodically conducted the press conference including key media assembled and moderated the process to be sure it went without incident. When I was brought upstairs to meet the

Beatles, I immediately spotted Tony conferring with Brian, and shortly thereafter he came over to make my acquaintance. Tony was the consummate professional, keeping all the moving parts of the huge Beatles machine in tune.

After the initial meeting at the Warwick, I didn't connect with Tony again during his time with the Beatles. When I went to London in 1967, he wasn't at NEMS the day I visited or at Chapel Street for the brief hello with Brian. I followed his winding career in the trades and was always happy to see his name mentioned during the ensuing years.

In January 1993, my husband was invited to moderate a panel sponsored by the International Association of Entertainment Lawyers about a book he wrote, *Enforcement of Copyright & Related Rights Affecting the Music Industry*, at MIDEM in Cannes, France. MIDEM is an annual music industry conference akin to the Cannes Film Market. Since my husband was conducting business, I had plenty of time to walk the conference within Cannes's Palais des Festivals and learn about the planned fundraiser for AIDS research combined with an all-star tribute to Marvin Gaye to be held during MIDEM. The gala was big news.

One afternoon I was in the Palais and came upon Los Angeles-based DJ Rick Dees of KIIS-FM broadcasting live from the conference floor to LA, where it was around 7 in the morning. Rick was handing out T-shirts and talking about the Marvin Gaye tribute that he would host. I stopped to say hello, though I had not met him before, but thought being far from home it should be OK to meet a fellow Los Angeleno. That's when I spotted Tony Barrow.

I raced over to Tony so excited to see him and blabbered about our last meeting at the Warwick. Did he remember me?

Being a proper English gentleman, he said, "Of course I remember you . . . the young fan with the leaking glass that helped out with the other fan breaking in through the window."

I had forgotten about the girl climbing the thirty-three floors.

I sat down with Tony and had the pleasure of hearing some of his insights about touring with the Beatles. Tony asked if I ever saw Pam and Sue from the fan club in New York, or Bernice. No, I hadn't for many years. I mentioned my trip to London and my disappointment at the fan club meeting; he just shook his head in acknowledgment. Then I told him about my visit to EMI/Abbey Road Studios and seeing George Martin and Geoff Emerick.

"You know George Martin is here at the Palais; have you seen him yet?"

"No," I replied, "I didn't know that he was here."

Tony took me at once by the hand and led me to George Martin's stand.

George Martin and his managing director, John Burgess, were at MIDEM to launch their new Chrysalis/Air Studio headquarters, which recently had moved from Oxford Street to a state-of-the-art recording facility at Lyndhurst Hall in Hampstead, a former Methodist church. In addition, Mr. Martin was to be honored by Cannes Mayor Michel Mouillot at a special luncheon at his home. (Interestingly, Mayor Mouillot was arrested a few years later for corruption.) George Martin had established Air Studio as a multimedia recording complex and staging facility for live television and concerts.

Again, I reminded Mr. Martin about our correspondence and meeting with my mom when Abbey Road was still known as EMI Studios. Mr. Martin had immediate recall of the meeting. I had something new to add—I had met his son, Gilles, when he visited mutual friends in Los Angeles and recounted the infamous "rubbish" incident at the Warwick Hotel press conference. Tony Barrow backed me up with all the details, even adding some I didn't know. According to Tony, from the time I left the Warwick Hotel suite after meeting the Beatles, John Lennon forever made fun of me, even imitating the scene of water dripping out of my handbag and the horror my face showed when he asked to inspect my bag further. Hearing this confirmation of what I always suspected hurt, but I hid it well.

This impromptu meeting was joyous, and Mr. Martin gave me a press folder announcing Lyndhurst Hall; if I ever had television work to do in the United Kingdom, his facility was available. Walking away with press materials in hand reminded me of the old days—a new addition to my Beatles collection.

PARTY OF THE DECADE

We were forewarned that Mike McCartney was planning a huge blowout for his fiftieth birthday: a year out we already knew that something big would happen in Liverpool in January 1994. Liverpool in January? No one in her right mind visits Liverpool in January. I convinced my family that with the proper clothing it would feel like the Bahamas. Our first trip to visit Mike had been in June, and the temperature was so cold then that my husband had bought a jacket there to fight the wind and cold. January weather would pose a problem, but not even rain, ice, freezing temperatures, or snow would keep me from Mike's celebration.

I was in a weird place concerning work. I had left the ABC TV daily television show, *Home*, I had worked on for several years to become media director for a large public relations firm in downtown Los Angeles. I took the job for two reasons—first, a new executive producer had come on the ABC show, ruining the production in my opinion, and he didn't like me. Second, the former host of the *Home* show, Robb Weller, with a new creative business partner, Gary Grossman, was starting a production company producing for cable TV. I always liked Robb and thought that if given an opportunity, I would work with him in a second.

That chance presented itself. Not to conflict with the ABC show, I left to work for the public relations firm until Weller/Grossman Productions was up and running. The company proved successful, and I worked there for seventeen amazing years. We produced more than nine thousand episodes of television for thirty-six broadcast and cable networks, including launching HGTV and the National Geographic Channel in the United States, and winning Emmy awards.

Mike's party was falling right between moving from the public relations firm to Weller/Grossman. It was awkward because I would take vacation time, then return to the public relations company to give my notice. In the interim, the executive producer of *Home* was now gone, and the original executive producer had returned and wanted me back. Three jobs were mine to have. But my choice still was the production company.

Mike's birthday is on January 7, so we made a winter holiday out of it and visited friends who lived in a charming village in Kent. Kent would be Christmas-card perfection over the holidays, on to London to see in the New Year, and then hop on the train to Liverpool.

On Christmas Day 1993 we boarded a TWA jet that flew us to Gatwick via St. Louis. It was always exciting to return to England, even in December, and to spot the rolling hills and green countryside from our seats as the plane descended at sunrise. This time it was even better with the expectation of a wonderful birthday celebration. With time being short, we decided to take a British Midlands flight to Manchester and pick up a rental car to Liverpool.

It was a quick flight and a forty-five-minute drive from Manchester to Merseyside. When we pulled up at Mike's house, preparations were already underway. Their expansive front lawn was covered with a large, sturdy white tent that could withstand the cold and wind gusts. We were immediately put to work blowing up white and black balloons: the theme of the party was based on Mike's best-selling book, *Mike Macs Whites and Blacks and One Color*. Everyone was told to come wearing only black-and-white clothing. We joined the McCartneys, decorating for two days, stopping only to have something to eat or run inside to warm up. It was fun.

Not only was I excited to be included in the party but to meet Barb Paulsen. Barb, based in Cleveland, Ohio, was president of Mike's fan club for years, and over the years we had spent hours talking on the phone. The name of the club was "The Mike McCartney Depreciation Society." Barb also wrote "Gear Box," a publication named after Mike's professional name since the 1960s—Mike McGear. He used that name, as he frequently proclaimed, to protect the innocent.

On this trip guests stayed at a local Travelodge adjacent to the roundabout I had first seen riding in the backseat of Mr. and Mrs. Harrison's car. No matter how many years have passed, and how many times we have stayed there, I always feel the spirit of that first visit. When I see the roundabout, it signals that we've arrived.

Mike's big day had finally arrived. With decorations and other preparations completed, we headed back to the Travelodge to don our three new black-and-white outfits. Barb drove to the McCartneys' with us, to find family members already partying big-time. The band was going through a short sound check. Now how does a McCartney find a band? Well . . . the answer is very simple . . . The Chip Shop Boys, a local Liverpool band comprising musicians who had played all the clubs with the Beatles from the '60s.

Friends and family arrived, many from Mike's past and longtime friends of his family. Members of Scaffold, coworkers from Andre

Bernard's hair studio, cousins, and neighbors all gathered under the tent. It was a sea of black and white until Mike made his spectacular entry in a colorful outfit; he was the one color. It was so much fun to be there.

My daughter, Katie, and Mike's sons were in charge of taking coats and putting them in a safe place. Kate is super-efficient, and that night she organized a system to easily tag and locate each coat, making for easy departures from the party. Plenty of drink and food was served. The party festivities were taking off just as Paul and Linda entered the marquee without fanfare, just like all the other guests. They had driven up that day from the south of England and were staying in their Liverpool home just a few blocks from Mike's—the same house that Paul had bought for his dad and Mike, where Mr. and Mrs. Harrison had brought me to meet Jim and Angela McCartney. After Jim McCartney's death in 1976, Paul took ownership of the home, Rembrandt, so he would always have a base when visiting family.

Everyone was super happy to see Paul and Linda, and their cousins and Mike greeted them appropriately. The famous couple seemed like just another two people at the party as they began to wander through the crowd, both enjoying the music. When I saw Paul standing alone, I went up to him. He seemed very happy to see me and gave me a kiss on the cheek and a huge, welcoming hug.

Paul said, "It is important that you are here. I know that Mike wanted you here with us. I'm glad you made it."

Paul was curious how we were holding up in the cold weather. He glanced at my husband and chuckled, seeing him shivering even though he was in a black wool suit. "Not exactly LA," Paul commented. We shared a good laugh and just stood together, taking in the action.

It felt great to be there without the usual hype—there was no better moment.

The music blasted loudly, and the Merseyside Constable's office sent someone to say that neighbors were complaining about the noise even though Mike had specifically invited them all to avoid this problem. Immediately after the officer left, Linda moved behind the band's speakers and put the music up even louder as the Chip Shop Boys took their place onstage. At the first notes, Mike and Paul jumped onto the riser with the band. We were all transported back to Paul and Mike as the young Everly Brothers playing the Butlin's stage, introduced by cousin Mike Robbins as the host of a National Talent Contest. The brothers broke into song—many songs—harmonizing, with all the partygoers gathering around and joining in. It was easy to forget that a superstar was two feet away.

When Paul and Mike broke into "I Saw Her Standing There," I did something that I had couldn't resist—reach for my camera. It was an electric moment to be captured for posterity. Throughout the near sixty years, I haven't taken advantage of my camera and the unique opportunities that were presented. I looked for reasons why I was so graciously included in Beatles Fan Club events, rarified behind-the-scenes activities, and eventually family gatherings. I always attributed my invites to the confidentiality, to my discretion in not bringing out the camera and trying to impose myself on anyone. That is why writing this book has been a very soul-searching and conflicted project.

But watching with the McCartney clan and friends at the birthday party, I had to capture this rare moment of the brothers singing together. I snapped a series of photos and quickly put the camera away.

The Merseyside Constable showed up a second time, with the same complaints, but he understood the situation. The chief constable wanted to join in the party when he realized that Paul and Linda were there, too. At that moment Linda ducked behind the speakers again. She was the one who kept turning up the sound.

When Linda realized that I had seen her sneak behind the sound system, she came over to talk. We shared a good laugh about what she had been doing and, for the first time, I think we appreciated each other's sense of defying the system.

"Your daughter is a doer," she said.

"What do you mean?" I asked.

"Can't you see how she organized everything; she took our coats when we came in the house, gave me this number (holding up a number written by Kate on a snippet of paper) so I could easily get my coat back . . . brought us something to drink when we were inside sitting on the couch . . . she's a doer! None of the other kids would do that," Linda admitted.

I thanked Linda for the compliment. We talked briefly about her children, none of whom were there that evening. They were all home, and tomorrow she and Paul would drive back. Linda mentioned the television segments we did together, and out of nowhere said I should have joined the family for Chinese food that evening. That was a detail I had forgotten, but she remembered. We stood together in silence for easily five or six minutes, just observing the activity under the tent. As I slowly edged away, not wanting to push things any farther, Linda pulled me back by the arm to say, "We're glad you made it here."

"I am, too," I replied with a smile.

Linda added, "Not to be missed."

The party went on until 5 a.m., with breakfast for all back at Mike's house in just a few hours. As my husband, Kate, and Barb all jumped into the car to return to the Travelodge, my husband headed to the wrong side of the car, forgetting that we're in England. He finally figured it out and got into the driver's seat, but we couldn't see out—the windshield was entirely iced over. Now, my husband is a San Diego native. He had never seen ice on a windshield and did not know how to clear it away. I jumped out of the car and taught him while Barb and Kate huddled under a blanket in the car. The defroster slowly melted the thick ice, revealing Paul and Linda, arm in arm, framed in glistening ice as they walked to their car.

"The party of the decade," Paul McCartney proclaimed in the morning as everyone gathered at Mike's house to deconstruct the evening.

I COULD HAVE LIVED THERE, TOO!

When we were in Liverpool to celebrate Mike McCartney's birthday, we drove by 20 Forthlin Road, the home where Paul and Mike were raised and where several of the Beatles' earliest songs were written. Fortunately, through Mike's photographs, we can get a good look at life in the McCartney household back in time. In one of Mike's iconic photos, John and Paul are sitting before the fireplace composing "I Saw Her Standing There." Other photos of the back garden became the cover of Paul's record "Chaos and Creation in the Backyard." Shots show Paul climbing down the drainpipe, as he frequently did, escaping from the second-story window undetected. The McCartney family moved into the house in 1955 and lived there until 1965, when Paul purchased for his dad and Mike a lovely Tudor-style home across the River Mersey on the Wirral Peninsula.

Forthlin Road is a terrace house—one where a row of identical houses share side walls, much like what we in the States call townhouses, with an upstairs and downstairs. This building design became popular beginning in the 1920s in England, and one had to qualify by income and profession to move into these homes.

We drove over to Forthlin Road not just for the nostalgia but because we were told the house was for currently for sale. Asking price was £70,000. I wanted to buy it. I shared the news with Mike when we got back home, and he encouraged me. I contacted the representative; learning that an American was interested, the asking price immediately went up £20,000. After much consideration, I was deterred from the purchase; the property was too far from where I lived to properly care for it.

Shortly thereafter, the historical importance of 20 Forthlin Road caught the attention of the National Trust of England, Scotland, and Wales, which purchased the house to be preserved as a national landmark. In 2000, when we were in Liverpool for my fiftieth birthday celebration, Mike took us to see the indoor reconstruction of the house based on his early family photographs. Mike's iconic photographs are displayed throughout the property, a primary reason no photography is permitted within its confines. The National Trust offers tours of the property along with 251 Menlove Avenue fondly known as "Mendips." John Lennon lived at Mendips with his Aunt Mimi and Uncle George Smith, a home purchased a few years after Forthlin Road with the assistance of Yoko Ono. Several other houses in and around Liverpool where any of the Beatles lived, including George and Ringo's childhood homes, have sold for double the area's median price. One woman from London purchased George Harrison's childhood home to turn it into a Beatles house for rent.

Never would I have turned Forthlin Road into a commercial enterprise, but what an addition to my memorabilia collection. As we toured Forthlin Road we ended in the kitchen, where the caretaker fixed us all a cup of tea. Visions of mother Mary stirring the family scouse on the stove crept into my head. That image was awesome.

YOU CAN'T DO THAT

After I returned from Liverpool and Mike's grand birthday celebration, Walter Shenson and I met for lunch at our usual spot, Don Hernando's in the Beverly Wilshire Hotel across the street from his office. Walter was striking the *dangerously* thoughtful pose I came to recognize immediately as a prelude to something intriguing. He told me about his idea to produce a documentary on the making of *A Hard Day's Night*.

Never one to say no to Walter's ideas, I agreed that it would be informative to understand the mechanics of what comprised this already classic film directly from the people involved in the film's production. Walter suggested that I should share a few anecdotes. Because I had taught two classes on the Beatles at UCLA and knew many fans, Walter wanted to be sure the market was there for the documentary. Failure was not in his dictionary.

In addition, what prompted this idea was that people associated with the Beatles were getting older. Walter wanted to document their memories in an hour-long retrospective that examined the underlying importance of how the Beatles influenced and changed culture. Walter hired David Leaf, a producer and writer, to put together the script and conduct the interviews. Later in his career David wrote the marvelous *The U.S. vs. John Lennon* and a well-received biography on Brian Wilson.

The documentary *You Can't Do That! The Making of "A Hard Day's Night"* was hosted by Phil Collins who, as a young London lad, was seen in the film's opening shots at the train station chasing after the Beatles. The objective was to gain insight into the film's importance and influence from experts of the era ranging from Roger Ebert to Roger McGuinn of the Byrds. Walter encouraged me to be part of the project by including an interview I gave on how I organized the fans for the highly promoted 1964 US premiere of the film by sleeping on the sidewalk adjacent to the box office on Broadway in front of the Astor Theatre.

David conducted my interview in the living room surrounded by memorabilia from the original release with additional items Walter had made for the 1982 rerelease of the movie. The interview went well, but by the released version, most of my interview was on the cutting room floor. When I watched the documentary, I cringed when I admitted on camera to seeing *A Hard Day's Night* approximately twenty-five times. Walter's blue Rolls-Royce did belong to me.

HOUSE OF BLUES/HOUSE ON FIRE

After our many visits to Liverpool, Mike McCartney and family came for a California holiday in April 1995. His three boys were a perfect age to travel, so they rented a time share in the rustic town of Ramona, hidden in the hills of San Diego County for a week before coming to stay with us. Ramona was best known in the 1960s as the training camp for boxers George Foreman and Muhammad Ali. During the Beatles' first trip in February 1964, while at the Deauville Hotel in Miami for their second Sullivan show appearance, they had time to spar with Muhammad Ali when he was still known as Cassius Clay. He probably perfected those moves in Ramona.

After a few days, my family and I drove to Ramona, and we all stayed overnight in the time share. We had a big pajama party. The following day we drove to the border with Mexico and walked across the bridge and by taxi took in the sights of Tijuana. We stopped at the Hard Rock Café, only to find a poster from the popular 1960s UK TV show *Juke Box Jury* featuring the Beatles! This location closed around 2010 due to the dismal economy in Mexico, along with fears of drug wars in the area.

We caravanned back, staying the night in the Mediterranean-like seaside town of La Jolla, and drove the next day to Los Angeles. The days were packed with fun touring the landmarks—Universal, posing at the foot of the Hollywood sign, and Santa Monica/Venice/Malibu beach.

Mike had one request while in Los Angeles: to see Isaac Tigrett. Isaac was cofounder of both the Hard Rock Café and the House of Blues. The McCartneys knew the Hard Rock Café well because the original was in London. Now Isaac was living in Los Angeles to oversee his newest venture, the House of Blues on Sunset Boulevard. We were invited to join Isaac for dinner in the private Foundation Room followed by the show. It was important for Mike to see Isaac, who had been married to Ringo's ex-wife, Maureen Cox Starkey, until her death from leukemia the year before. Mike wanted to convey his condolences and show support for Isaac from Liverpool scousers.

When we arrived, Isaac was waiting for us in the Foundation Room. We enjoyed drinks and had just started our main course when we received a phone call from our daughter: our house was on fire, and we needed to return immediately. Isaac ran ahead of us to the parking lot, shouting to the valets to get our car. We waited, nervously. When Isaac thought the valet wasn't moving fast enough, he tore ahead, grabbing our keys and bringing the car himself to the valet stand. Isaac jumped out and we jumped in as fast as we could, racing down Sunset to Doheny and home.

When we arrived home, two fire engines and one paramedic unit were in front of our house. The next-door neighbor, Dorothy, was holding Mike's youngest son in her arms. Our nanny was caring for the other three children. I raced into the bathroom; the smoke was still filling the room. The bathroom floor was black, and you could see that flames had edged up the walls.

It seems that all the kids had taken their evening shower. My daughter, who was twelve years old, decided that she should dry the boys' hair. By the time she got to the youngest boy, the dryer overheated and sparked. Seeing the sparks fly, she got frightened, dropping the hairdryer on the floor, and ignited the throw rug.

Fortunately, the damage was minor. I envisioned the next day's headlines had the fire been worse, and I still cringe at the thought. The evening went down as "the night of the 'House of Blues' fire." Every time we are together, the fire is part of the conversation.

TURNING FIFTY

There was no better way to celebrate my fiftieth birthday than to join my extended family in Liverpool. I came from a small family—I had a few cousins on my dad's side on the East Coast, with whom at the time I had little contact; no one was left on my mom's side. I couldn't decide how best to see the next fifty years in, so my husband suggested looking at what had been the biggest influence in my life: no mystery there—the Beatles! I phoned Mike and proposed that I bring my husband, daughter, and her high-school boyfriend to Liverpool for the celebration. They thought it a fun idea, so we made plans.

A few days later Mike called, and when I heard his voice, I immediately thought that the trip was off. No. On his end, the McCartney family had gotten together and decided it would be fun to celebrate at the home of Ian and Jackie Harris, Mike's cousins and son of Auntie Gin, the family matriarch. The home that Ian had grown up in was always the party house because Auntie Gin and her husband, Harry Harris, encouraged everyone to hang out there.

Mike first photographed the Beatles in color back in 1958 at Ian and Jackie's wedding. The photograph is iconic; a fourteen-year-old George, fifteen-year-old Paul, and sixteen-year-old John with instruments were joined by the infamous Dennis holding a pint of Guinness. Dennis Littler was cousin Ian's best friend; legend says he had his own band and would bring his guitar over to Auntie Gin's to play. The Beatles had at one time asked to join Dennis's band, but Dennis thought them too young, and he passed. Dennis sadly passed away in 2022.

Ian, now deceased, and Jackie have the most fabulous large family, raised in a charming house right alongside the River Mersey. We had been to dinners and gatherings at Ian and Jackie's before, and I loved the idea of having my birthday at their house. Meals were a free-for-all—children, friends, and all invited would descend upon their home. We had to learn not to wait politely for an invitation. When the food was put on the table, you had to go for it, or you could find yourself with nothing to eat. Food time at the Harrises' was legendary, so much so that both times when I produced Linda's cooking segments, we couldn't help but reference how fast you had to get to the table at their house to get food.

We arrived in Liverpool on a cold March morning and checked into the now-familiar Travelodge. We were tired from the long trip from Los Angeles, changing planes in Chicago, and on to Manchester.

Turning fifty didn't seem so bad after all because it involved spending time with close friends. Knowing that this was my daughter's boyfriend's first visit to Liverpool, Mike gave us the royal tour. It was an unforgettable drive, seeing the city's iconic spots with commentary provided by Mike. Kate's boyfriend, though, seemed to constantly fall asleep, missing the tour and all of Mike's insights. He didn't realize that when you get to Liverpool, you hit the ground running.

The evening of my birthday everyone gathered at the Harrises' home, decorated with birthday bunting. Their children, as many as could be rounded up, along with the rest of the Mike McCartney clan, descended upon the Harris home. We ate, laughed, and had a fabulous time culminating in a birthday cake and me making a wish. It wasn't the standard wish for the future, but a personal thank-you to this wonderful family who had welcomed this young screaming girl at the Sullivan show dreaming about how she could get to meet the Beatles. That no longer seemed important.

After Liverpool we spent a few days in London before returning to Los Angeles. I wanted to send something special to the Harrises for their kindness. I knew they all loved to eat well, so we ordered a side of ham, accompanied by various mustards, from Fortnum & Mason, to be delivered to their door. The ham was a big sensation. Even today when I see the Harrises, the first thing everyone in the family talks about is the ham. Well . . . it is great to be remembered for something.

MR. AND MRS. HARRISON'S SON

It started out a day like most others in late November driving to work in Sherman Oaks over Coldwater Canyon with the sunlight streaming through the towering pine trees. I had returned the previous evening from a business trip to New York City. I may have not appreciated the sunlight in the past, but on this morning, everything was particularly clear and vibrant. It was just over two months after the 9/11 attacks, and New York and our country were suffering. Grand Central Terminal's concourse still housed bulletin boards where notes, letters, signs, and cards were randomly posted—have you seen my dad?; my sister is missing; my son didn't come home last night. Their desperation was indescribable, and heartbreaking; now, weeks later, we knew the answers to their questions. At the A&E meeting I attended, the network executive shared that three students at her child's Manhattan school had each lost a parent.

Returning to Los Angeles, I resolved like many other Americans to appreciate every day. On this Thursday morning driving to work over Coldwater Canyon to the San Fernando Valley, I took special notice of the trees, the sunlight and the stream of nonstop traffic headed into the LA Basin. I passed familiar streets and places, Coldwater Park where our daughter played as a child, Lindacrest; Cherokee; Tree People, where I enjoy taking walks at the top of Mulholland; and the descent into Studio City. The world seemed at peace for a moment, and I was thankful to return to the daily routine. Hours later it would be shattered again.

When I got home that evening, I heard that George Harrison had passed away with his family at his side. Although it was widely known that George was seriously ill, his death was shocking. Where, exactly when, what were the circumstances? Slowly the details came out. George reportedly died at 1971 Coldwater Cañon in Beverly Hills (the street is spelled Cañon in Beverly Hills but is renamed Coldwater Canyon in Los Angeles). I had just driven Coldwater that day in both directions, morning and evening, and saw nothing unusual. I knew the road very well, enough to know that no such address existed.

About three weeks prior to his passing, George knew the end was near. His wife, Olivia, who was from Los Angeles, had her support system and family here. Paul visited George in New York City letting him know that he had a place close to Olivia's family where he could receive the necessary care. It was at this house at 1:20 p.m., November 29, 2001, George died.

The following day a crew from ABC *World News Tonight* with Peter Jennings brought cameras to my workplace and interviewed me about George for that evening's newscast. Gary Grossman, co-owner of the TV production company where I worked, prepped a room for the interview; and his business partner and my friend, Robb Weller, helped to calm my nerves before the cameras started to roll.

I shared my remembrances of George at the Sullivan show and of him pleading with the New York City police officer to let the young fan remain in the Warwick suite to meet the Beatles. I spoke about his loving immediate family, especially Mr. and Mrs. Harrison, who had been my support through so much; and how I cherished the pieces of George's clothing that Mrs. Harrison had included in her letters along with updates on his travels and career from a mom's perspective.

The selection of 1971 Coldwater was disturbing, and I wondered how this happened. Through various sources I learned that security maven Gavin de Becker came up with the idea of using an incorrect address to protect the Harrison family. De Becker had been around for years, hired to provide security services to celebrities including Dolly Parton, Jeff Bezos, and others.

De Becker is an intriguing personality in his own right; in the '80s he codesigned the MOSAIC Threat Assessment System used to screen threats to members of the US Congress, the Supreme Court, and the CIA.

Choosing 1971 Coldwater is even more interesting. The residence where George passed is located not far from there, close to two adjacent properties that were home to Debbie Reynolds and Carrie Fisher. De Becker and Carrie Fisher, although two years apart in age, knew each other from high school; de Becker even delivered a eulogy at Carrie Fisher's memorial service. He was very familiar with Carrie's address, and de Becker knew that house number on Coldwater did not exist. It was a very convenient solution.

FIFTY YEARS AFTER

PART 1—THE INTERVIEW

It was while I was sitting in producer Andrew Solt's Sunset Boulevard office in early 2010 that he first mentioned the upcoming fiftieth anniversary of the Beatles on *The Ed Sullivan Show*. Andrew's comment wasn't wasted on me. I had already been thinking about the anniversary. The reason for my visit to the production office was to discuss with Andrew my participation in the DVD reissue of all four of the Beatles' 1964 and 1965 appearances on *The Ed Sullivan Show*. The DVDs, released by Universal Music, would include not only the Beatles' performances from the master but also the show in its entirety, including commercials. Without hesitation I agreed. Andrew sent me to meet Sujata Murthy and her team, who were working on the release at Universal Music. We went to lunch as a group, and they were eager to hear my Beatles story. By the time we returned to their office, they were convinced I could more than adequately handle any Beatles question. I would make myself available to promote the DVDs, and I left pleased, to be part of the project.

The drill was this: I would do a few early morning drive-time radio interviews via phone. I wouldn't have to leave my house at 4 a.m. Pacific Time, just be awake enough to participate in these interviews across the country. Only about eight were scheduled. That was no problem until the eight turned into thirty-five interviews over several days. Some were scheduled with radio syndicates where the interview was broadcast on more than 350 stations. And at 6:20 a.m., it wasn't easy to grant WMGK, a Philadelphia classic rock station, its special request to sing "We Love You Beatles!" or to play a Beatles trivia game on KKCD Omaha. Other requests came in from as far away as Valencia, Spain, and Nova Scotia, Canada. Although my days started early during that two-week span, it was great fun to reminisce about being in the audience for the Beatles' first appearance on *The Ed Sullivan Show*. The DVD went double platinum.

I had gotten to know Andrew in the late '80s while securing some of Mike McCartney's early photographs of John Lennon for *Imagine*, the feature documentary on John's life that Andrew produced with David

Wolper. At the premiere and launch party, Andrew—in a miraculous feat—brought both Yoko Ono and Cynthia Lennon together for a rare joint appearance. From then on, I knew that Andrew could accomplish the impossible.

When Andrew talked about the fiftieth anniversary of the Beatles' first appearance on *The Ed Sullivan Show*, I could sense that something grand was in the works. Andrew's production company, SOFA Entertainment, owned the complete Sullivan library; the Beatles' appearances figured prominently with those of Elvis, The Doors, Richard Pryor, and the Italian mouse, Topo Gigio. Andrew's astute purchase of the Sullivan catalog in 1990 amazed insiders when they learned that owner Bob Precht had sold this historic archive.

Back in 1983, I was still working at CBS Television City when I received a letter from Bob Precht, a longtime producer of *The Ed Sullivan Show*. He had learned of my Beatles connection via the entertainment president at CBS, Bob Daly, and his wife, Nancy. It was under Bob Daly's 1977 move West from CBS New York to Los Angeles that I found myself suddenly transferred to Television City. The Dalys in the day were among Los Angeles's most in-demand couples, but the marriage fell apart. After a very public and shocking divorce Bob, who left CBS to become the head honcho at Warner Bros., eventually married Carole Bayer Sager. A philanthropist and children's advocate, Nancy married and later separated from former Los Angeles mayor Richard Riordan. Sadly, Nancy died a very somber death from pancreatic cancer at just age sixty-eight. A true loss especially for her beloved family and the hundreds of children she worked tirelessly to support. I remember her as Nancy MacNeil from Brooklyn who worked as a secretary at CBS.

While married, Bob and Nancy were great friends with Bob Precht and his wife. Mr. Precht still owned the Sullivan shows under his banner, Sullivan Productions, and was married to Ed Sullivan's only child, Betty. He wanted to discuss ideas regarding the upcoming February 1984 twentieth anniversary of the Beatles' appearance on the Sullivan show. We met at his impressive Beverly Hills home on North Linden Drive and discussed the possibilities, including a television special, but we soon discovered that CBS wasn't keen on doing anything music related. Just one year earlier my CBS colleague Paul Dobbs and I had worked with Stevie Wonder developing an hour-long special that Stevie would host. But the network rejected it for the same reason—anticipated poor ratings. Ultimately, no official Sullivan/Beatles project marked the twentieth anniversary.

In early fall of 2013, Andrew asked if he could give my name to Augie Max Vargas from Ken Ehrlich Productions, who was working on a fiftieth anniversary Beatles tribute show. There had been a mention in *Variety*

SULLIVAN PRODUCTIONS, INC.

January 7, 1983

Ms. Debbie Gendler
Assistant to the Vice President
Feature Films
CBS Entertainment
7800 Beverly Boulevard
Los Angeles, California 90036

Dear Debbie:

I have been following, with interest, your work on
the Beatles music. I hope the material we provided
was of some help to you.

With an eye toward 1984 and the 20th Anniversary of
the Beatles arrival in the U.S., I have been thinking
of some kind of Special. Your expertise and thoughts,
I'm sure would be helpful in developing the notion.

At your convenience, please call me.

Sincerely,

Bob Precht

BP/rh

Bob Precht, executive producer of *The Ed Sullivan Show* and Ed's son-in-law,
contacted me to strategize with him regarding a twentieth-anniversary salute to the
Beatles' first appearance on the show. CBS passed.
AUTHOR'S COLLECTION

that Ehrlich and AEG would produce a special in association with the Beatles and Apple. *The Night That Changed America* would be taped in Los Angeles the evening after the 2014 Grammy Awards.

Honored to be included, I told Andrew yes. "I'm always happy to relive my Sullivan adventures."

For several years I rarely mentioned the Sullivan show. It just never seemed appropriate to most conversations about the Beatles or television history. Every ten years, on an anniversary of the broadcast, there would be an interview or two, then nothing. If someone asked, I would talk about the excitement of being in the studio audience and the circumstances surrounding how I became involved in the explosion of Beatlemania. As time moved on, I grew more hesitant to mention the show because the people I told would introduce me ever after as a screaming teen. It always felt like it was a put-down.

But the fiftieth anniversary would be a major event, and from that perspective I wanted to be included. It was time to share how I found my way to a ticket for the Sullivan show, my involvement with Beatles Fan Club, meeting the Beatles and their families, and examining how a simple letter unfolded into an eyewitness account of four guys who came to America and changed our world.

Augie Max Vargas phoned a few days later and came to my office/ trailer on the Universal backlot for a preinterview. I was working on a daily daytime television show that taped on Denver Street in the heart of Western town. It was fun sitting around the conference table, discussing all things Beatle. After a few minutes, the trailer began to shake. Usually, I would forewarn my guests because the trailer sat adjacent to the famed Earthquake ride. Already desensitized to the shaking, I had neglected to warn him that we are reminded at five-minute intervals that we are in California.

A tape date for the interview was set right before Thanksgiving at the Universal Sheraton. Augie reserved two suites convenient to my work. He mentioned that he had located a few other audience members from that February night. Augie described them. Brigitte, her sister, Ann; and Patty, a fan also from New Jersey, would be interviewed. Patty was not just from New Jersey, but Wyckoff, the town next to where I grew up. I found out a few months later that she and her mom knew my dad. I don't remember ever making the connection that he knew another teen who was in the Sullivan audience.

At the time, only a few of the television producers I worked with knew my Beatles' history. Some remembered when I brought Yoko Ono on to promote the United Nations–sponsored event where the song "Imagine" was simultaneously played around the world to honor John Lennon's birthday. Others recollected Linda McCartney twice promoting her new home-style vegetarian cookbooks. Even fewer remembered Michael McCartney joining me at work for the day when he was staying at my house in Los Angeles.

But for most of the young staff, the Beatles seem as relatable as Rudy Vallée was to us in the '60s. Tainted by the biz, they couldn't understand all the excitement over my interview for the CBS Grammy special. If I had talked about Sam Smith's debut, they would have been jazzed. Being interviewed about sitting in a television studio fifty years earlier made me a rock relic.

When I arrived at the Universal Sheraton, Augie immediately introduced me to Vince Calandra. Vince had worked on the Sullivan show and had even stood in at the Saturday dress rehearsal for George Harrison after he fell ill when they arrived in New York. Everyone I work with in Los Angeles knows Vince. At one time, Vince and I held the same job title for the same executive producer, Vince on *The Mike Douglas Show*, me on ABC's *Home* and then Hallmark's *Home & Family* Show. It was fun to compare stories with Vince. He had brought along a sweet Paul and Linda McCartney autographed photo to share. As I was making a fuss over Vince, Augie called me into the next room. It was time.

Lights were set up all around. People were checking and double-checking audio levels, shadows, and camera angles. I got settled in the chair. The interviewer was the cohost of *Entertainment Tonight*, Kevin Frazier. Initially, I felt confident about Kevin—he had interviewed the biggest celebrities in town—but the questions he led with were superficial and meaningless. "Was there a lot of excitement at the Sullivan show?" "Did you scream?" Each question was crafted for a sound bite, rather than the answers I had prepared from the preinterview with Augie on the Beatles' sociological influences for a generation and beyond.

I wanted to explain from my perspective how this night changed America: our culture, our dress, our music, our politics, ultimately pitting families and friends across ideological divides that in some cases have taken decades to repair. Beatlemania brought us out of a deep, national sorrow and into a period in which culture and politics intertwined with an emerging resurgence of youthful energy and passion. Kevin simply read down a list of predictable questions without substance or genuine interest. I tried to answer his questions with the hope that the best was yet to come. Then came the final question: Kevin, smiling, looking self-assured, as though he was heading for an exclusive, asked, "Who's your favorite Beatle?"

I rose from the chair, frustrated and disappointed, as Vince Calandra took my place. Vince is a terrific storyteller, and I hoped his comments would be treated with more respect. I couldn't get the "Who's your favorite Beatle?" question out of my head. I was concerned. Was this the defining moment of the interview?

Casting a smile to Vince, I walked to the adjacent Green Room to collect my belongings. Seated in makeup chairs were Charlie Brill and Mitzi McCall. I was surprised to see the comedy duo and didn't know what to say other than hello. Both Mitzi and Charlie had been listening to my interview and seemed to be amused. Mitzi motioned me over to her makeup chair and grabbed my hand. She was warm and truly sparkled, and she sincerely was taken with my comments about the show.

With no sensitivity, I divulged how the audience wanted them off the stage during Sullivan because they were taking valuable time away from the Beatles. Mitzi, with perfect comedic timing, said, "You weren't the only ones. It was the beginning of the end of our career." The makeup crew laughed. Mitzi and Charlie told me about being backstage with the Beatles. They were trying to go over lines for their routine when someone knocked on their door. When Mitzi opened it there, stood John Lennon. He asked for a dime to get a Coke from the machine.

Before I left, Mitzi gave me a hug and squeezed my hand. There is a special bond among all of us who shared that electric night. Today, I am proud to call Charlie and Mitzi friends.

FIFTY YEARS AFTER

PART 2—THE LEGACY

Two months later, I squeezed my husband's hand tightly as we entered the West Hall of the sprawling Los Angeles Convention Center ready to be part of the CBS show taping. Together with the pretaped interviews, this "live" tribute special would be edited and then broadcast on Sunday night, February 9—exactly fifty years to the day when the Beatles first appeared on the Sullivan show. With VIP treatment we found our seats near the stage. Vince was already there, one row behind us; Bill Bohnert, who designed the famous set, sat to Vince's left. Andrew Solt and his family, brimming with pride over the Sullivan shows he gets to call his own, was farther back.

I leaned forward and seated on the aisle was a blonde woman. She said, "I was one of the girls in the audience that night." It was Ann, Brigitte's sister! Ann and her husband flew from Florida to Los Angeles to attend the taping. What a great night this was turning out to be. How happy I was to meet her; I finally had a Beatles sister, someone who had experienced the excitement, the insanity, the craziness we all shared in CBS Studio 50.

Over my left shoulder there was a small commotion: Yoko and Sean, Olivia and Dhani, Paul and Nancy, Ringo and Barbara with Barbara's sister, Marjorie, and her husband, Joe Walsh, were taking their seats. Fifty years earlier I would not have imagined being so close to the heart of what remained of the Beatles. John was gone, George was gone. We had shared the devastating losses, but tonight we were together celebrating a seminal event. Only seven of us including Ringo and Paul at the Convention Center had been at the Sullivan show on February 9. I felt honored to be included.

As the show started, it was impossible to concentrate solely on the performances onstage. I couldn't take my eyes off the guests of honor. It was spectacular to watch Yoko and Paul, Nancy and Olivia, Ringo and Barbara getting into it, moving in their seats, singing the words to the songs they had sung so many times before, now being performed by the likes of

Katy Perry, Pharrell Williams, Ed Sheeran, and Dave Grohl. The energy felt comfortable like the Sullivan audience fifty years before; all together, bouncing in our seats while mouthing the words to "She Loves You" and screaming simultaneously. That night our idols were just like us.

It was a long show—a very long show. Stevie Wonder had to do two takes; lighting caused delays. Cirque de Soleil required extra time setting up their Beatles' *Love* aerial performance. After the tribute part of the show ended, Ringo performed, followed by Paul, and then they joined together in song, culminating with everyone singing "Hey Jude." The Convention Center swayed in a sea of unity. It was magical.

And eerily familiar. In my head, I could still hear Ed Sullivan's voice instructing the audience to get home safely. A small crowd was gathering around Yoko. As the Convention Center emptied, I could feel the lingering sadness of an empty, suddenly still CBS Studio 50 stage. At age thirteen I had wanted more, and I knew in my heart that these four guys were forever.

Two weeks elapsed between the taping of the show and the airdate, and my Beatles sisters and I didn't know whether our interviews would make it to the final cut. Our producer Augie kept managing expectations by saying that the show was running long, and I knew what that meant in television terms. We were on the cutting-room floor.

February 9 finally arrived. Earlier in the day, I had friends over to celebrate the anniversary, and at 8 p.m. my husband and I were ready. Almost immediately, my mobile buzzed with text messages; my Beatles sister on the East Coast was telling me that we made it. I focused on the TV screen; yes, there was Brigitte, then Ann, then Patty, and me. My voice could be heard talking over film footage of the crowds at the theater, and then some sound bites followed by a few more questions. And then, oh no, the question, "Who's your favorite Beatle?"

If you watch the show carefully, you can see me hesitate, uncomfortable, but looking straight ahead at the camera, I responded, "Yes, I did have one, but I will never say." The producers and editors needed to keep the response in the program.

For several days following the show's airing, people were asking, "OK, so you can tell *me*, who's your favorite Beatle?" Friends, friends of friends, casual acquaintances all tried to figure out which Beatle was my favorite. At work, one gal was positive my favorite was John, while another said it had to be Paul, but the person sitting next to me was confident my fave was George. Then I added when the Beatles first arrived in the United States, Ringo was the most popular. A few people changed their vote. Is this my Beatles legacy?

When Andrew Solt called me three nights after *The Night That Changed America* aired, I shouldn't have been surprised. We chatted endlessly, like we always did.

At the end, Andrew sarcastically said, "Paul has watched the entire show three times already."

Honestly impressed, I responded, "Really . . . wow."

"He has just one question—he wants to know who's your favorite Beatle?"

"Who's my favorite Beatle, after fifty years? Andrew, this just isn't making any sense. Tell him to call me," I said jokingly.

LBJ HOSTS THE BEATLES

According to Accuweather, it was 98 degrees but felt like 102 in Austin. I had gone to Texas to see the *Ladies and Gentlemen . . . The Beatles!* touring exhibit that was excerpted from the CBS special *The Night That Changed America: A Grammy Salute to the Beatles* on the fiftieth anniversary of their first appearance on *The Ed Sullivan Show*. Forty-two million people across the country had watched it. I was thrilled to finally attend the exhibition that had been on tour immediately after the television special aired. Previous three month stops included Lincoln Center's Performing Arts Center Library, Mall of America, Miami, and the Woody Guthrie Center in Tulsa, where thousands of people filed through the exhibits and saw the tape of Brigitte, Ann, Patty, and me sharing our Sullivan adventures. The exhibit at the LBJ Presidential Library in Austin had been open only one month when I phoned Anne Wheeler, the communications director. Anne told me that one thousand interested individuals lined up for opening day. I let Anne know that my husband and I were flying to Austin to see the exhibit; she kindly set aside two tickets.

It was exciting to finally see the exhibit eighteen months after the TV show. A museum docent approached us, welcoming us to the library and gave us a quick overview. I shared with her the reason for our visit and frankly, I was beginning to question whether I was really part of the exhibit—if she worked there and didn't know me, maybe the content had changed.

At that instant, she launched into her own recollection of seeing the Beatles perform in Toronto in 1966 at the Maple Leaf Garden. People love to talk their own Beatles stories and I always rejoice in the retelling of their remembrances. The docent shared that her husband was the true "Beatles fan" but never saw the group perform live. She, on the other hand, got to see them in concert. It equaled out.

The docent had one final question: "Who was your favorite Beatle?" I really had to laugh because I knew that she had never walked through the exhibit. I suggested she join me inside because I answered her question in my interview. After coming this far, I was anxious to see the exhibit. As we were edging away from the Beatles discussion, another worker passed by, shouting out loudly, "I recognize you from the interview." My husband and I appreciated the big Texas welcome.

Having lived only on the two coasts, I don't "get" Texas. The irony of having the exhibit at the LBJ library was perplexing. Texas is where President Kennedy was assassinated. The Beatles' reception in the States may have proved very different if not for the trauma that all of America and the world had experienced on November 22, 1963. I think my generation, then in their teens, took it particularly hard because we looked to JFK as the new generation of politicians.

If LBJ had not inherited the presidency, maybe Beatlemania would not have swept the States, offering us relief for the depression and disbelief following the assassination. Many historians and sociologists allude to this now widely accepted theory as an explanation why Beatles fans so fiercely and vocally dedicated themselves to the group. These four guys from Liverpool helped us heal with the belief that life can still be optimistic and joyful.

With the Beatles exhibit downstairs and the LBJ permanent collection on several upstairs floors, it became evident that much of the cultural revolution that started with the Beatles formed the backdrop for the LBJ White House years. By 1968, when LBJ decided not to seek reelection, the Beatles, as a cohesive entity publicly had started to live their separate lives.

Walking into the CBS Grammy exhibit was surreal. People were queued up intently studying the displays, reading about the Beatles—fans and museumgoers exhibiting their love for the Beatles. Parents shared with their adult children and grandchildren where they were when the group came to America. Everyone brought their own experiences and thoughts, talking about their teenage bedrooms as they viewed the display of a typical Beatles fan's bedroom.

I wish they had shown my room. Some people were sitting on a bench and others standing watching, laughing intent on what my Beatles sisters and I were sharing about the dynamics of being in the audience. I took a seat next to one woman who seemed to be mesmerized by the content. The interviews played on a ten-minute loop; as I watched, I was listening closely to peoples' comments.

No one made the connection between me at this exhibit and me being interviewed until one young woman with her husband and baby approached me.

"That's you talking, isn't it?" she asked.

Although she was too young to have seen the Beatles perform as a group, she immediately shared how ten years earlier at age eighteen, she had visited Liverpool and had gone to the Cavern Club. This young mom was so enthusiastic that she asked me to pose with her family for a photo.

Another young couple visiting from Albuquerque struck up a conversation wanting to hear more, and a few other people gathered as I responded to questions. A couple from New Orleans wanted to hear additional details, so we walked to the memorabilia displays and discussed the items that were vital to the life of a Beatles fan. They agreed that this personal tour was the most interesting part of the exhibit. People wanted to learn more, to reminisce, to sense the impact of the band and to simply reflect on the good times the Beatles presented.

Later in the day I noticed a very young couple move from gazing at the Beatles bedroom closer to the screen. When the Beatles started singing, they began to dance, a special moment not lost on other visitors. Behind me stood a man and a woman in their late forties. The woman was chattering away, and I could pick up a few words. She had attended one of Paul McCartney's concerts and when she saw Paul tilt his head in a certain way in the clip, she excitedly clued her companion in saying, "You see how he moved his head? He did the same thing when I saw him in concert two years ago. All these years . . . that's our Paul."

The words "our Paul" kept playing in my head all the way back to Los Angeles. There is an intimacy about the people we follow today—the one-on-one experience that speaks directly to us. For this fan, he is "her Paul."

As Beatlemania took shape, no one associated with the group was really an adult. Everyone was in uncharted territory. The Beatles were still kids; Brian was the elder, passing away at only age thirty-two having already lived a lifetime. That is why they are *ours*, growing up alongside us and forging the way. Through the Beatles we learned about life—saw the burgeoning power of the media, witnessed unfathomable breakups, experienced the sadness of death way too early, and came to understand that life brings its own distinctions. Fresh in my memory are embedded visions of Ringo and Barbara, Olivia, Yoko, Paul, and Nancy at the Los Angeles Convention Center together for this momentous event celebrating fifty years of coming to America and gripping the nation on *The Ed Sullivan Show*. They are us and we are them and we are all together (to quote some famous lyrics).

Living in Beverly Hills presents occasional surprise sightings. I've spotted Ringo walking alone down Bedford Drive in Beverly Hills. Though I wanted to talk to him, I stayed on the opposite side of the street, feeling the sweetness of a bygone era. Would I ever have imagined sixty years before when, at age fourteen, I held a sign "Ringo for President" that I would be standing in this spot? I did walk down to Santa Monica Boulevard on a Saturday in late 2019 when Ringo, who is a Beverly Hills resident, unveiled to the city a statue of his hand with his trademark peace sign. It is now displayed in Beverly Gardens Park and, on July 7 at noon each year, he celebrates his birthday beside the statue.

Similarly, I've had Paul and Nancy sightings on Santa Monica Boulevard near the Beverly Hilton; hiking at Tree People at the top of Coldwater Canyon; or walking in the park at Coldwater; or Paul enjoying dinner at Madeo's on Beverly Boulevard with friends Martin Short and Lorne Michaels. And when their schedules coincide, seeing Ringo and Paul leaving Mr. Chow's. The Beatles were a group phenomenon that will never happen again. It was a special time in history a convergence of so many ingredients that made us feel they were all ours, all we would ever need, and the good times would last forever.

I had had enough "Beatling" for the day.

The visit to Austin and the exhibit served its purpose. In January it would be traveling to yet another city, where fans and the curious would revel in the times. As we were about to leave, I overheard a woman wondering to her companion why I wouldn't disclose who was my favorite Beatle. Not realizing that I was standing right next to her, she wanted to know the reason. Does it really matter?

The Beatles fiftieth anniversary Grammy tribute has traveled as far as Japan where thousands experienced it. Nearly ten years later, in 2023, the exhibit landed at the Grammy Museum in Newark, New Jersey. Interest in the John, Paul, George, and Ringo phenomenon will continue for as long as the Beatles' music warms our hearts and excites our sensibilities—in other words . . . forever.

EIGHT DAYS A WEEK PLUS TWO YEARS

To keep this book updated would be tedious both to write and read. Much has happened since I wrote what was intended to be the final chapter.

Two years after the CBS special aired, it was announced that the Grammy exhibit would be coming to Los Angeles. I had the honor of speaking twice at the Grammy Museum when the exhibit, now called *Ladies and Gentlemen . . . The Beatles!*, was in high gear. Beatles events have led me from one amazing experience to another, and I meet other fans who at the evening's end want to hear more of my adventures.

Gay Linvill, Beatles aficionado, brought me to the attention of noted Beatles historian Mark Lewisohn, who interviewed me via FaceTime for his newest work on the Beatles. Mark already knew about me through ancient Beatles documents and a book on Brian Epstein, where I was referenced. He lived up to his reputation as the noted Beatles historian: his knowledge is vast, and his books are packed with vital info for every person interested in the Beatles.

I received a supreme honor when I was approached to be included in Ron Howard and Brian Grazer's feature documentary, *The Beatles: Eight Days A Week—The Touring Years*. I was first contacted by a producer in late 2014, regarding my attendance at the Sullivan show.

I was very excited to be a part of this newly announced Beatles project being produced in conjunction with Apple Corps. After the initial email and phone call, months passed with no communication. Then unexpectedly one afternoon at work I received a phone call from Paul Crowder, one of the producers of the documentary. I was still under consideration for a possible interview.

Before we hung up, I asked Paul, "Are you related to Alan Crowder?" I could sense that Paul was somewhat taken aback.

"Yes, he was my dad."

I had met his dad back in New York City in the mid-'70s when he was Paul McCartney's manager at a photographic exhibit. I had sensed that Alan Crowder was a gentleman; Paul Crowder seemed likewise.

Nothing associated with the Beatles Empire ever came easily or without extensive strategizing and planning. It had been many years since the old days, and my skills were rusty. I wanted to be part of this project as I believed it would do extraordinarily well based on Ron Howard's integrity and cinematic skills and, obviously, the subject matter.

Months passed again with no communication. Then I read that the film was being screened in Cannes at the annual film market for buyers. With the movie seemingly done, I moved on.

Six months passed, and again I was surprised when the supervising producer for the film, Marc Ambrose, called to tell me to hang in there. The time for my interview was near. What? The crew was going to London to conduct interviews in early January 2016, and when they returned, it would be my turn. That was eighteen months after I was first contacted.

January came and went. Marc called again, asking for my schedule for the following month. Days later the film's writer Mark Monroe phoned, and we had a lengthy chat regarding details of my Beatles life. Finally, February arrived, early March, and still no call. At the end of the month, the phone rang: April 4 was confirmed. Be at the London West Hollywood for the interview at 6 p.m. Not to worry—hair and makeup were available.

I had a lot to do—schedule a hair appointment, talk to the makeup team at work, select my clothes. I was all set for the 4th, and then the phone rang. Could I do the interview the very next day, March 30, at 4:30 p.m. at the London?

I had been to the London a few times for BAFTA events, but not for an interview of this importance. When I arrived, cameras were set to roll. I was directed to a chair, and the lights were adjusted because I decided to wear my glasses at my husband's suggestion. I was especially happy to see a female cinematographer operating one of the cameras.

Ninety minutes later it was over. Mark Monroe's questions were incisive, in sharp contrast to Kevin Frazier's a few years back. They also shot some B-roll of the memorabilia and letters I brought along, and it was a wrap.

As I started to leave, Jeff Jones came over to thank me. I didn't know he was watching. Jeff had replaced Neil Aspinall years earlier at Apple Corps and currently runs the company from both New York and its headquarters in London. I was flustered at first, but then I went for it. The old spirit was returning. I told Jeff I was working on this manuscript. Based on my interview, he felt I was uniquely qualified to write this book, having been at more Beatles concerts in the United States than probably anyone else (besides Ringo and Paul) he had met. I added that when the book was completed, I would get him a copy.

Nodding, he agreed, handed me his business card, and started to tell me about the Grateful Dead, his favorite band.

Ron Howard's documentary was released in September 2016, and I was invited to join the suits at the talent agency CAA in Century City to see the finished product. Larry David was there. So was Stevie Wonder. As always, I was happy to see Andrew Solt and family seated two rows away. At the reception afterward, I spotted Gene Simmons with his wife, Shannon Tweed, and daughter Sophie.

The interview, although not in the body of the documentary, landed in the accompanying DVD package under the heading "Three Fans."

> The most interesting part for me [of Ron Howard's film *The Beatles: The Touring Years*] was the bonus feature about the 3 fans who were there at the beginning of the US hysteria. I liked hearing their stories.
>
> Alex D., San Antonio, TX
> February 8, 2017
> Steve Hoffman's Music Forums

SUNDAYS AT 8; MONDAYS AT 10

In the end, where you finish is sometimes where you start.

After forty-seven years working in television, I was ready to call it quits. I had planned to leave my position on a Hallmark Channel morning television series at the end of the year, but in August I was told that I was among several on the staff not being asked back for the show's next season beginning in September. The person giving me the news was in tears. I was angered by the abruptness but joyful about the freedom.

Free time was very short-lived. Andrew Solt asked me to stop by his office: I knew what that meant. Andrew had a music project that was well underway and needed some additional research for interviews. I didn't want work-related responsibility, but Andrew assured me this would be only twenty hours per week. I can never say "no" to Andrew. His kindness and trust in my abilities was more important than being a person of leisure watching *Midsomer Murders*. So, the work began. And then more work, and even more.

With a new streaming deal with Universal Music for *The Ed Sullivan Show*, Andrew and his son, Josh, now president of SOFA Entertainment, asked me to remain on the project. Every Monday at 10 a.m., we're on Zoom talking Ed, Beatles, and the thousands of performers who graced the Sullivan stage beginning in 1948 to its final episode in 1971.

Apparently, my work and interests haven't changed since age thirteen when I excitedly took a seat in the Sullivan theater waiting to see them standing there. Now sixty years later, I am still in a seat but in front of my desktop seeing the Beatles who are still standing there. I may not be screaming, bouncing, and ready to pass out, but I'm still feeling the love. Life has come full circle.

INDEX

Photo insert images are indicated by *p1, p2, p3, etc.*

ABOUT THE AUTHOR

Debbie Gendler is a four-time Emmy®-nominated talent and development executive and producer formerly at CBS (New York and Los Angeles) and ABC. She also served as Women in Film's (LA) first executive director. A magna cum laude graduate of Boston University's College of Communication, Debbie is responsible for developing more than nine thousand episodes of television with Weller/Grossman Productions for thirty-six broadcast and cable networks, including the launches of HGTV and the National Geographic channel in the United States. Identifying talent and building show concepts is Debbie's expertise; she introduced many of today's notable hosts and experts to networks.

As an "original" Beatles fan—in the studio audience for the group's first appearance on *The Ed Sullivan Show*—she has given countless interviews on television, radio, and podcasts, including a Grammy salute to the Beatles on the fiftieth anniversary of that appearance, *The Night That Changed America.* Her interview traveled around the world as part of a Grammy exhibit and on the accompanying DVD to Ron Howard's documentary on the Beatles. She was also featured in a front-page story on the Beatles in the *New York Times.* Now, sixty years later, Debbie is a research consultant and coproducer at SOFA Entertainment, owner of *The Ed Sullivan Show.*

She enjoys the non-housewife life with her husband in Beverly Hills, California.

Do you have a Beatle story to share? Please email me at
debbie@ISawThemStandingThere.com.
I'd love to hear your adventure.